Christianity: Endangered or Extinct?

A People's History of Christianity
(in the Mode of Howard Zinn's A People's History of the United States)
Volume 1: The Gathering Storm

RODGER CRAGUN
& THOMAS KESSLER

WIPF & STOCK · Eugene, Oregon

Wipf and Stock Publishers
199 W 8th Ave, Suite 3
Eugene, OR 97401

Christianity: Endangered or Extinct?
A People's History of Christianity (in the Mode of Howard Zinn's
A People's History of the United States)
By Cragun, Rodger L. and Kessler, Thomas
Copyright©2014 by Cragun, Rodger L.
ISBN 13: 978-1-5326-6366-6
Publication date 7/19/2018
Previously published by Outskirts Press, 2014

Contents

Introduction i
   The Religion of Love—Essence of Early Christianity i
   Unfortunate Decision of the Twelve Apostles v
   Some of the Church's True Gems vii

Chapter 1: Marcion: The Shipbuilder in the Storm 1
   Marcion of Sinope 1
   "Sailor Marcion" 2
   Dire Situation in Rome and Marcion's Donation 4
   Diversity in the Roman Church at Marcion's Time 6
   Class Stratification and Hierarchical Development 7
   The Value Lesson of *The Shepherd of Hermas* 9
   "Supreme Leadership" Has Not Yet Developed 12
   The Primacy of Honor within the Community 13
   Valentinus 15
   Marcion, Valentinus, the Shepherd of Hermas,
      and the Developing Hierarchy 18
   Marcion and the Church Fathers 19
   Modern Reassessment of Marcion 30
   Heresy and Identity in Antiquity 30

Chapter 2: Marcion's Place in a Violent World 32
   Marcion Faces the Violence around Him 34

Violence: The Romans, the Christians, and the Jews 39
Marcion and Gnosticism 42
Marcion: Anti-Old Testament, Not Anti-Jew 44
Who was the Heretic? 46
Class Struggle within the Formation of Christian Belief 47
Marcion and the Formation of Scripture 49
Marcion and the Alien God of the New Testament 57
Conclusion 60

Chapter 3: The Spirit Blows Anew, Pentecost for Women
as well as Men 62
Comparison of the Women in the First and Second Pentecost 62
Setting for the New Group's Beginnings..................................... 63
Asia Minor, Center of Early Christianity 64
Life in Early Montanist Communities 64
The Spirit of Millenarianism and Montanism 65
Marcus Aurelius and Disaster 67
Justinian's Persecution of the Montanists.................................... 70
Who Were These "Montanists"? 73
Prophesies of the Montanists and Other Discoveries 75

Chapter 4: The Spirit Blows in Africa, Tertullian and the Carthage
Community 81
The Vigor of the Carthage Montanist Community 82
Tertullian's Intimate Account of the Vibrant Carthage Montanist
    Community 83
Summary of Tertullian's Life 85
Tertullian, Christian, Catholic, and Montanist 85
Tertullian the Unifier 87
Tertullian's Defense of the Montanists 88
Tertullian the Rhetorician 91
Tertullian's Use of Scripture 91
Tertullian's Relationship with Women 92
The Catholic Church and the Montanists 93
Tertullian's References 94
Conclusion 95

Chapter 5: The Torrents of Condemnation Come Cascading Down ... 97
    The Synod of Laodicea and the Council of Constantinople 97
    Witness of Tertullian to the Slanders of the Church 99
    Emperor Constantine and the Montanists..................................... 100
    Objections to the Early Montanists by Their Peers 101
    Epiphanius's Statements against the Montanists 106
    Epiphanius's Statements Related to the Statements of Others 108
    Attacks on the Montanists by Others of the Age 112
    Appraisal of Attacks 113
    Women in a Male-Dominated Church.. 113
    Women, Bishops, Πρεσβυτεροι, and the
        Uncomfortable in the Church.. 115
    Montanists Perceived as Fanatics 116
    Montanists, True Followers or Divisive Element? 116
    The Scourge of Greek Philosophy in the Church 117

Chapter 6: The Storm Intensifies: Arius, Athanasius, and
    the Age of Arrogance... 119
    Enter Arius.. 121
    Enter Athanasius 121
    The Tumultuous Era of Arius and Athanasius 122
    Persecution of Diocletian 122
    Constantine and the Changing Times of Christianity 124
    The War of Words.. 125
    Migration of Rural North African Christians into Alexandria...... 125
    Constantinian Changes in Church Structures 127
    The Rise of Athanasius... 127
    Essential Arianism.. 128
    Essential Athanasianism 129
    The Genesis of the Dispute.. 130
    Council of Nicaea 132
    The Social Background for Arius' and Athanasius' Views 139

Chapter 7: Ambrose, the Captain of the Ship................................... 141
    Family Background 141
    Ambrose and the Power Matrix 144

Arian Hysteria of Ambrose's Time 145
Crumbling Empire 148
Ammianus Marcellinus, Pagan Telling the Truth 150
Power Struggle for the Papacy 153
The Chaos of Power 156
Julian, the Christian Pagan 157
Accession of Ambrose as Bishop 158
General/Governor as Bishop 160
Unraveling of the Empire Continues 161
The Portian Basilica 162
Gratian's War and *De Fide* 163
De Fide, Not Truth, But Rhetoric 168
Ambrose, The Emperor's "Father in the Faith" 168
The "Council" of Aquileia 169
The Murder of Gratian 170
The Pagan Altar of Victory 171
The Burning of the Jewish Synagogue 171
Ambrose and the Pope 173
The New Asceticism 174
Ambrose and Slavery 176

Chapter 8: Augustine Versus the Donatists 180
Influence of Augustine 180
The Donatists of North Africa: An Ancient
    Christian Independence Movement 182
The Donatists and the Great Persecution 183
Bishop Donatus of Niger 184
Constantine and the Donatists 184
The Life of Augustine 186
Patricius, the Absent Father 187
Monica, the Controlling Mother 187
Augustine, the Bishop 188
The Gulf between the Bishop and His People 189
Augustine's Attack on the Donatists 190
Augustine's Monastery 193
Augustine's Basilica 194

Augustine before His God 194
Augustine, a "Kinder and Gentler" Bishop? 195
Augustine and the Teachings of the Donatists 202
Augustine and the Nonviolence of the Donatists 203
Summary 205

Chapter 9: Augustine Changes the Course of the Church 207
    The Council of Nicaea and the Transformation of the Church 209
    Augustine, Prime Corrupter of the Jesus Movement 210
    Augustine's Theology of Empire 211
    The Sincerity of Augustine 214
    Augustine's Writings without the Teachings of Jesus 215
    Augustine's Writings without the Teachings of Jesus 217
    "Turning the Other Cheek" 218
    Loving One's Enemy 220
    The Gospel of John 225
    Greek Philosophy 227
    The "Word" of God and the Greek "Word" 229
    The Philosophers' Concept of the Soul 231
    Augustine's Love 233
    Augustine and Nicodemus 236
    Augustine: the Priest as Broker of Eternal Life 239

Chapter 10: The Consequences of Domination in the Christian
    Church from the Second to the Twenty-first Century 241
    The Problem as It Is Experienced by the Roman
        Catholic Church: 244
    Denial within the System 245
    Projection 251
    The Power Problem in the Historical Church 251
    The All-Present Reality of Sexuality 258
    The History of Sexual Abuse within the Church 260
    The Answer of Jesus—Be a Servant: Paulo Friere 263

Introduction

"History is written by the victorious, the liars, the strongest, and the most determined. Truth is found most often in the silence, in the quiet places"

Kate Mosse.

The Religion of Love—Essence of Early Christianity

No religion in the history of the world has spoken about love as much as Christianity. Jesus, in the Synoptic Gospels, asserts that the whole law is summed up in two commandments: "Love the Lord your God with all your heart and with all your soul and with all your mind," and "Love your neighbor as yourself." (Matthew 22:37, 39; Mark 12:30–31; cf. Luke10:25–28) This was the essence of the Old Testament Law. But for Jesus, love went even beyond loving one's neighbor. In Matthew 5:43–44, Jesus is recorded as saying: "You have heard it was said love your neighbor and hate your enemy, but I tell you, love your enemies and pray for those who persecute you."

Love was to be the essence of Jesus' community. John 13:34–35 records Jesus as saying "A new command I give you: love one another. By this all men will know that you are my disciples, if you love one another." And John records Jesus pleading with his Father for future followers: ". . . [T]hat all may be one, Father, just as you are in me and I in you. May they also be in us so that the world may believe that you sent me." (John

17:20–21) The First Epistle of John reads, ". . . let us love one another, for love comes from God. Everyone who loves has been born of God . . . because God is love." (1 John 4:7–8)

Paul, after giving his famous poem on love, states: "And now these three remain: faith, hope, and love. But the greatest of these is love" (1 Corinthians 13:13 NIV).

Why all this love? John's Gospel says it best: "For God so loved the world that he gave his one and only Son, that whoever believes in him shall not perish but have life eternal." (John 3:16)

It is indeed love between the brothers and sisters that made Christianity successful in the Roman Empire. In *The Rise of Christianity*, sociologist Rodney Stark establishes that as a poor people's movement, Christianity encouraged sharing material goods, hard work, and services; and caring for the sick, the widowed, and the orphaned. Furthermore, he stipulates that women played an essential role in the movement in contrast to pagan women who were considered not much better than slaves. In his analysis, Stark asserts that it was not so much otherworldly miraculous activity that propelled Christianity but down-to-earth loving service. Slaves, women, poor people, and foreigners flocked to Christianity. (Stark 1997,157)

In short, in the empire, a poor pagan could very well starve unless a Christian found him in time. Poor Christians could expect their brothers and sisters to not only provide food, but also care for them in their need. Similarly to Stark, New Testament scholars Bruce Malina and Richard Rohrbaugh, in their *Social Scientific Study of the Gospel of John*, place in context of the social milieu that being born-again was not so much a spiritual transformation but rather a social transformation. Sons and daughters who were disinherited or forced out of their families would be born anew by "water and spirit" into a new family, a Christian fellowship. Malina and Rohrbaugh make the same point about slavery. They stipulate that a slave torn from his or her people in a far off land wherever he or she was in the Roman Empire would be truly born again into the Christian Family. (Malina and Rohrbaugh 1997. 8–89)

While love was the essence of the movement that Jesus founded, the historical record of those who claim to be the followers of Jesus has hardly been one that has reflected love of God, love for each other, and unity in the Spirit. It certainly has not reflected love of enemies. Rather, after the death of the apostles and the first witnesses to Jesus, the Christian church soon fell into vindictive behavior. Violence, of course, was the last sandal to drop and from then on the Jesus Movement was in jeopardy.

The Religion of Love Disintegrating— The Model for These Books

Our work is an attempt to document and to analyze the disintegration of the movement that Jesus founded so that we might contribute in some small way to the reestablishment of that movement. We believe deeply that despite the disastrous record that Christianity has had in the last 20 centuries, the Jesus Movement has something to contribute to the furthering of life on this planet.

The methodology, documentation, and analysis through which we conduct our research are different from the methodologies utilized by Christian historians of previous eras. A secular historian, Howard Zinn, a theologian and biblical scholar, Elisabeth Schüssler Fiorenza, and a French psychologist, Michel Foucault, shape our methodology.

Zinn (1922–2010), professor of political science Boston University, published a monumental work titled *A People's History of the United States* in 1980. Substitute "*Christianity*" for "*the United States*" and you have a near-perfect description of our book. Zinn's book is "a history disrespectful of governments and respectful of people's movements of resistance." Both works are biased in the direction of the poor people who are oppressed, and against the rich and powerful. Both histories report that the dominant class deceives and oppresses the poor. Both histories report that the voice of the common person has been shut out of the history books, the major media, the standard textbooks, and the voices of presidents, politicians, popes, cardinals, bishops, and scholars recorded. The elite in every age, including our own, have attempted to keep the common citizenry passive and powerless and dependent on "some new savior," a president, a new bishop, or a new pope to bring them justice. (Zinn 2003, 570; Zinn and Armove 2004, 24)

Christianity also needs a counterforce in the face of mitered popes, bishops, scholarly theologians, and self-serving and self-righteous Christians. What Zinn has done for the poor, Native Americans, African Americans, the worker, and women in United States history, we are attempting to do for the oppressed in Christian Church history.

As Howard Zinn reported about the voices of the poor in secular history, Harvard theologian and biblical scholar Elisabeth Schüssler Fiorenza has led the world in attempting to reestablish women's voices lost within the graveyard of male-dominated history. In her classic work, *In Memory of Her*, Fiorenza points out that in the passion account of the Gospel of Mark there is an incident where a woman anoints Jesus' feet (Mark 14:6–9) and Jesus says: "Truly I tell you, wherever the gospel is preached throughout the world, what she has done will be told, in memory of her." (Mark 14:9) In reality, things did not turn out the way Jesus insisted it would. Fiorenza reminds us that we do not even know the woman's name, but two of the twelve, Judas who betrayed Jesus, and Peter who denied Jesus, are engraved in our memories because of their gender, whereas the woman disciple who anointed Jesus for his mission is forgotten. Fiorenza leaves "theological certainty" and she aims at "retrieval" of the memory of the woman for the sake of women in Christianity (Schüssler-Fiorenza 1994, in toto).

This, too, is our venture and our quest. *In Christianity: Endangered or Extinct? A People's History of Christianity*, we likewise will bring out women's voices, but we will also deal with a multitude of persons and groups who were inordinately scorned and were considered the dregs of the dominant Christian religion. Conversely, we deal with those "saints" who were superabundantly or needlessly praised.

Within this perspective, the third influential voice is French psychologist, philosopher, historian Michel Foucault (1926–1984). He has much to offer to the discussions in these pages with his discursive analysis. We find that his approach is helpful in getting behind the language of the church fathers to see the oppression that existed in their wake.

The "laboratory of power," as Foucault calls it, has placed some in high positions of respect according to their often-perverted ideals and value systems. Those who exist as underlings in those systems become "docile bodies," according to Foucault. At the same time, others do not fit and even dare to resist the mold, which those in the power positions establish as the norm, and they are denigrated and even destroyed.

This work attempts to sort through the lives of the Christians who lived before us. We do so in order to ground ourselves, establish *a situs in re*, "a position in reality," that enables us to model as best as we can the life and words of Jesus. At the same time, we hope to restore justice to many Christians of merit who were denigrated and/or forced into oblivion, and establish that they indeed had been part of the Jesus Movement.

If the Christian religion is to have meaning in today's world, it is necessary that it be grounded solidly on reality. Our intention, as we write, is not merely a negative one. We do not merely want to knock down the established order; we want to do the grounding. We feel that it is necessary to critically evaluate the spurious value systems that have become set in ecclesiastical stone, and also the lives of some of the established "saints." We also feel that we must elevate others who have been sorely abused.

Unfortunate Decision of the Twelve Apostles

Besides the silencing of women in the New Testament, other indications of the disintegration of the Jesus Movement exist within the New Testament. It does not take a historical-critical method to perceive it. Evidence is found in the literal interpretation of a story in the book of Acts. The story tells of a seemingly innocuous decision of the apostles:

> In those days when the number of disciples was increasing, the Hellenist Jews among them complained against the Hebraic Jews because their widows were being overlooked in the daily distribution of food. So the Twelve gathered all the disciples together and said, "It would not be right for us to neglect the ministry of the word of God in order to wait on tables. Brothers and sisters, choose seven men from among you who are known to be full of the Spirit and wisdom. We will turn this responsibility over to them and will give attention to prayer and the ministry of the word." (Acts 6:1–5a)

Here were apostles who were taught by Jesus:

" . . . You know that the rulers of the Gentiles lord it over them, and their high officials exercise authority over them. Not so with you. Instead, whoever wants to become great among you must be your servant, and whoever wants to be first must be your slave—just as the Son of Man did not come to be served, but to serve, and to give his life as a ransom for many." (Matthew 20:25b–28)

In this text it is clear that the apostles were to serve each other and all their brothers and sisters. They were taught by Jesus to wash one another's feet (John 13:1–12). They were taught also to distribute the loaves (Matthew 14:13–21; Mark 6:34–44; Mark 8:1–10; Luke 9:10–17; John 6:1–13) when Jesus multiplied them. Perhaps they probably complained at the time that Jesus gave them this menial task.

Then surprisingly in Acts they said, "It was not right" for them "to wait on tables" lest they "neglect prayer and the ministry of the word" (Acts 6:1–5). The Greek word for "waiting on tables" is the same word for "being a servant" (διακονια). The apostles had made a major change in Jesus' message to them. Waiting on tables—serving—was part of Jesus' command to them.

Outside of commenting on this one situation, our work will not deal with the apostles or any other persons in the first century. We know that something remarkable happened after the death of Jesus, and his disciples carried the message of this remarkable event far and wide with vitality and conviction. Many of them gave their lives for him.

But like every other human being, the apostles were only flesh and blood, and they were as prone to error as the rest of us. We believe that the decision made in Acts was a terrible error, an honest mistake. Regrettably, that one decision reflects undercurrents which, in future years, would take hold, would become entrenched, and would suck the church down.

Some biblical critics question the historicity of the incident described in Acts 6. But in the history of Christianity, the incident intuits precisely what happened in the Jesus Movement. The job of serving the people was given to others, allowing "churchmen" to sit around in fancy robes and hats and meditate on, and argue about, theological matters.

The written text of Acts 6 is the first clear indication of the eventual fall of the church.

In our research, as we will document in these volumes, the following elements plague the Church. First, a group of men took initial control. Second, they separated themselves from others through meditation and dogma. Third, they exercised control over the whole church insisting that they alone had the answers concerning dogma and morality. These men decided not only what happened in the church, but also what was true and what was not true in Christianity, what was heresy and what was not, and who would suffer because they were heretics and who would not. Their arrogance, perceived infallibility, self-righteousness, and lack of communication with the real world drove the Church into its present state of near destruction.

Those who left the distribution of bread to others to concentrate on serving the "Word of God" became increasingly not disciples amazed by the person of Jesus, but an elite force, which became increasingly judgmental. Gradually, they demanded more and more respect from the laity, and they donned elaborate garments and put on airs that set them apart from the "common" Christian.

Then they began to answer to no one but to a hierarchy of their own making, a hierarchy that now demands recognition not of the presence of Jesus, but of the indispensability and ascending "infallibility" of these churchmen.

We begin in this volume with the rejects of Christian history: Marcion of Sinope, a ship builder; the Montanist women; the Arians and the Donatists. These are people who, from our research, were closer to Jesus than was the evolving, dominant Christian elite.

Some of the Church's True Gems

As we will show, the fact that the history of the church has been dominated by a number of power-hungry people does not diminish the fact that every age has known humble Christian clerics, clergy, nuns, and laypeople who have dedicated themselves to being servants, as Jesus would have them be. They are well-known and appreciated up to this very day. Every age has had its Francis of Assisi, Mother Teresa of Calcutta, Dietrich Bonhoeffer, John Wesley, Jan Hus, Peter Chelčický, Andreas Karlstadt,

Alexander Mack, Sojourner Truth, Dorothy Day, Rosa Parks, Martin Luther King Jr., etc.

These volumes are not about sincerity or the lack of it, or good intentions or the lack of them. We do not doubt that many of the church fathers, Athanasius, Arius, Ambrose, Augustine, Martin Luther, Calvin, and many others, may have been sincere. We do not doubt, either, that others, even by their own words, were not sincere in their Christian belief.

1

Marcion: The Shipbuilder in the Storm

Marcion of Sinope

Early in its history, the poison of intolerance flooded Christianity. As it will be apparent throughout this book, intolerance continued to flood church structure.

Marcion of Sinope (ca 85 CE–160 CE) was one of the many to experience the torrents of the wrath of the church fathers. Marcion is unknown to most Christians today. Yet for centuries, he unjustly was the prototype of heresy for the church's establishment. He was the tallest tree in the forest constantly attracting the lightning bolts of angry churchmen. He was the scapegoat for unacknowledged problems that had developed within the Church. But he had a much more important role than that of passive target and victim. He was a theologian of merit, a true biblical theologian.

In order to understand Marcion, it is necessary for us to first spend time in this chapter not expounding on Marcion himself, but on the culture and the social setting of his times, a setting which is in many ways foreign to us. Only then can we appreciate Marcion's place in the total picture.

In earlier days, the church suffered from disputes. Peter and Paul disputed over dining with Gentiles (Galatians 2:11–14). Paul and Barnabas had a "sharp" dispute and actually parted ways (Acts 15:39). Scholars find indications in the record of history that Paul and James showed signs of having an ongoing dispute. However, in all these cases they always considered one another brothers. They refrained from condemning each other. On the other hand, Marcion's Christian theological peers ostracized Marcion, who deeply considered himself a member in good standing in the Christian church, and they drove him into oblivion.

The overwhelming opinion of scholars today is that the early Christian Church was composed of a great variety of communities and shades of Christian beliefs. After the destruction of Jerusalem, the apostles scattered. We have no indication in the historical record that they ever again had contact with one another. There is evidence that Andrew went as far as Georgia, between the Black Sea and the Caspian Sea (see Georgia Apostolic Church Archives), Thomas went as far as India, and Bartholomew and Thaddeus went to Armenia and Asia Minor.

As the religion spread, it developed various liturgies and practices, different voices all expressing the one Jesus. These voices expressed the faith in the varying languages and customs of the people encountered. One faith developed into many different forms.

"Sailor Marcion"

Marcion from Sinope was one of these many voices speaking for Jesus in the second century. Because early Christian authorities and scholars either destroyed or never transmitted his writings to the next generation, historians today can glean little primary evidence about Marcion's life. But piecing together the data given to us by his adversaries, whose works did survive, Marcion comes across as a likeable and intelligent Christian, as well as a good theologian. Few Christians in this early period are as interesting and personable as Marcion. Few had as reputable a belief system.

Concerning some things we are almost certain: Marcion was born into a Christian family of Sinope in Asia Minor around 85 CE. His father was the bishop of Sinope and most likely the founder of the Christian church there. Alongside the Christian community in Sinope was a highly sophisticated Jewish community. Joseph Hoffmann in *Marcion: On the Restitution of Christianity* points out that Jews settled in Sinope as far back as the second century BCE, and that the scriptures used in the Christian

MARCION: THE SHIPBUILDER IN THE STORM

church were most likely a very literal and accurate rendition of the Old Testament (Hoffmann 1984, 4–5).

Born and raised in the most important commercial city on the Black Sea, Marcion was naturally drawn to the maritime world. A person with above-average talents and skills, he became a successful merchant, an accomplishment we would not ordinarily expect from a scholar of the scriptures. The church fathers, Rhodo and Tertullian, refer to him as "Sailor Marcion." But the name most often used for Marcion in Greek, ναυκλερον, implied much more than "sailor"—it implied "ship owner." Marcion was much more than just another sailor employed on someone's boat. He had many employees and owned a whole fleet of ships that sailed the Black, the Caspian, the Aegean, and the Mediterranean seas. From these enterprises Marcion became a wealthy man.

Merchant fleet owners were given the greatest respect in Roman society. Rome compensated them richly because they brought food and other resources into the empire. Accordingly, Rome exempted them from certain taxes and granted them positions of honor (Lampe 2003, 242–44).

Because of his huge income, Marcion was able to give generous donations. He also had the leisure time of a rich man. He used this time to study theology and proselytize his beliefs.

Marcion's detractors reported that the church at Sinope excommunicated him. But the evidence for such statements is suspect. If this were true, it would have been a painful blow. The people of Sinope were his own people. They were his friends, his relatives, his business partners, and his father was the bishop. Marcion would have left Sinope in a bad state of mind and spirit.

At any rate, more than likely, Marcion sailed through the empire establishing churches. We assume that he arrived in Rome around 140 CE. Peter Lampe asserts that, according to Jerome, before Marcion got to Rome he sent a woman ahead of him to prepare for his arrival (Lampe 2003, 244). While this is only a hint, with hardly any more evidence, in light of Schüssler Fiorenza's research, this hint is like a prick of conscience echoing in the tomes of history. With Catholic Church's attempts to blot out the existence of women, an anomaly such as a woman being the advance person for the mission has a great credibility. In most segments of the Jesus Movement, which later Catholics would label "heretical," women were important in leadership roles.[1] So it may be that within the Marcion movement women likewise played a leadership role.

Before the Catholic oppression beginning with Constantine (CE 312), the Marcionites may have been the largest group of Christians. Justin Martyr asserted that Marcion " with the aid of devils has caused many to speak blasphemies in every nation" (*1 Apology* 26, *ANF* 1, 170 CCEL). Tertullian claimed that Marcion and the Marcionites made churches like "wasps making combs" (*Against Marcion*, IV.5 *ANF* 3,350. CCEL). The Emperors Constantine, Theodosius, and Justinian all tried to repress them from the years 315 to 565. Cyril of Jerusalem (ca 315–386) warned visitors to Jerusalem that if they did not ask for a Catholic church, they would more than likely be directed to a Marcionite church, because Marcionites were apparently the predominant group of Christians even in Jerusalem (Hoffmann 1984,19).

Dire Situation in Rome and Marcion's Donation

While in Rome, Marcion shared a large amount of money, 200,000 cisterces (thousands of U.S. dollars) to fund the Christians' work with the poor of the city. This is evidence that Marcion was a generous man. Even his adversaries never charged him with greed.

In an attempt to cleanse the historical record, Tertullian (ca 160–ca 220) reported that the Roman Church returned Marcion's gift after he was "excommunicated" (Tertullian, *On Prescription against Heretics*, XXX, *ANF* 3, 257. CCEL). From many angles, Tertullian's statement is improbable. The fact that Marcion remained in Rome for 6 years is reason enough to challenge Tertullian. Why would the church have waited so long to give back the money? Furthermore, any statement concerning an excommunication of Marcion while he was in Rome is spurious. Tertullian lived in Carthage across the Mediterranean Sea. He could not be expected to know the details of the happenings in Rome.

But there is even more evidence that the Roman church never returned the money. The Roman scene was catastrophic. The overwhelming population was dismally poor and oppressed, living in squalid conditions. The aristocracy, composed of less than 5 percent of the population, maintained

---

[1] This will be very apparent in the next sections dealing with the Montanists, and then, later with the Bogomils, the Cathars, and then with the Waldensians.

MARCION: THE SHIPBUILDER IN THE STORM

its wealth by forced labor. Anyone outside of the circle of family, clan, and friends of the aristocracy were seen as mere supports to their good lifestyle. Thus, the bulk of the population was either slaves or surviving on the edge of slavery.

Within this grinding oppression, the church committed itself to helping the poor. It certainly was in no position to refuse money from any fellow Christian. Sociologist Rodney Stark argues that the strength of the Church was in its compassion. Christianity became an earnest response to the misery, devastation, and fear that characterized the life of the poor in the cities of the empire. To the homeless and poor, Christianity offered a constant helping hand. To the orphans and widows, it gave a loving family. To victims of plagues, fires, and earthquakes, Christianity offered nursing care. (Stark 1994,161)

The following comments from *The Apology of Aristides*, written in the first half of the second century, confirm these assertions:

> Falsehood is not found among them; and they love one another. From widows they do not turn away their esteem; orphans they deliver from anyone who treats them harshly. Those who have give to those who have not, without boasting ... And if they hear that one of their number is imprisoned or afflicted on account of the name of their Messiah, all of them anxiously minister to his needs, and if it is possible to redeem him they set him free. And if there is among them any that is poor and needy, and if they have no spare food, they fast two or three days in order to supply to the needy their lack of food. They observe the precepts of their Messiah with much care, living justly and soberly as the Lord their God commanded them. Every morning and every hour they give thanks and praise to God for His loving-kindnesses toward them; and for their food and their drink they offer thanksgiving to Him ... (*Apology of Aristides*, XV, ANF9, 276-77. CCEL)

After all that is written about Marcion, we do not believe that he had the heart to take back his money. From the church's position we cannot believe that, after 6 years, any of the money was even left.

Jesus said, "By their fruit you will recognize them" (Matthew 7:16).

CHRISTIANITY: ENDANGERED OR EXTINCT?

In the rough times, Marcion's generosity was a strong indication that his heart was based in Jesus.

Diversity in the Roman Church at Marcion's Time

The Rome that Marcion entered was not the Rome we know today. It was not the Rome with multiple, huge cathedrals and large church buildings with well-dressed clergy moving in and out. Roman Christians at the time would have laughed at such an idea. Christians gathered in 15 to 20 homes around the city. These were their churches. Each group consisted of no more than 100 members. The total number of Christians in Rome at the time, then, was no more than 1,500 to 2,000 (Thomassen. 2004, 246). Nowhere are these Christian house groups called churches (εκκλησια).

In previous eras, the analysis of church historians concerning the milieu of Christianity was found in textual evidence from the writings of such men as Ignatius, Justin Martyr, Irenaeus, and other historically respected fathers of the church, with some consideration given to pagan literature and archaeological findings. Today, many church historians use a rich variety of tools to analyze the early Christian community. They still look at the indicators given above, but they also utilize other tools, such as sociological analysis, the discursive analysis of Foucault, and feminist studies to ferret behind the written word in order to construct a more accurate understanding of the texts of history.

From a sociological and archeological perspective, James Jeffers, in *Conflict at Rome: Social Order and Hierarchy in Early Christianity*, gives an excellent description of the abysmal conditions in Rome. As with most scholars, Jeffers assumes that Christians first attended the Jewish synagogues, and then gathered for their specifically Christian worship in their homes. However, after they were blatantly expelled with curses from the synagogues, they were forced to meet only in their homes.

Most of these homes were tenement buildings for the poor, not the villas of the rich, with center gardens to enjoy. They were hovels in poor condition, one neighbor living in close proximity to other neighbors. Jeffers points out that the public buildings and the mansions of the wealthy took up over half the 16 miles of Rome, and the million or more poor people had to live within the 8 or less square miles (Jeffers 1991, 4).

MARCION: THE SHIPBUILDER IN THE STORM

These 8 square miles did not have aqueducts or sewage systems. Sewage ran down the center of the streets, and people had to get their water from a common well. It is hard to imagine the squalid conditions in which the mass of people lived. Jeffers asserts that they lived in multistoried buildings with one or two rooms where they slept, cooked, and socialized. They cooked on a common wood or charcoal-burning stove with no ventilation. Most of the time, as we can expect in such situations, several families shared one residence. Life expectancy was incredibly short.

People were afraid to go out at night for fear of being robbed. A small attachment of Roman soldiers policed the wealthy properties and kept an ear open for pending riots, but if a person who was not part of the elite population was mugged or if his or her relatives were killed, it was up to them to track down the offender and achieve justice (Jeffers 1991, 5).

Class Stratification and Hierarchical Development

As in the Jewish synagogue, class and ethnicity divided the groups of Christians. Justin Martyr and his group of Christians met over the Bath of Myrtinus. (Jeffers 1991, 42). Because Justin was a "philosopher," he probably met with more prosperous Christians. Another group met in a warehouse of the imperial family of Flavius Clemens and Flavia Domitilla. Jeffers speculates that Clement of Rome, the author of *The Epistle of I Clement*, was a leader in this group. He was "either a slave of the Imperial family of Flavius Clemens and Flavia Domitilla or a recently freed slave." He most likely received his name Clement from his master, as was the custom in slaveholding societies (Jeffers 1991, 48). According to Jeffers, this was a small group of Christians who enjoyed the protection and status of being members of the elite Roman household. Slaves and ex-slaves of an imperial household considered themselves better than the other slaves, whom they considered uncouth and illiterate. From this position of recognition, Clement became one of the prime promoters of hierarchy in the church.

Recent scholarship on Clement of Rome would support Jeffers's position. Clement shows a level of education not often found at that time in the city of Rome. His utilization of the Greek language is excellent.

While there is no way to determine the actual event that precipitated the writing of The First Epistle of Clement to the Corinthians, it is clear

CHRISTIANITY: ENDANGERED OR EXTINCT?

from the text Clement vehemently opposed what he claims is the removal of the elders of the Corinthian church by unnamed persons. Clement accuses these unnamed upstarts of being guilty of gluttony and drunkenness (1 Clement 3:1). Such charges border on the ridiculous. If anything Christians of the first and second century would most uniformly be noted for temperance. What is even more incredible than these charges is what Clement claimed was the result of this gluttony and drunkenness:

> Hence flowed jealousy and envy, strife and sedition, persecution and disorder, war and captivity. So the worthless rose up against the honored, those of no reputation against such as were renowned, the foolish against the wise, the young against those advanced in years. (I Clement 3:2, *ANF1*, 5. CCEL)

Christians of the fourth and fifth centuries certainly could be guilty of "sedition," "persecution", "war and captivity." We have, however, no indications that Christians of the first and second centuries would have ever had attitudes that would lead to such activities, and every indication that such activities would have been abhorrent to them.

In this passage Clement reveals the fact that he is from the elite classes, and that he was well educated. He was using rhetoric, the chief instrument of oral persuasion used by the dominant class. Rhetoric was the basis of the education of the elite males of the Roman Empire. Averil Cameron asserts that after Augustus Caesar established the empire in 30 BCE changes were introduced into the manner of presenting and explaining ideas. Writing and speaking were promoted as the means to enhance the empire, oneself, and one's cause. Aristotelian logic was laid aside like a worn-out toga. In its place, words were used blatantly to degrade one's opponent. (Cameron 1991, 30ff.)

Truth was not necessarily part of rhetoric's methodology. In fact, as in the case of 1st Clement, truth would get in the way of the task of rhetoric. The task of rhetoric was to vilify one's opponent in the worst possible terms. This was precisely what Clement was doing. He was vilifying his fellow Christians on a grand scale, driving home the point, utilizing couplets, synonyms, and the best rhetoric of the time. Clement is not supporting any Jesus Movement-related values in his explanation, but he is

MARCION: THE SHIPBUILDER IN THE STORM

concerned about the Roman Empire's values of peace and harmony, meaning lack of discord and the submission of those of lesser status to those in power. Clement's concern is with the "uppitiness" arising in the hearts of poorer church members. He was not concerned that these elders had to be removed because they were causing division in the body of Christ, but rather that "worthless rabble" were rising up against the honored, those of no reputation were rising up against the renowned, the foolish were rising up against the wise, and young people were rising up against those advanced in years. Within elite Roman society, not necessarily the community of Jesus, all these were considered unacceptable social behaviors.

The accusation that Clement raises is that the problems arose out of "jealousy and envy." This is the precise charge that the Emperor Constantine will raise against Alexander and Arius in the Nicene struggle of 325.[2] In classical society, the elite in society were always concerned that the lower classes were filled with "jealousy and envy." This justified the violence utilized to keep the poor and oppressed in their place and stifle any movements toward revolution against the rich and prosperous.

Anthropologists have long pointed out that within this society many of the rituals and etiquette were geared to maintaining divisions while keeping tensions down. I Clement is a document coming from a person from an elitist Christian community in Rome, a person who was intent on maintaining the status quo in society.

The important point here is that in Marcion's time, c.140-180, a group of elitist Christians were attempting to take control of the Jesus movement. Whereas in previous generations the well-off and the poor Christians shared equally, now a definite social and economic gradation of Christians was taking place.

The Value Lesson of *The Shepherd of Hermas*

The fact that this social and economic gradation is taking place is the predominant complaint in the remarkable but not well-known work, *The Shepherd of Hermas*. Despite present day unfamiliarity with *The Shepherd of Hermas*, it was held in the highest respect and was considered to be part of the Holy Scriptures by the second and third century church fathers, Irenaeus (c. 130-c. 202), Clement of Alexandria (c. 150-c. 215),

---

[2] See Chapter 7 of this volume

CHRISTIANITY: ENDANGERED OR EXTINCT?

Tertullian (c. 160-c. 220) and Origen (c. 185- c. 254). *The Shepherd of Hermas* is an apocalyptic, visionary work written in Rome by Hermas, a freed slave in the middle of the second century. This places him in Rome at the same time frame with Clement, Justin, and Marcion. Unlike Clement, a slave who thought of himself as an elite person, the Shepherd of Hermas thought of himself as a simple slave who was loved by his mistress, Rhoda. It is very clear from the various messengers of God that appear to Hermas that God was very upset with the elite in the Roman Church who were becoming arrogant and not sharing their abundance with the poor. (see particularly Carolyn Osiek 1983, 20ff; Osiek 1999, 2) One of the most poignant, revealing passages of *The Shepherd of Hermas* is the following message from the Woman Church Angel:

> Give ear unto me, O Sons: I have brought you up in much simplicity, and guilelessness, and chastity, on account of the mercy of the Lord, who has dropped His righteousness down upon you, that ye may be made righteous and holy from all your iniquity and depravity; but you do not wish to rest from your iniquity. Now, therefore, listen to me, and be at peace one with another, and visit each other, and bear each other's burdens, and do not partake of God's creatures alone, but give abundantly of them to the needy. For some through the abundance of their food produce weakness in their flesh, and thus corrupt their flesh; while the flesh of others who have no food is corrupted, because they have not sufficient nourishment. And on this account their bodies waste away. This intemperance in eating is thus injurious to you who have abundance and do not distribute among those who are needy. Give heed to the judgment that is to come. Ye, therefore, who are high in position, seek out the hungry as long as the tower is not yet finished; for after the tower is finished, you will wish to do good, but will find no opportunity. Give heed, therefore, ye who glory in your wealth, lest those who are needy should groan, and their groans should ascend to the Lord, and ye be shut out with all your goods beyond the gate of the tower. Wherefore I now say to you who preside over the Church and love the first seats, "Be not like to drug-mixers. For the drug-mixers carry their

drugs in boxes, but ye carry your drug and poison in your heart. (*Shepherd of Hermas*, Vision III, IX, ANF 2, 16. CCEL)

Here the peace that is envisioned by the angel is much different than the peace promoted by Clement. For Clement, peace arises from the absence of discord and the subjection of the lowly to those in positions of honor and wisdom. For the angel, peace comes from "looking after one another." In effect, the angel is saying, "Do not help only yourself—fooling yourself into thinking that you are the best of God's creatures, but share with one another." She warns those "in honor" that their position in life will not enrich them, but the "venom or poison" in their hearts will judge them.

Both *I Clement* and *The Shepherd of Hermas* agree on one point: a class system has developed within Roman Christianity. Clement represents those Christians who believe that because of their prestige they are entitled to priority. Hermas complained that some Christians "glory" in their wealth and ignore the plight of their poorer brothers and sisters.

Within that class system there is another element that is important in understanding Marcion. This element is the importance of literacy. According to Carolyn Osiek, Jack Goody establishes in *The Interface between the Written and the Oral* that when writing was introduced, those who could write and who could read dominated over the population that was illiterate. (Osiek 1999, 13)

Who then was the most literate in the society of Marcion's age? It was, first of all, the philosophers. This, indeed, was what Justin Martyr, Irenaeus, and Tertullian were. Another philosopher, condemned by Marcion's detractors as Marcion's co-heretic, was Valentinus, who, according to Jeffers, had a congregation that met in a villa outside of Rome. This would suggest that his group of Christians in Rome was also elite and prosperous (Jeffers 1991, 40). Valentinus, too, was a learned and prosperous man. Lampe even asserts that Valentinus most likely had more than one prosperous congregation (Lampe. 2003, 359–65).

We, likewise, must conclude that because Marcion was noted for establishing congregations, he, too, most likely established his own congregation within Rome. This community could have attracted a relatively large group in comparison to other congregations simply because of his ability to provide substantial financial support for the community. He, too, was a learned man, but he lived a life more in accord with the Shepherd of Hermas.

"Supreme Leadership" Has Not Yet Developed

Within these Christian communities in Rome, the strong central "supreme leadership" had not yet evolved. The leaders who existed in this early Christian milieu were called presbyters (πρεσβυτεροι), or bishops (επισκοποι), but no distinction in rank yet existed among them (Thomassen 2004, 246).

Church doctrine was not yet codified in a single, unvarying code. W. H. C. Frend, the preeminent church historian, stated that in Rome there was a very wide difference in thought among Christians (Frend 1984, 146; cf. M. A. Williams 1996, passim). Correspondingly, the literature that came out of the Roman Christian groups at the time showed a varied degree of tolerance. Clement, Irenaeus, Justin Martyr and Tatian would represent the least tolerant and most hierarchical group. Marcion and his followers; Prepon, Apelles, and Syneros; Ptolemy and Heracleon; a woman philosopher/theologian by the name of Marcellina, and the Shepherd of Hermas may have been the most tolerant. Valentinus and his followers have represented a level of tolerance that was in between both of those groups of Christians. All of these people were in Rome at the same time because it was the center of the empire and the world, and because of their perception that this would be the center of the church, which they desired to influence.

From Africa, across the Mediterranean, Tertullian (ca 160–ca 230) complained about the diversity in the Roman church: Tertullian charged that their general conduct was "empty, earthly, and human containing no *gravitas* [intensity], no *auctoritas* [responsibility], no *disciplina* [system for promoting true knowledge]." At their meetings, he claimed, one even found pagan outsiders (ethnici) in attendance; they made no effort, he wrote, to keep the secrets of the religion from the unbelievers. "The pearls, fake though they be, are thrown to dogs and swine" (*De praescriptione haereticorum* XLI.1–2, CSEL 70).

Among this wide variety of views, Marcion's theology did not stand out. Even if Marcion's views were considered a bit different during the 6

MARCION: THE SHIPBUILDER IN THE STORM

years that he was in Rome, they were more than likely at least tolerated, for it takes a great deal of exaggeration to see the growing church in Rome as monolithic.

It is traditionally held that Marcion's beliefs were incompatible with the church and that the church excommunicated him. However, Einar Thomassen writes that the reality was just the opposite. In a Harvard Divinity School lecture, Thomassen concludes that Marcion was not excommunicated, but resigned from the church of Rome in protest. He states "... Marcion was in Rome, urging his message of the true Christian faith. Christianity," he insisted, "is a new religion, different from both Judaism and paganism." According to Thomassen, in the summer of 144 Marcion invited the "presbyters and teachers" of the capital to debate the interpretation of Luke 5:36–37, the text concerning not putting new wine into old wineskins. Marcion was not able to convince them, and he left Rome on his own freewill. He was not kicked out (Thomassen 2004, 242–43).

Sebastian Moll, in *The Arch-Heretic Marcion*, presents a slightly different perspective. He suggests that Marcion was not so much trying to persuade the other group leaders as he was challenging them for having perverted the Jesus Movement (Moll 2010, passim, particularly 124–25). While we find Moll's reasoning particularly compelling, we do not conclude with him that Marcion was heretical.

The Primacy of Honor within the Community

Most likely it was not Marcion's theological exposition that was the heart of the problem. Here was a full-bloomed struggle for power. To get a more accurate assessment of the situation, we must examine the social milieu of the area around the Mediterranean. The main concern was not the integrity of the Gospel message, or what Jesus' message was or was not. The main concern was this: who would ascend to the position of honor within the Roman Christian community? Cultural historians and anthropologists have long stipulated that the chief operating social forces within the ancient Mediterranean world were the emotions of honor and shame.

In penetrating, essential appraisal of the Mediterranean culture, Professor Zeba Crook, Bruce J. Malina, and Richard L. Rohrbaugh greatly enhance our understanding of those who live around the Mediterranean

CHRISTIANITY: ENDANGERED OR EXTINCT?

Sea in these early centuries (See Crook 2009, 591f.; Malina and Rohrbaugh 2003, 370–71).

Crook writes that honor and shame work together and independently. She insists that they work differently in different locations, but in the Mediterranean area, past and present, honor and shame are pivotal (Crook 2009, 591f.).

Malina and Rohrbaugh clarify that honor is simply public reputation. If a person makes the wrong decision on the matter and claims more honor than the public is willing to give, he or she plays the thief or the fool. If a person hangs onto the honor, he or she has achieved the very essence of social life. Honor is essential to Mediterranean life (Malina/Rohrbaugh, 2003, 370–71). Crook gives a good summary of the power dynamics of the Roman culture:

- First, there was great sensitivity to daily living. People were terribly concerned in their activities outside of their family relations about their honor;
- Second, if there was an insult the family would have to decide on how to respond to that insult.
- "[T]hird, challenges and replies can only be made among social equals: peasants cannot threaten the honor of the king. A peasant might be beheaded for insulting the king, but that is insubordination, not as a defense of honor" (Crook 2009, 611).

This analysis is crucial for understanding the social dynamics of what transpired in the Christian community of the second century. It will be the underlying struggle occurring in every chapter in this volume.

In the Introduction, we state that the decision of the apostles in Acts 6 to become "servants of the word" marked the departure from Jesus' teaching that the disciples were to be the servants of one another. As a consequence, the disciples or the leaders of the congregations became dogmatists or theologians.

With this in perspective, the philosophers, now theologians, Polycarp, Justin Martyr, and Irenaeus believed that because of their high status in Roman society as philosophers, they should rightfully be in the same honored position within the church. They wore their philosopher's robes with great pride, but then into their midst came Marcion without philosophers' robe. He had no right to speak about theology (philosophy). Furthermore, this layman had the gall to challenge them to lay aside their philosophy and get back to the true Gospel. But people listened to him and accepted what he said. The philosophers probably reasoned that it was because he had money to buy their attention, and what's more he had a charming personality which may have meant to these philosophers that this layman was leading the congregation away from "the true philosophy."

Marcion's popularity and influence certainly was the prominent, main issue, as he stood intelligent and personable in the midst of proud philosophers. They felt it was their right and duty to control the thinking and agenda of that Roman Christian community. This desire to control resulted in their forming dogma from their philosophy. Dogma became a subterfuge for disguising real issues. Those real issues gradually and eventually strangled the church.

Valentinus

Valentinus (ca 100–ca 160) was in Rome about the same time as Marcion. He, however, is not historically as notorious as Marcion but was treated just as shabbily by the church fathers. Although there is no theological connection between the two, the history of Valentinus helps us understand what happened to Marcion.

Valentinus, like Marcion, walked away from the church of Rome because of his conflict with the hierarchical element in the church. In the minds of the church fathers, he shared the title of arch-heretic with Marcion. However, here the likeness ceases.

He remained in Rome for many years, certainly more than 15, perhaps for as long as 20 or 30 years. The fact that he remained for a longer time than Marcion would tend to indicate that he received much more acceptance than Marcion. This is the conclusion of Professor C. G. Stead in a paper titled "In Search of Valentinus," delivered at The International Conference on Gnosticism. Stead asserts that the evidence found in the church fathers did not support their charge of heresy. "The problem," he states, "is that the fragments of Valentinus taken by themselves, would give no ground for supposing anything but a Platonizing biblical theologian of some originality whose work hardly strayed beyond still undefined limits of Christian orthodoxy . . ." (Stead 1980, 75). Likewise Professor Simone Petrement, in *The Separate God: The Christian Origins of Gnosticism*, argues that for Valentinus, Platonism brought him close to the thinking of Augustine in the fifth century.

The church father who wrote the most about both Marcion and Valentinus was Tertullian, who knew the two only by hearsay. Tertullian, early in his Christian life, was capable of writing enflaming and derogatory words about anyone from hearsay evidence. After high waves and storms, he picked up any driftwood out of the seaweed, which floated from Rome to Carthage.

Thomassen writes about Tertullian's comments concerning Valentinus:

> Tertullian's contradictions suggest that he did not possess any clear information that Valentinus had been excommunicated, or even condemned by the Christian leadership. On the contrary [from] Tertullian's shifting statements—Valentinus himself left the church, he did not reveal his heretical views until a later stage in his career, it was only among Valentinus's students that Valentinianism became clearly heretical—may have been conjectures made in the absence of reliable data." (Thomassen 2004, 244)

However, in Tertullian's early days as rhetorician, "reliable data" was not necessary. He was interested only in painting the opposition in the worst possible terms and winning support for himself.

In the course of becoming a voice of influence in the church in Rome, Valentinus could have met and discussed theology with Marcion. However, there is no mention in the historical record that they even knew each other. We speculate that Marcion rejected the intrusion of Greek philosophy into the religion of Jesus, and Valentinus was just another of these philosophic corrupters of Christianity. Thus, Marcion ran headlong into the storm created by Polycarp, Justin Martyr, and Irenaeus, and perhaps even Valentinus.

The storm that they created, however, was not based on any earthly, or for that matter, heavenly reality. Justin, who was in Rome for the longest period, only mentions the Valentinians one time (*Dialogue with Trypho*, xxxv, *ANF* 1, 212), and he has two brief statements against Marcion (*The First Apology*, xxvi, lviii. *ANF* 1. 171, 182).

In all of Irenaeus's writings, he hardly mentions Marcion. In his "Preface," Irenaeus states that when he wrote about the Valentinians he was basing his comments not so much on Valentinus' ideas, but primarily on the ideas of Ptolemaeus, Valentinus' disciple (*Against Heresies*. 1, Preface 1,2, *ANF* 1, 315). More than likely, Irenaeus had little, if any, contact with Valentinus himself. Furthermore, there is no reliable evidence that any church authority in Rome condemned Valentinus or the Valentinians, or Marcion or the Marcionites at the time of their stay.

From his own words, Irenaeus was not a reliable witness. He blended both Marcion's and Valentinus's thought—a position which is untenable. He stated that both believed in "the false Father" of the Old Testament (*Against Heresies*, 4.6.4 ANF 1). He also condemned both in that they "blaspheme the Creator" (*Against Heresies*, 5.26.2, ANF 1.). We, thus, glean that Irenaeus was ignorant of the positions of Marcion and Valentinus, which were, in fact, much different.

According to Williams, Irenaeus condemns both Marcion and Valentinus with the same stroke of the pen that he condemns the Gnostics. Williams asserts that Irenaeus did not understand Gnostics either, for he believed that all heretics were Gnostics (M. A. Williams 1996, 36).[3] In fact and in reality, the recent findings of the Nag Hammadi Gnostic manuscripts give us a more objective view of the Gnostics unencumbered by the biases of the church fathers. Gnostics believed simply that salvation came through knowledge, which saved a person from the clutches of the material world—not a horrendous belief at all. Professor Petrement underscores this. She turns a corner from traditional church history when she states that the knowledge of the Gnostics was not human reason, but the knowledge, which is praised by churchmen throughout the ages. It is closer to faith. The early Gnostics spoke of faith as much as they spoke of knowledge, and surprisingly, made little distinction between the two (Petrement, 1984, 129).

At any rate, from the days of the German scholar Adolph von Harnack (1851–1930), most scholars acknowledge that Marcion was not

---

[3] Williams is here agreeing with Norbert Brox in "Γνωρτικοι als Haresiologischer Terminus" ZNW 57 (1967): 105–14.

a Gnostic. And Harnack lived in an era before the Nag Hammadi Gnostic manuscripts were found.

Marcion, Valentinus, the Shepherd of Hermas, and the Developing Hierarchy

Truly, Marcion and the Shepherd of Hermas were reformers.[4] They were echoing the words of Jesus calling for church unity in a badly divided church in Rome. The church, they believed and preached, was a spiritual seed, an entity above and beyond the cosmos, which came to earth in the one body of Christ. Likewise, the harmony that existed in the sphere, reigns above us in the heavens of divine fullness, where the eternal beings manifest unity through actions of grace and thanks, and through the singing of hymns (Thomassen 2004, 249–54).

It is a given that there is seldom only one reason for a person's actions. Thomassen is probably right in asserting that Marcion's main reason for exiting Rome was dismay over the lack of unity. We do not think he is right in asserting that Valentinus and the Valentinians left for the same reason. We think that Lampe and Stead are more accurate in suggesting that Valentinus lost out in the power struggle over the seat of the bishopric of Rome (Lampe 2003, 242–46; Stead 1980, 75). Also, Lampe suggests that both Marcion and Valentinus left Rome because Victor was asserting "the mono-episcopal system of the papacy" (Lampe 2003, 246), something that would have caused both of them consternation.

While we may never know what really happened, we think Stead's reasoning fits in well with the existing information. It would seem that Valentinus's Neo-Platonism fit well with the church fathers and that there would have been no doctrinal reasons for them to be upset with Valentinus. Furthermore, the fact that Valentinus was in Rome for a much-longer time would indicate that he was not an unsettling person to the early leadership, and would have been in line for the bishopric of Rome.

On the other hand, from everything that we know, Marcion, upset with the Platonizing of the Gospel by the church fathers, left to proclaim The True Gospel of Jesus. The fact that Marcion was upset with the

---

[4] Thomassen also includes Valentinus as a reformer, but we, with Steade and Petrement, think that he was a Platonist (see above), and we accept with Stead that he left Rome disillusioned over being passed over for bishop.

MARCION: THE SHIPBUILDER IN THE STORM

Platonists explains why we see no intrinsic connection between Valentinus and Marcion. According to Thomassen, Marcion and the Marcionites did not condemn those who did not follow them. They simply believed that these others had not yet received the true message of Jesus (Thomassen 2004, 254–55).

In contrast, the philosophers of the established society used their prestige as the educated elite to dam up and control the flow of the Jesus Movement. They formed a church on the foundations of hierarchy and subservience learned in the Platonic schools, foundations which were more to the likings of Roman emperors, current and future bishops, future popes, and various religious hierarchs, than they were to Jesus.

Marcion stuck to his firm intention of following Jesus. He founded churches, and not separate schools of Christianity.

The dam had broken. The essence of the movement of Jesus—caring for one another, tolerating one another's humanity, and loving one's enemies—was gradually swept away in the hierarchy of the age. Intolerance gushed into the Christian community. Petty differences became tidal waves. The church constructed huge breakers, which resisted differences of thought and change. Intolerance swept the church into the swamps of inhumanity and into the cesspools of divisiveness, which has lasted to our own day. Today, there are nearly 3,000 different Christian churches at clear variance with one another, often intolerant of one another's positions on theology and beliefs.

Marcion and the Church Fathers

1. JUSTIN MARTYR (100–165 CE)

One of the philosophers who was intolerant of Marcion was Justin Martyr, an eccentric man in the church of Rome. He was a "freelance philosopher with no ecclesiastical position," according to Einar Thomassen, with no "significant influence" in church matters in the evolving Roman church. He was "a withdrawn philosopher" without extensive ties to fellow Christians. Thomassen suggests that Justin could not be a good source of information for what other Christians thought. When he started to pinpoint heretical groups, he was suspect of expressing his own opinion, not that of a widespread group of Christians in Rome. When he was interrogated before his martyrdom, he admitted: "I have lived above the bath of Myrtinus, . . . and I have known no other meeting place. Whoever wished to come to my dwelling was welcome to do so, and I would give him the word of truth." Thomassen indicates that Justin Martyr's writings were preserved and utilized by future church fathers to enhance their own ideas. (Thomassen 2004, 242)

Besides the discussions that Marcion raised, there were, most likely, other discussions, even vehement discussions, within the Roman church.[5] But these were never recorded. There were many other priorities to occupy the church like the persecutors, the poor, the migrants, the hungry, etc. Furthermore, most of the Christians in Rome, even their presbyters, their leaders, were not writers or even, for that matter, literate.

Light on Justin from a Rabbi

While in his day, Justin may have lacked societal instincts and influence in the church of the time, he, according to Rabbi Daniel Boyarin in "Justin Martyr Invents Judaism," did much to define Christianity as an entity apart from Judaism. Furthermore, the Judaism that Justin describes is not a true picture of Judaism according to Boyarin (Boyarin 2001, 35ff.).[6] But Boyarin asserts that Justin does not stop with Judaism. His invention of Judaism also precipitated the invention of his own vision of Christianity (Boyarin 2001, 35ff.).

Boyarin's evidence is significant. He stipulates that Justin was responsible for introducing into Christianity the concept of heresy (Boyarin 2001, 12). For this alone, Justin deflated the inclusive Gospel message and sent it plummeting downward to the point that even Jesus would not recognize it.

---

[5] We know that Valentinus's ideas were discussed, but, as Thomassen stated earlier, the church did not excommunicate him. We know that a person by the name of Hermas was in a leadership role in the church. However, we do not know how much support his thought, as indicated in *The Shepherd of Hermas*, was received by the churches.

[6] Boyarin asserts that Justin took the Hebrew word *'Am 'Ha'ares*, which meant people of the earth, or unclean, uncouth person, and used the word to describe a person who was not in accord with the true faith, or as we would say today, a "heretic." At one time in the early Christian period, when doctrine was not yet defined, *haeresis* meant "choice," the accepting of a different school of thought. All the various schools spoken of, however, were Christian. (See Walter Bauer, *Orthodoxy and Heresy in Earliest Christianity*, 2nd German ed., translated by George Strecker, Philadelphia Seminar on Christian Origins. Philadelphia: Fortress Press, 1971); also, Marcel Simon. "From Greek hairesis to Christian Heresy," Early Christian Literature and the Classical Intellectual Tradition: In Honorem Robert M. Grant, ed. William R. Schoedel and Robert L. Wilken, 101–16, Theologie Historique, 54. Paris: Editions Beauchesne, 1979).

MARCION: THE SHIPBUILDER IN THE STORM

As far as the Christian faith is concerned, Justin's sins go deeper. Justin reached his lowest point when he went so far as to identify Plato as a Christian. He indicated that he found elements of the Gospel in Plato's works. He wrote in his *Hortatory Address to the Greeks*:

> Here Plato seems to me to have learnt from the prophets not only the doctrine of the judgment, but also of the resurrection.... For his saying that the soul is judged along with the body, proves nothing more clearly than he believed the doctrine of the resurrection. (Chapter XXV, ii, *ANF* 1, 283 CCEL)

Marcion would have found this to be beyond belief. No Christian today, no theologian, would accept this as an orthodox statement. As much as Justin would have liked to unite his life as a follower of Plato with his life as a follower of Jesus, his Plato who lived in ca 427–347 BCE had no knowledge of the Jesus who was to come 400 years later. Plato's philosophy is found in ideas, which emanate from God, and it has nothing in common with the life, death, and resurrection of Jesus. Most Christians of the first and second century who experienced the hardships of Christian living would have thought that Justin was not only stretching reality to the breaking point, but also cheapening the faith.

In his introduction to Justin Martyr's works in *The Ante-Nicene Fathers*, Cleveland Coxe commends Justin's blending of philosophy and Christianity. He claimed:

> He wore his philosopher's gown after his conversion as a token that he had attained the only true philosophy [that of Plato and the Greeks]. And seeing, that, after the conflicts and tests of ages, it is the only philosophy that lasts and lives and triumphs, its discoverer deserves the homage of mankind. (*ANF* 1, 160. CCEL)

Even Adolph von Harnack speaks positively of Justin's blending of Greek philosophy and Christianity:

> As Catholicism, from every point of view, is the result of the blending of ideas from antiquity, so the Catholic dogmatic, as it was developed after the second or third century on the basis of the

CHRISTIANITY: ENDANGERED OR EXTINCT?

Logos doctrine, is Christianity conceived and formulated from the standpoint of Greek philosophy of religion…The union of Christian religion with a definite phase of human knowledge and culture may be lamented in the interest of the Christian religion. But lamentations become here ill-founded assumptions, as absolutely everything that we have and value is due to the alliance that Christianity and antiquity concluded in such a way that neither was able to prevail over the other. (Harnack 1922, 1976, 13–14)

Coxe, in a footnote to the works of Justin, affirms Harnack's positive assessment of the influence of Greek philosophy on Christianity when he states that Justin's thought "… survives in the pulpits of Christendom—Greek, Latin, Anglican, Lutheran, etc.—to this day, in slightly different forms" (*ANF*, 1, 160.CCEL). While their picture of the influence of philosophy on Christianity is accurate, the reality is far from sanguine. Rodger Cragun gives a different picture:

Professor Harnack [first] published this work in 1886 when Germany as a united nation was in its youth and beginning to flex its muscles. Industrialism was growing by leaps and bounds, and wealth was multiplying exponentially. I cannot help but wonder, if Harnack had lived to 1945 and had seen all of Europe devastated, whether he would have had such a positive assessment of the amalgamation of Greek thought and Christianity. I would like to have been able to say to Harnack that much of 'everything that we have and value' has provided much devastation and pain in the world and that the 'alliance of Christianity and antiquity' has allowed people like Otto von Bismarck, King Wilhelm, and German Lutherans and Catholics to live schismatic lives and inflict havoc on God's world. In essence the absorption of Greek philosophical thought into Christianity has meant the subversion of Christianity and the transformation of it from the kingdom of God to the kingdom of this world. (Cragun 1996, 158)

MARCION: THE SHIPBUILDER IN THE STORM

Certainly Greek philosophy is not destructive in itself. It is not evil. If it does not merit Christian standing ovations, it also does not merit its condemnation. The advancement of civilization owes much to Plato, Aristotle, Archimedes, and the other great Greek philosophers. The point is—Greek philosophy can hold but a candle to Jesus. Contrary to the words of Justin, Plato neither spoke the words of Jesus, nor could he stand side by side with Jesus as coequals. Marcion agreed.

Marcion, Victim of Rhetoric

Clement of Rome, Justin, Tertullian, Hippolytus, and Epiphanius were well educated and trained in rhetoric. As we stated above, rhetoric in writing and speaking was used to promote and enhance the empire, oneself, and one's cause. Aristotelian logic was laid aside like a worn-out toga. In its place, words were used blatantly to degrade one's opponent. Justin Martyr was a prime example. In good rhetorical fashion in his *First Apology*, Justin wrote the following about Marcion:

> And there is Marcion, a man of Pontus, who even to this day is alive and teaching his disciples to believe in some other God greater than the creator. And he, by the aid of the devils, has caused many of every nation to speak blasphemies, and to deny that God is the maker of this universe by stating that some other being, greater than the creator has done greater works. All who take their opinions from these men are, as before said, called Christians.... This man many have believed as if he alone knows the truth and they laugh at us even though they have no proof of what they say. They are carried away irrationally as lambs by a wolf and they become the prey of atheistic doctrines and devils.... (1. xxvi, lviii, *ANF* 1, 171, 182 CCEL)

2. TERTULLIAN (CA. 160-CA. 220)

Later, Tertullian, from Carthage in North Africa, shows just how far a rhetorician could go to defame a perceived opponent. Tertullian used caustic sarcasm to attack Marcion. He first attacked the very place

CHRISTIANITY: ENDANGERED OR EXTINCT?

where Marcion lived on the Black Sea. He wrote in graphic and derogatory terms:

> The Euxine Sea, as it is called, is self-contradictory in its nature and deceptive in its name. It is not what a civilized person would call an uxorial or hospitable sea. It is situated in the poorest of places, severed from our more civilized waters, and it carries a certain stigma of a barbarous character. (Against Marcion. I .1, *ANF* 3, 271CCEL)

Tertullian does not here attack Marcion's ideas, but the place from which he came. This is like writing off Ernest Hemingway because he came from Cicero, Illinois, or, for that matter, questioning whether anything good can come out of Nazareth, as Nathaniel first said about Jesus in John 1:46. It makes no sense, but it is typical of the rhetoric of the empire. Tertullian goes on in the same vein:

> The fiercest nations inhabit it... They have no fixed abode; their life has no germ of civilization; they indulge their lustful desires without restraint, and their bodies are for the most part naked.... They cut up the dead bodies of their parents, and they devour them with their sheep at their feasts...Their women do not show the gentleness of the fair sex. They show no modesty. They uncover their breasts in order to suspend their battle-axes from them, and they prefer warfare to marriage. (Tertullian, *Against Marcion*, I.1, *ANF* 3, 271. CCEL)

How could any person in this present day read these words without breaking into hysterical laughter? No comic could do better. But Tertullian was one of the best rhetoricians. While we find his comments humorous, he was serious, and the church took him seriously![7] We can only wonder what the bishop of Sinope, Marcion's own father, would have thought of Tertullian's description of the moral condition of his diocese.

---

[7] In the next chapter, we will see that the church later declared Tertullian a heretic, yet they base most of their thinking about Marcion on Tertullian's reasoning.

MARCION: THE SHIPBUILDER IN THE STORM

Tertullian even took on the climate of the place in order to make Marcion look like a barbarian:

> The climate of the place shows the same unruly nature. The daytime is never clear; the sun is never cheerful; the sky is always cloudy; the whole year is wintry. The only wind that blows is the angry north wind.... All things are disruptive—all stiff with cold....

Tertullian goes on:

> Nothing however in Pontus is so barbarous and sad as the fact that Marcion was born there. He was fouler than any Scythian, . . . more inhuman than the Massagite, more audacious than an Amazon, darker than the Pontic cloud, colder than its winter, more brittle than its ice....Nay, more, the true Prometheus, Almighty God, is mangled by Marcion's blasphemies. Marcion is more savage than even the beasts of the barbarous region. (Tertullian, Against Marcion, I.1, *ANF* 3, 271. CCEL)

This was typical of the discourse of the philosophers who became Christian theologians. They placed themselves on a slippery slope leading to Christian and even human degradation. Both Justin Martyr and Tertullian wrote their words about a man whom they knew only through hearsay and through his only known work, now extinct, *Antithesis*.

3. HIPPOLYTUS (CA 170–CA 236)

Hippolytus, another of Marcion's detractors, lambasted Marcion by saying he was a disciple of Empedocles (Hippolytus, *Refutation of All Heresies* III. VII. xvii–xviii, *ANF5*, 110-112). Empedocles lived in 492–430 BCE, and he was a light for his own time, but not for Marcion's time. Linking Marcion to a pre-Christian Greek philosopher was another stretch of reality. There is no evidence that Marcion had philosophical training. If anything, Marcion reacted negatively to the intrusion of philosophy into Christianity.

CHRISTIANITY: ENDANGERED OR EXTINCT?

Here is just a sample of what Hippolytus said,

> But Marcion, a native of Pontus, far more frantic than these (heretics), omitting the majority of the tenets of the greater number (of speculators), (and) advancing into a doctrine still more unabashed, supposed (the existence of) two originating causes of the universe, alleging one of them to be a certain good (principle), but the other an evil one. And himself imagining that he was introducing some novel (opinion), founded a school full of folly, and attended by men of a sensual mode of life, inasmuch as he himself was one of lustful propensities. (*Refutation of All Heresies*, III. VII, xvii, ANF 5, 110)

As Marcion was not a philosopher, nor had he any relations with philosophers, there is not any evidence that he founded a school of any sort. Furthermore, as we shall see there is no evidence that he had "lustful propensities."

4. Epiphanius, bishop of Cyrenia (350–403)

Approximately 150 years later, Epiphanius picked up on Hippolytus's accusation and in good rhetorical fashion, took it to the back alley:

> He was by birth Pontic. That is from . . . Sinope...From the first part of his life he practiced virginity. For he was an ascetic and the son of a bishop of our holy Catholic church. But in the course of time, unfortunately, he met a virgin, deceived her, and drew both her and himself down from that in which they had put their hopes. Having seduced her, he was expelled from the Church by his own father. For his father was illustrious on account of his piety, had a great concern for the Church, and was outstanding in his exercise of the Episcopal office. Time and again, Marcion begged and beseeched his father for a chance to repent, but did not get it...(*Panarion* XIII. 42, 1. 3–4. 144)

Even in our own times with our electronic tools, we struggle to discern historical events with accuracy. How could Epiphanius know so much about the intimate details of Marcion's life when Marcion lived 200 years before him? Beyond the rhetoric, which we find on the written page, we have no reason to believe in Marcion's sexual immorality. Robert Smith Wilson points out that "it is significant that in all the remarks written about Marcion by other fathers of the church, no one—not Irenaeus, not Rodon, not the Alexandrians, not Eusebius, and not even Tertullian—ever mentions such a thing" (Wilson 1933, 46). Furthermore, John Knox states in *Marcion and The New Testament*: "If there had been grounds for the accusation, Tertullian would have known about it, and if he had known about it, he was not the kind of man to be silent about it" (Knox 1942, 2).

Jennifer Wright Knust, in *Abandoned to Lust: Sexual Slander in Ancient Christianity*, asserts that accusing opponents of sexual indiscretions was standard practice for the fathers. She states that the fathers defined "virtue in such a way that they, and they alone, were capable of sexual self-mastery; everyone else was said to be incurably debauched" (Knust, 2006, 3–4). Consistent with Knust's thought, the fathers flung these charges in what they perceived as "fierce struggles for identity, prestige, and power." "These accusations," according to Knust, "do not offer straightforward evidence of sexual practice; rather, they indicate a conflict between the author and those whom he maligned (Knust 2006, 6)."

Knust well-defines the attitude of Hippolytus and Epiphanius in these words: "Engaging in a 'solemn act of naming,' the followers of Jesus sought to define their group by representing themselves as sexually virtuous and their enemies as sexually degenerate. In the process, a 'Christian' became someone who exhibits self-mastery" (Knust 2006, 10). So Marcion, in the church fathers' minds, was simply degenerate, and this fit nicely with the horrid charges they pinned on him.

Recent Tributes to Marcion

In the recorded history of the Catholic Church, Marcion was clearly the more influential of the two "arch-heretics." In *The Rise of Christianity*, Frend summed up Marcion's activities:

> Tertullian declared that Marcion planted churches "as wasps make nests." His heretical tradition "filled the whole world." In fact, apart from Rome and Carthage, we hear of Marcionite churches in

CHRISTIANITY: ENDANGERED OR EXTINCT?

Nicomedia on the Asiatic side of the Sea of Marmara, at Smyrna, in Phrygia, Gortyna, at Antioch, and, above all, in northern and eastern Syria... (Frend 1984, 215–16; see also Thomassen 2004, 253)

Frend further stipulates that Marcion claimed no special position among his church members. He gave converts his version of the New Testament, and let the Lord do the rest (Frend 1984, 216). Further, F. L. Cross in *The Early Christian Fathers* points that the sect Marcion started "spread rapidly and was one of the greatest challenges that Catholic Christianity ever had to face" (Cross 1932, 40).

Probably the scholar who was most responsible for raising Marcion's stock from the dregs of the ecclesiastical dump was the great German historian and theologian, Adolph von Harnack, in his classic work, *The Gospel of the Alien God (Marcion, das Evangelium vom fremdem Gott*, 1921, 1990). His defense of Marcion is still accepted by scholars today. Due to his research we know that the only part of Marcion's work *Antithesis* to survive is the first sentence. This sentence is celebrated for its praise of the Gospel. Seldom in history has anyone praised the Gospel so well: "O wonder beyond wonders, rapture, power and amazement is it, that one can say nothing at all about the Gospel, nor even conceive of it, nor compare it with anything" (*Antithesis* 1, 1). In this, he sounded like Francis of Assisi, Martin Luther, and Karl Barth.

Harnack points out that Tertullian quoted Marcion as saying: "One work is sufficient for our God; he has delivered man by his supreme and most excellent goodness, which is preferable to [the creation of], all the locusts [symbol for the Old Testament]." For Marcion, redemption was so complete that he did not think that anything could be added. What came before was empty and meaningless in comparison.

In his attempts to rescue Marcion from the ash heaps of history, Harnack makes the following points which most contemporary scholars accept as valid descriptions of Marcion's thought:

1. Marcion never proposed, nor did he intend to propose, a complete doctrinal system.
2. Even though Irenaeus, Tertullian, and Hippolytus accused Marcion of being a Gnostic, Marcion refused to appeal to any

MARCION: THE SHIPBUILDER IN THE STORM

special knowledge "gnosis" granted to him. He was then not a Gnostic. He saw himself no better than others, striving to struggle with his own human mind and spirit to understand Jesus and the meaning of the new Christian era.

3. He was a theologian strictly rooted in the scriptures. His sources were exclusively the Gospel of Luke and Paul's epistles. His doctrinal interventions into the text are minimal.
4. In the churches that he formed after his excommunications, different doctrinal principles were freely and easily explored by the members of those churches without causing divisions or splits in his church.
5. He stuck exclusively to the literal sense when quoting scripture. He never drifted into allegory or any other sense of scripture.
6. He never indulged in philosophy, which he considered "vain deceit." He was strongly against the Logos theology of the Greeks (Harnack 1921, 1990, 65–92, our summary).

Certainly Marcion was not guilty of wrapping Christianity in the cloak of pagan Greek philosophy, but certainly his detractors were. Their Christianity was established on a concept of truth based on abstractions which Jesus, in his Palestinian, Aramaic culture, would have found totally foreign and nonsensical. For example, they, like Plato and Aristotle, thought that to be in error in thought was to wallow in the worst of sins. For Jesus, sin was much more than error in thinking. Sin was a matter of the heart and proceeded from the corruption of being.

These philosopher/theologians equated Jesus with the logos of Greek philosophy, certainly a contention that is impossible to equate with Jesus' own actions and words. Of course, in the minds of the church fathers, their reasoning was without error and divinely inspired. The sad fact is their thought has permeated and shaped Christian theology for thousands of years. (See Cragun 1996, 145–50)

The question then must be: if heretics existed in Marcion's time, who were the heretics—Marcion or his detractors? If Marcion was a heretic, he certainly lived in good, accepted company. No, we can say it much better: Marcion was a sincere and faithful follower of Jesus, and his detractors were good Platonic philosophers who led the church away from Jesus.

Modern Reassessment of Marcion

In the last two to three decades, scholars have been introducing some earthshaking conclusions. Before we get to that analysis, there are some conclusions about Marcion which we can be fairly certain are accurate:

1. Marcion was a Christian in a time when there were some extreme consequences for being Christian. Otherwise, he could very easily have lost his life and found himself on one of those crosses he saw standing around the Mediterranean Sea. We must conclude that he was sincere.
2. He was willing to share his immense wealth with his brothers and sisters in Christ Jesus.
3. He was intensely committed to the Gospel and its implications for this life.

Today, some of the research that is coming out suggests that many of the assumptions about Marcion are being questioned. But the end result of the research suggests that Marcion was not an extreme fanatic at all, and certainly not a heretic.

Heresy and Identity in Antiquity

The charge of "heresy" was a a common theme of the rhetoric of the fathers. By this time, the fathers threw the label around like mud in a pigpen. In his characteristic good humor, John Knox wrote:

> All the great Christian teachers of the period—the authors of the Fourth Gospel, of Hebrews and of Revelations, Ignatius, Polycarp, Clement, Papias, Marcion, Tatian, and many others—were orthodox or heretical, according to the point of view of the critic. (Knox 1942, 4)

Then Knox quips: "One may claim that in a sense this is always true. 'Orthodoxy' is always 'our own doxy....'" (Knox 1942, 4). Analysis of heresy in the present day has taken on much deeper analysis thanks indeed to much of the insights of Michel Foucault. With Foucault, it is never what

MARCION: THE SHIPBUILDER IN THE STORM

is said that is important, but the power behind what is said. What is seen today simply as a difference of opinion on issues, heresy, in today's sociological analysis, is seen as an essential threat to the life of the community. William Arnal, in "Doxa, Heresy, and Self-Construction," explains well:

> ... [W]hat is really at issue for both the heretic and those who aim to suppress heresy is a way of living, a set of structured assumptions built into social practice to the benefit of particular groups of people, which heretical ideas or, better, expressions threaten to disrupt. It is for this reason that genuine heresy elicits such a strong repressive reaction... (Arnal 2008, 62)

What we see in early Christian literature, certainly in Ignatius and Barnabas, is the setting of boundaries between Judaism and Christianity. Jewish literature shows a similar setting of boundaries in the expulsion of Christians from Judaism. The writings of I Clement, Justin Martyr, Hippolytus, and Irenaeus are attempts to blend the radical egalitarian Jesus Movement within the classic Roman civilization. This is to say that what was happening was the evolution, or better the devolution of the movement. Most original characteristics of the Jesus Movement were still gasping their last breaths within the new hierarchical, philosophical movement. Certainly, compassion and love of enemy still existed within the community, but the cultural transformation was well on its way. The mores of the dominant culture were becoming the mores of the Jesus Movement. This transformation was what Marcion faced and could not accept.

2

Marcion's Place in a Violent World

In the last Chapter we dealt with the interactions of Marcion and the "church fathers." We pointed out that it was not Marcion who changed the Jesus Movement, but rather the "church fathers" that corrupted the Church by wrapping it in Greek philosophy. We thus suggested that, while Marcion may have been a heretic, the "church fathers" more than likely were greater heretics. However, in the power dynamics of the dominant society, the "church fathers" were more representative of the thought of the elite of the dominant society. The "church fathers" were thus able to make Christianity more palatable to those in power. Consequently, the "church fathers" were the victors. They recorded history and branded Marcion as the "arch-heretic".

In this chapter we will point to the fact that increasing number of scholars believe that Marcion might have been much closer to traditional "orthodox" views than most church historians and the "church fathers" have portrayed him. The major heresy that the church fathers imputed to Marcion was a belief in two gods, the god of the Old Testament and the God of Jesus and salvation. We will suggest that, if he had these beliefs, they more than likely arouse out of the extreme violence in the Roman Empire. Because of novels and movies most contemporary people have a concept of the violence in the Roman Empire. They can easily imagine a picture of the coliseum with gladiators slaughtering Christians; they imagine emperors, in a victory celebration, parading captive slaves into Rome. While some of these perceptions are accurate, they only present an

MARCION'S PLACE IN A VIOLENT WORLD

aspect of the empire that can be conveniently glamorized or dramatized. G. E. M. de Ste. Croix drives home the true, stark realities in the Roman Empire in *The Class Struggle in the Ancient Greek World*. He abundantly documents that it was only through violence and the threat of violence that the Roman Empire and the elite, wealthy citizenry could cling to their power. The slaughter of 400 slaves after the murder of their master, a Roman senator, by a single slave, shows the horrendous brutality in the Roman Empire. De Ste. Croix quotes Roman senator and lawyer Gaius Cassius: "You will not restrain that scum except by terror." (de Ste. Croix 1981, 245)

In the second through the fourth centuries, the empire was in rapid decline, and the elite were increasingly worried about losing their luxurious lifestyle. As with the prosecution of the slaves above, any groups that showed any sign of dissent against the Roman elite were savagely put down. Due to their significant differences from the elite Roman culture, Christians were considered to be one of those groups marked for severe treatment.

From his trips around the Black Sea and the Mediterranean Sea, Marcion, the paramount sailor, would have known firsthand and by word-of-mouth the misery that Christians were facing. One of the best indications of the threat to Christians that Marcion saw was highlighted in a letter sent to Emperor Trajan around 111–112 CE by Pliny the Younger (61–113 CE), the governor of Pontus, the province from which Marcion came. Pliny wrote:

> ... [I]n the case of those who were denounced to me as Christians, I have observed the following procedure: I interrogated these as to whether they were Christians; those who confessed I interrogated a second and third time, threatening them with punishment; those who persisted I ordered executed. (*Pliny's Letters* Volume 2, 10:96–97, *Loeb Classics*, Vol. 55, 401)

Of course, when he says "interrogated," he means interrogated *through torture*. The emperor responded to Pliny that he was acting properly.

It is well accepted today that in the empire, persecutions of Christians were sporadic, not universal. But at the same time, persecutions were more than flies on the noses of Christians. Tertullian complained: "If the Tiber floods to the walls, if the Nile floods not the fields, if the sky gives no rain, if the earth shakes, if there is famine or pestilence, immediately comes the cry 'The Christians to the Lion!'" (*Apology*, 40, 48 *ANF* 3. CCEL)

Seen in this light, the Christian position was precarious. Marcion was well aware of all of this. The Romans lined the roads to all the major cities with the crosses on which hung the revolutionaries and even those who were merely suspected of revolutionary activities.

Marcion Faces the Violence around Him

In the last chapter, in the discussion over the struggle for power in the Jesus Movement, we left out any mention of how violence played a roll in that struggle. In our discussions so far involving Marcion, we have not reported that Irenaeus, Justin Martyr, and Polycarp acted "violently" toward Marcion, nor did we report that they and the other Christians constantly threatened violence against Marcion and his followers.

It is true that the stark physical violence of the Roman Empire had not yet intruded itself upon the Jesus movement, but it was lurking around the corner in the male dominance that was grasping for control of the movement. As we reported in the introduction, the incident in Acts 6: 1-4, where the "apostles" assert that they should be about prayer and being servants of the Word, represented the apostles elevating themselves over their brothers or sisters. More than likely this act of elevation of "the apostles" portrays the situation within the church several generations removed from the first disciples. Certain males, like the philosophers whom we have been discussing in relationship to Marcion, may have felt that such a story would help solidify their leadership roles.

Most feminist scholars, such as Elisabeth Schüssler Fiorenza, Paula Fredriksen, Elisabeth Clark and a host of others, prove that in the early Jesus movement women were very much in leadership roles. Furthermore, noted Historical Jesus scholars, John Dominic Crossan and Jonathan L. Reed, assert that contrary to many modern feminists, who consider Paul the arch villain, Paul, himself, was very much an egalitarian. The problem that the feminists have with Paul is, according to Crossan and Reed, derived from pseudo-Pauline epistles (1&2, Timothy, Ephesians, Colossians, 2 Thessalonians, and Titus), and the later textual editing of genuine Pauline epistles. (Crossan and Reed 2004, 105-120) As we saw in the last chapter, women must have played an active role in Marcion's church. In the same time frame as Marcion, and in Asia minor, women, called Montanists by their detractors, and whom we will discuss in the next three chapters, played a leading role within the Jesus Movement.

The question must be raised: if the Jesus movement was so egalitarian, how is it possible for the Christian Church to become so oppressive to women? We think Michel Foucault has some help in answering this question. In *Knowledge and Power* he states:

> ...power is not to be taken to be a phenomenon of one individual's consolidated and homogeneous domination over others, or that of one group or class over others. What, by contrast, should always be kept in mind is that power... is not that which makes the difference between those who exclusively possess and retain it, and those who do not have it and submit to it. Power must by analysed as something which circulates, or rather something which only functions in the form of a chain. It is never localised here or there, never in anybody's hands, never appropriated as a commodity or piece of wealth. Power is employed and exercised through a net-like organization...They [individuals] are not only its inert or consenting target; they are always also the elements of its articulation. In other words, individuals are the vehicles of power, not its points of application.(Foucault 2003, 98)

This is a very profound and a summary statement of much of Foucault's thought. Looked at from our *People's History of Christianity* perspective it must be stated that women or other oppress groups, such as the Marcionites, Montanists, Arians or any other "despised" group of the dominant "orthodox" church, were never simply passive receptors of oppression. Their routes to silence or their acceptance of their inferior status has never been easy and never been complete.

The evidence that the voices of women particularly were never totally suppressed is latent within the texts of the New Testament. As we have pointed out scholars like Schüssler Fiorenza, Crossan, Reed and many others have found indications of egalitarianism of Jesus' followers within the texts. This is despite the fact that these texts were edited, compiled and redacted by persons (males) in the elite, dominant class whose interest in their self-promotion was to cover up the fact that there were any other opinions or that those opinions were evil in the first place. The problem is that the church "net of power" that was developed had many different "threads" in it from women, heretics and the poor, which are now just being examined by the scholars.

Foucault states that when societies become oppressive, and when those oppressors are overcome, their conquerors in turn will become oppressors. Jesus himself said: Cast out one devil and seven others will replace it. Foucault asserts that those who make the rules make them in their own favor:

> The nature of these rules allows violence to be inflicted on violence and the resurgence of new forces that are sufficiently strong to dominate those in power. Rules are empty in themselves, violent and un-finalized; they are impersonal and can be bent to any purpose. The successes of history belong to those who are capable of seizing these rules, to replace those who had used them, to disguise themselves so as to pervert them, invert their meaning, and redirect them against those who had initially imposed them; controlling this complex mechanism, they will make it function so as to overcome the rulers through their own rules.[8]

Foucault calls this type of maneuvering "power discourse." Philip Esler in "God's Honor and Rome's Triumph," relates Foucault's thought to ancient Rome and the Jews:

> This type of ideology or power/discourse can be seen in the outlook of the Romans. Accompanying their vast imperial subjugation was an imperial ideology. It is expressed unashamedly by the Augustan poet Virgil in the Aeneid in a passage which describes one aspect of it as *parcere subiectis et debellare superbos* (6.853). I paraphrase: "Grovel and live; resist and die." (Esler 1995, 240)

---

[8] Cited in Esler (1995. 240).

MARCION'S PLACE IN A VIOLENT WORLD

Foucault shows that the power of the victor creates a counterforce in the vanquished and is expressed in resistance (Foucault 1980, 109–44; see volume 1, *History of Sexuality* in toto). Esler points out this resistance in certain Jewish apocryphal works. From 2 Baruch, he quotes: "The last ruler that is alive will be bound, whereas the entire host will be destroyed, and they will carry him on Mount Zion, and my anointed one will convict him of all his wicked deeds . . . And after these things, he will kill him. . ."

Then Esler goes on:

> This scene plainly constitutes a parody of the Roman triumph. What the Romans dealt out to the Jews will be paid back to them with interest. In Foucault's terms, we have here an inversion of the Roman processes of violence and their re-direction against those who had originally imposed them. The rulers will be overcome by their own rules. The Messiah will visit the Roman ideology of debellare superbos upon Rome itself. Rome's triumph will become God's. At the heart of the artistic achievement of 2 Baruch, therefore, lies an on-going conflict, a progression from combat to combat installed in a mythological framework spanning the remote past and the distant future. (Esler 1995, 255)

Such discourse is found in 2 Baruch, the Qumran documents- particularly the War Scroll- and likewise in many books of the New Testament- particularly *The Book of Revelation*. It is interesting to note that the Gospels of John and Matthew have the most passages of retribution whereas the Gospel of Luke, which was Marcion's Gospel (see below), has the least passages calling for retribution. Matthew and John were written 50 to 70 years after Jesus' death and resurrection. The fact that there is so much retribution in them may indicate a transformation of the Jesus Movement from a movement where love of enemy and forgiveness of sins predominated, into a discourse of domination, where getting even had begun to permeate. For instance, Matthew 22 reads:

> Then he sent some more servants and said, 'Tell those who have been invited that I have prepared my dinner: My oxen and fattened cattle have been butchered, and everything is ready. Come to the wedding banquet.' But they paid no attention and went

off—one to his field, another to his business. The rest seized his servants, mistreated them and killed them. The king was enraged. He sent his army and destroyed those murderers and burned their city. Then he said to his servants, 'The wedding banquet is ready, but those I invited did not deserve to come. So go to the street corners and invite to the banquet anyone you find.' So the servants went out into the streets and gathered all the people they could find, the bad as well as the good, and the wedding hall was filled with guests. But when the king came in to see the guests, he noticed a man there who was not wearing wedding clothes. He asked, 'How did you get in here without wedding clothes, friend?' The man was speechless. Then the king told the attendants, 'Tie him hand and foot, and throw him outside, into the darkness, where there will be weeping and gnashing of teeth.' "For many are invited, but few are chosen." (Matthew 22:4-42)

Depending on one's theological perspective, verse seven could have had two different interpretations. Either Jesus was predicting the destruction of Jerusalem, or the Christian (Jewish) editor, angered at his fellow Jews' rejection of Jesus as the Messiah, saw the destruction of Jerusalem as not only Rome's chastisement of Israel for its insurrection, but also divine wrath. Neither perspective, that of the prophecy or the editor's interpretation, square with Jesus' final request: "Father, forgive them, for they do not know what they are doing (Luke 23:34)." We would assume then, that if Jerusalem was destroyed because the Jews did not come to Jesus' banquet, that God did not grant Jesus' final prayer.

The important point here is not that the Christians were devising retribution for the Jews or the Romans. They, by far, were not in a position to reign down retribution upon anybody, but they, in their anger for the violence inflicted on them, were looking forward to the day when that violence would be poured out on their enemies. That day would come when Emperor Constantine became a "Christian." This, of course, was not the way of Jesus. But the way of the world was beginning to predominate within the church. One could have wished it were different, but if violence immersed the Roman Empire, it is not surprising that it influenced the religion of the Roman Empire.

MARCION'S PLACE IN A VIOLENT WORLD

As we have pointed out, well-educated philosophers from the upper echelons of society dominated the power struggle going on within the Jesus Movement. They were not the poor, the slaves, and the lower elements of the Roman society, who were, in truth, the heart and soul of the Jesus Movement. They were rather philosophers who had learned well the empire's attitudes toward control and subjugation.

We would like to believe that somehow the Christian faith of these people might have changed their attitude toward those who differed with them. But their own record does not support that belief. Jesus had very little, if any, impact on their attitudes certainly and primarily toward Marcion. They used a tool of the empire's elite, rhetoric, to attempt to shame and destroy him. Marcion had no chance once the philosophers took the reins of Jesus' community. Marcion especially stood mystified, shaking his head in the face of such arrogance.

This was no way for them to treat a Christian brother, and a Christian brother is exactly what Marcion was. We cannot underscore enough the fact that in Marcion's day, to be a follower of Jesus was life threatening. It took considerable courage for Marcion to be a Christian. Furthermore, as we stated, there was considerable evidence from Marcion's generosity and attitude that he was a true follower of Jesus.

Despite the fact that Justin Martyr, Irenaeus, Hippolytus, and Clement were not in the position within society to wield the tools of physical violence, their rhetoric was violent. If they would have had the opportunity and weapons, they more than likely have violently suppressed Marcion and any other perceived threat to their power.

This verbal, psychological violence fomented the physical violence of Ambrose toward the Arians and Goths, of Augustine toward the Donatists, and of the inquisitions and crusades, and of the later wars of the Roman Catholics and Protestants. The incidences of Christians inflicting violence on other Christians and non-Christians have always been a sad commentary on the degeneration of the Jesus movement.

Violence: The Romans, the Christians, and the Jews

With the Roman Empire's ever-increasing internal and external struggles in the first, second, and third centuries, the need to control dissenting groups became paramount. While Jews being strict monotheists and culturally different might have been considered dissenters, the Romans had accepted the Jews as a legal and ancient group. Judaism was bestowed that acceptance in 47 BC. In that year, Julius Caesar defeated Pompey and gained control of the Roman Empire. Hyrancus II, a Maccabbean high priest and king of the Jews, had thrown his support and that of his people to Julius Caesar. Because of the allegiance of the Jews, Julius Caesar granted the Jews complete religious freedom.

Being strict monotheists Jews were seen as different from all other groups and nationalities within the Roman Empire, but Roman law protected those differences. On the other hand, despite the fact that Jesus and his disciples were Jews Christianity was seen as an innovation because the Jews denied that the Christians belonged to their religion.

Christians, however, such as Paul, Ignatius, and Barnabas tried to position Christianity as "the true Israel." All three wrote serious diatribes against Judaism.[9] They did not convince Nero (54–68) and Domitian (81–96), who accepted the religion of the Jews as legal. These emperors were not fooled by the negative slams of the Christians. Rather, they accepted the contentions of the Jews that Christianity was an innovation and therefore illegal. This really created problems for the Christians in that being monotheists like the Jews they would not participate in the pagan rituals, but not having the protection of the law, they were subject to constant harassment and persecution on their own account.

Keeping the overwhelming threat of violence in the Roman Empire in mind, Marcion was aware of any problem for Christianity that arose because of its relationship with Judaism. In the first century, Christianity struggled because it was perceived as an "innovation" threatening the empire.

In the last part of the first century, the emperors' patience with the Jews ran out. The religious tolerance, granted them by Julius Caesar, seemed to the emperors to be the pretext for revolution. Consequently, the emperors began to contravene Julius Caesar's promise of religious freedom, and increasingly violated and impeded the Jewish religious practices. The end result was that the Jews revolted all the more. Of course, this meant that Rome had to increase its repressive methods and thus waged war on the Jews from 60 CE to 136. Between the years of 60 CE – 72 CE

---

[9] These fathers, unlike Marcion, were never considered heretics by the church.

MARCION'S PLACE IN A VIOLENT WORLD

the Jews carried out one of their fieriest rebellions. This was one of the most protracted and expensive revolutions with which the Roman Empire had to deal. Emperor Vespasian (69–79 CE), as Consular general led the Roman forces from 66-72, crushed the rebellion, destroyed Jerusalem, and the Temple, of which only the Wailing Wall remains today. Vespasian took control of the temple tax stipulated in Exodus 30:13 to be collected by the high priest. He enraged the Jews by diverting the tax to the temple of Jupiter.

This tax was so offensive to the Jews of the Diaspora that in 115 CE, revolts on a huge scale broke out in Jewish communities across the Roman Empire. Trajan, the emperor at the time and a master military strategist, ruthlessly suppressed the revolts. A prime example of Trajan's retribution was the total destruction of the city of Cyrenaica after a major Jewish revolt in 115-117 CE. Trajan was forced, in fact, to spend all of his 10 years as emperor repressing Jewish revolts. Many of them were in Asia Minor (Anatoli), the area around Pontus, where Marcion built his shipbuilding business (Grant 1997, 69–76).

In 132, another emperor, Hadrian, who was infuriated by the "ungrateful arrogance of the Jews," outlawed circumcision. The Jews were seething. This was more than any Jew could take. They rose up under a messianic figure by the name of Simon bar Kokhba. Professor Werner Eck in "The Bar Kokhba Revolt: the Roman Point of View," a lecture delivered at the Universities of Tel Aviv and Haifa, gave one of the best assessments of the bar Kokhba revolution. He said: "The revolt constituted a great challenge to the Roman military power and a mighty wound to Roman self-esteem and pride; a small province, or rather a small nation, dared revolt for a second (or even a third time) against mighty Rome, a revolt that lasted four years" (Eck 1999, 76).

Further compounding the problem, according to Eck, the revolt spread to Arabia and Syria. Rome needed to deploy its best generals and troops to suppress it (Eck 1999, 76–89). The bar Kokhba revolt was crushed in 135. Simon bar Kokhba and thousands of men, women, and children were massacred (see Eusebius, *Church History*, IV. vi. 1). For all practical purposes, the Jews were forced out of Palestine (Boyarin 2001, 427). The Roman tolerance for the Jews completely evaporated.

Marcion's view of Judaism must be considered in the context of an extremely violent, enraged Roman Empire. Most previous scholarship has dealt with Marcion's theology in isolation from this event. Marcion would have been well informed about the bar Kokhba Revolution, as well as the destruction of Cyrenaica and the other Jewish centers around the empire. He heard and might have even seen the horrors connected with the revolt. For the most part, his customers were Romans or Roman sympathizers, so he heard the curses they threw at the Jews. He gradually became convinced that any Christian connection or even perceived connection with the Jews was now extremely problematic. We hypothesized that, in his desire to protect the church, which he loved, he downplayed any connection with the Jews and the Old Testament.

Marcion and Gnosticism

In 1970, Professor Robert M. Grant wrote of Marcion: "His lack of enthusiasm for Judaism was increased by the disastrous Jewish revolt of 132–135; his rejection of the Jewish religion was characteristic of Gnosticism" (Grant 1970, 124). "Gnosticism" is one of the ghosts of religious history past. It is even difficult to describe it. In some ways, it is Marcion-like, in that it says that two gods exist, a "god" of the world (the god of the Old Testament) and the higher God.

The fathers saw this superficial similarity, and they beat Marcion into oblivion because of it. But the similarity between the Gnostics and Marcion stop here. The fathers should have looked deeper, but they did not.

Many Gnostics believed that creation took place by the workings of a series of "powers." These powers intended to keep the human soul entrapped in an evil body. Hidden wisdom or knowledge, given to only a select group of Gnostics, was necessary to save humans from the world. Outside that, the whole world and most of mankind was flawed. Life was absurd. And it was not the fault of humans. It was the fault of the Creator. Other ghosts, aeons, intermediate deific beings, float between the ultimate true God and ourselves, interjecting the Pleroma between God and ourselves so that humans could hardly even communicate with the true God.

All of this is a far cry from Marcion's beliefs.

While not seeing Marcion and Gnostics as similar, many scholars, influenced by the manuscripts of the Nag Hammadi Library, have come to believe that both Marcion and the Gnostics were negatively impacted by the bar Kokhba revolution. Stephen G. Wilson, in *Related Strangers: Jews and Christians, 70–170 CE*, asserts that the "relations" had already soured between the Jews and Christians, but with the bar Kochba rebellion, many Christians believed they needed to put distance between themselves and the Jews. (Wilson 2006, 219-221) This is precisely what we believe Marcion and the Marcionites did.

Wilson also believes that the bar Kochba rebellion and its resulting disaster was so threatening to many Jews that they had to reevaluate their beliefs. The end result of this reevaluation was the development of Gnosticism. (Wilson 2006, 16-19) While there is really no consensus on the origins of Gnosticism, Wilson is among a large group of scholars who believe that Gnosticism developed within Judaism and that some of that movement was then Christianized.

In a well-documented volume entitled, *Two Powers in Heaven: Early Rabbinic Reports about Christianity and Gnosticism*, Allen Segal asserts that the rabbis solidified their views on monotheism with their arguments with many groups over the two powers in heaven. The whole issue of two powers in heaven has a very complicated history which Segal lays out from rabbinical discussions of the two names of God, YHWH and Elohim, to the divine concepts of Justice and Mercy; the Qumran community with its concept of sons of light and sons of darkness; Rabbi Akiba who saw bar Kokhba as a divine Messiah; or Philo who developed a logos theology. But for Segal the rabbi's defining of their radical monotheism came with the argument with Christians and Gnostics over the fall of Jerusalem and the bar Kochba revolutions. Segal insists, however, that the struggle did not begin there, but it began —around the fall of Jerusalem. He wrote:

> Christians and others had taken the fall of Jerusalem as proof of the end of the Jewish dispensation. Such ideas were heinous to the majority of the Jewish community. A new set of standards was necessary to ensure survival . . . In asserting further control over the synagogue, the rabbis excluded any sectarian who compromised monotheism from participating in the service. This meant that Christians, among others, were excluded from Jewish life.

CHRISTIANITY: ENDANGERED OR EXTINCT?

> The growing emphasis on strict monotheism characterizes the rabbinic movement and sets it off from the other sects of its time. (Segal 2002, in toto, quote specific 264)

The Jewish rabbis clearly did not believe that Christians were strict monotheists. Trinitarian language later will state that three persons make up one Godhead. But this was formulated in the language of the Nicene Creed in 325 at the Council of Nicaea. Such language had not yet developed in Marcion's time. Segal is right to point out that the divinity of Jesus was strong in certain circles such as the Johannine community (Segal 200, 261–63). Most scholars today believe that Christians viewed the person of Jesus from a variety of perspectives (see Bauer below, p. 45), but most would have accepted the resurrection and some form of exalted state of Jesus. This exalted state, which Segal called "angelic," troubled the rabbis in their attempts to expunge "two powers in heaven" beliefs and make Judaism radically monotheistic (Segal 2002, 260–66). At any rate, these rabbis were undoubtedly anxious to get rid of this strange group of people and their beliefs.

Birger Pearson in *Gnosticism, Judaism and Egyptian Christianity* suggested, as others have, that Gnosticism arose from Jewish intellectuals in Alexandria, who, in reaction to the destruction of the Temple, Jerusalem, and the state of Israel, rejected the Old Testament and its gods. They took, however, the imagery of the Old Testament and reshaped it into a totally new religion (Pearson 2005, passim) In *What Is Gnosticism?*, Karen King hints that the genesis at least of some of Gnosticism might be the dire situation of "the socio-political condition of imperial violence" (King 2003,110–38; quote specifically 137).

Marcion: Anti-Old Testament, Not Anti-Jew

Harnack established in the nineteenth century that Marcion was not a Gnostic, and present-day scholars have accepted this as fact. Furthermore, it may have been that Marcion even held a moderate position regarding the Jews somewhere between those who were upset with the Jewish Gnostic denigration of Yahweh and those who were all-out Catholic anti-Semites. Indeed, the Gnostics totally rejected the God of the Old Testament as evil, and many of the church fathers, especially Tertullian, pinned this rejection on Marcion.

Rather, Stephen Wilson tersely describes the true difference between the predominant Catholic position at the time and that of Marcion regarding the Jews:

> ... the Marcionite said to the Jew: 'Keep your god, your scriptures... your law; consider them to be inferior, superseded by the gospel.' The Catholic said: 'We'll take your God... your scriptures, and some of your law; as for you, you are disinherited, cast into limbo." (Wilson, Stephen 2006, 220)

Considering how anti-Semitic Christianity became, Marcion's lack of hostility toward the Jews would have to be considered another strength of Marcion.

Marcion:
A Protest against the Degeneration
of the Jesus Movement

What we are seeing in the beginning ages of Catholicism should be disturbing to the contemporary Christian. Some obvious changes were happening in the church that transformed the church from the movement of Jesus, and these changes are seriously and negatively impacting Christianity even today.

- First, it became a male-dominated hierarchy.
- Second, it became wrapped in Platonic philosophy.
- Third, it became anti-Semitic.
- Fourth, it became a worldly power contrary to Jesus of Nazareth.
- Fifth, it espoused the very violence that killed Jesus.

All five of these elements of the degeneration of the Jesus Movement may in some way have contributed to Marcion being proclaimed an arch-heretic. The first two corrupting influences of male domination and Greek philosophy are intricately involved. Male domination certainly was a major factor within the cultural milieu of the Roman Empire.[10] Then, as we discussed above, the honored position of the philosopher put the businessman Marcion in contention. His theology became the target which all the Christian philosophers attacked again and again, not only when he was alive, but also after his death. The rhetoric with which they vilified Marcion was indicative of their need to control, and the anger and violence in "their hearts."

Reevaluation of Marcion's Contributions to Biblical Theology

WHO WAS THE HERETIC?

As much as Marcion was the lightning rod for the storms incited by the church fathers, he was not so much a heretic as he was a faithful follower of the Jesus Movement, and the church fathers may not have been so much the expounders of "orthodoxy" and defenders of the correct faith as they were corrupters of that faith. Here we must be careful that we are being correctly understood. We are not saying that Justin Martyr, Polycarp, Irenaeus, and Tertullian were not followers of Jesus. We are saying that they were corrupters of Christianity in that they wrapped Christianity in Greek philosophy, and this had disastrous effects upon the Jesus Movement. Marcion might have been a corrupter of the Jesus Movement by leaving Rome just when his influence was most needed, or for other subtle reasons unknown to us now, due to the fact that his works were destroyed. Certainly, in light of the damage that Greek philosophy has done, the church fathers departed from the Jesus Movement more than Marcion, but because they won in the power struggle, their brand of heresy became orthodoxy. There is enough reason to call into question the historical assumptions of the past. Furthermore, the evidence coming out of the Nag Hammadi documents has changed scholars' traditional thinking about Gnostics and, correspondingly, Marcion. Perhaps somewhere in Asia Minor another discovery, some text or texts or other archaeological finds, will shine even more light on the subject.

If the orthodoxy of Ignatius, Polycarp, Justin Martyr, and Irenaeus, all considered saints by the Catholic Church, were judged by the post-Nicene

---

[10] See Introduction discussion of gender and dominance, pp. v-vi.

standards, they would all be found to be heretical. These early fathers of the church would have been better advised not to harass Marcion and his followers, to accept them as brothers and sisters, and to accept the thought of Paul in 1 Corinthians 13:12, which states: "Now I know in part; then I shall know in fully, even as I am fully known."

Jesus and the movement that he fostered, within the grand perspective of the ages, is the most amazing phenomena in the history of humanity. When the church attempted to codify it within Greek philosophy and human reasoning, the results bordered on blasphemy. It would have been wonderful if these male philosophers had accepted the amazing and miraculous events of Jesus' life instead of trying to dissect them. In this day when scientists are finding it hard even to conceive of the outer circumferences of the universe, and when they are perceiving that there may be many galactic universes beyond our own, it would have been better if these philosophers had not tampered with the great mystery of Jesus in our very midst. If the only sentence to survive of Marcion's Antithesis is indicative of Marcion's total attitude toward the Gospel, it would have been a more helpful theology than that which was developed by Catholic theologians of the time: "O wonder beyond wonders, rapture, power and amazement is it, that one can say nothing at all about the Gospel, nor even conceive of it, nor compare it with anything" (*Antithesis* 1, 1).

Class Struggle within the Formation of Christian Belief

With one sentence existing of Marcion's work, a person might think that it would be impossible to draw any conclusions about what Marcion believed. In the above discussion, we have been dealing with the milieu in which Marcion lived and some of the opposition to Marcion. Here we will attempt to help excavate the thinking of Marcion with the aid of Marcion's opponents.

Most scholars today accept Walter Bauer's 1934 assessment that in the second century there was no such thing as orthodoxy, but there were a multitude of "doxies," or faith communities. Most of these faith communities by later standards would have been considered heretical, but in the areas of Asia Minor, Syria, and Egypt, they were considered the only Christianity the people knew. Therefore, they cannot be judged by later standards set by Roman and Greek philosophers. Bauer saw orthodoxy arising not out of Nazareth, but out of Rome. (Iricinschi and Sellentin 2008, 5) This is beyond dispute. Furthermore, it is in the struggle with Marcion that orthodoxy begins to take shape.

During the first and second centuries, there were very primitive creedal statements, but these were scripturally based texts. There was a great deal of fluidity within faith matters during this period. It is almost impossible for Christians in our dogma-ridden world to even imagine an era of unregimented belief such as that of the early-second century. Robert Smith Wilson asserts that theologians in the church at the beginning of the Marcion era had much freedom to explore in their theologies many facets of Jesus, the Christ. Marcion was doing what Paul, Luke, and many others had done before him; for his own age, he was using his intellect, his spirit, and his sincerity to try to understand Jesus and his church. (Wilson 1933, 19)

There was a problem that made this diversity of faith intolerable: the ever-increasing numbers of members of the upper classes were becoming Christian. For many of these persons of the dominant class such as Justin Martyr, Irenaeus, Polycarp, and Hippolytus, and those such as Clement who were dominant class "wannabes," the egalitarian and diverse nature in the Jesus Movement was insufferable. The sociologist Pierre Bourdieu has well described the process where the faith, "doxa," of the people was replaced by the faith of the dominant society and was now to be considered "orthodoxy." Bourdieu summarizes his views:

> The dominated classes have an interest in pushing back the limits of doxa and exposing the arbitrariness of the taken for granted; the dominant classes have an interest in defending the integrity of doxa or, short of this, of establishing in its place the necessarily imperfect substitute, orthodoxy . . . [Then] the arbitrary principles of the prevailing classification can appear as such and it thereafter becomes necessary to undertake the work of conscious systematization and expressed rationalization which marks the passage from doxa to orthodoxy. Orthodoxy, straight, or rather straightened . . .aims, without ever entirely succeeding, at restoring the primal state of innocence of doxa . . . (Bourdieu 1972, 1977, 170; cited Arnal 2008, 61)

MARCION'S PLACE IN A VIOLENT WORLD

In essence, orthodoxy was the means that the dominant society, indeed, the aristocracy, used to defuse and control the Jesus Movement. What is amazing, however, is in spite of the fact that Marcion obviously belonged to the upper classes, he was totally obsessed with trying to keep the Jesus Movement faithful to its founder.

Marcion and the Formation of Scripture

1. Marcion and the Gospels

It is difficult for us in the twenty-first century to imagine the power of the Jesus Movement during Marcion's time. The love and fellowship of the brothers and sisters in the Messiah, Jesus, was powerful. The memory and the spiritual presence of Jesus were strongly felt among his followers. The people in the Christian community savored Jesus' presence first in the oral stories about him, before anything was written about him. These stories were so powerful that little more was needed to sustain the new Christian movement. A good example is found in an early statement of Papias. Papias knew written Gospels. Yet, he preferred the words about Jesus which were passed from person to person.

Geoffrey Mark Hahnehan, in his carefully documented work, *The Muratorian Fragment and the Development of the Canon*, quotes Papias:

> If anyone ever came who had followed the presbyters, I questioned them in regard to the words of the presbyters, what Andrew or Peter or Philip or Thomas or James or John or Matthew, or any other of the Lord's disciples had said . . ., and the presbyter John, the disciples of the Lord, say. For I did not think that information in books would help so much as the word of a living and abiding voice. (H.E. 3.39.4; Hahnehan 1992,. 95)

Hahnehan states that this preference for the oral tradition is also evident in other Christian literature of the early second century:

> H. Koester has shown that the citations of gospel traditions among the Apostolic Fathers are more likely to be drawn from oral tradition than to be free quotations from written Gospels,

to which explicit appeals are made. Written Gospels probably became increasingly used as oral tradition began to dissipate and grow unreliable. Originally, they must have circulated individually and perhaps were used in isolation from each other, with only one such document being valued and used in any given Christian community. (Hahnehan 1992, 95)

Gradually, as the witnesses died, Christians had to rely more and more on the textual witness of their not-yet-defined canon of scripture. The question regarding which texts were inspired and which were not was yet to be answered in Marcion's day. Some texts, which were cherished as "scripture," never made it into the final canon of Scripture.[11] It is more than likely that Marcion played a significant role in the formation of the scriptures. Adolph Harnack wrote:

Marcion's proclamation of Christianity is intended to be nothing but biblical theology, that is, religious teaching which on the positive side is exclusively based upon the book that consists of the Gospel and the letters of Paul and on the negative side on that other book, which also is actually truthful, the Old Testament. Both books intend to be understood as mere writings, that is, their contents are fully contained in the letter of what is written. (Harnack 1924, 1990, 65)

Harnack, picking up on the church fathers' charges, believed Marcion edited the gospels and Paul's epistles, trying to eliminate traces of Judaism. In this matter, Sebastian Moll believed that Harnack was an "overzealous German Lutheran" (Moll 2010, 2–3). There are increasing number of scholars today who question whether Harnack was right in believing that Marcion edited the text. In this regard, most recently, Matthias Klinghardt of Dresden University has presented astounding evidence that the Marcionite text of the Gospel of Luke more than likely preceded the canonical Gospel of Luke. It would then follow that the composers of the canonical Gospel of Luke more than likely edited Marcion's Gospel.

---

[11] See Cragun 1996. 109–44. For much of the time up to 419 CE, *The Shepherd of Hermas* was considered Scripture whereas *The Apocalypse of John* was not

Indeed, Klinghardt asserts that the Gospel Marcion had in hand influenced the formation of both the Gospel of Matthew and the Gospel of Luke.[12] (Klinghardt 2010, 1–27)

Without knowing of Klinghardt's work, David Williams's analysis of quotes of Marcion's adversaries show that Marcion did not throw out other Gospels as Tertullian and others said, but actually utilized sections from what we now know as the Gospel of Matthew and Mark (Williams 1989, 481). Hahneman agrees. He states that Marcion probably did not reject other gospel traditions, but he adds that Marcion simply did not know other versions. He states that written Gospels, as we quoted above, must have circulated individually in isolation from one another, with only one Gospel being valued and used in any one community (Hahneman 1992, 95). Klinghardt argues that Marcion did know Mark and did utilize Mark, but that texts of Matthew were found in the Gospel Marcion had in hand, not in another existing Gospel (Klinghardt 2010, 11–27).

Furthermore, among these texts quoted by Tertullian and Epiphanius, Williams found reference to a Gospel passage which identifies Jesus as "Son of David," another referring to "Moses and the prophets," and another which quotes Jesus as saying that he fervently desired to celebrate the Passover with his apostles (Williams 1989, 481). These passages hint that Marcion might not have been as anti-Jewish or as anti-Old Testament as the church fathers made him out to be.

Joseph P. Tyson agrees with Klinghardt that Marcion did not edit out the first three chapters of the Gospel of Luke. Tyson believes that *The Gospel of Luke* that Marcion had began with what we now recognize as chapter three verse one. Thus, it did not contain the nativity narratives. Tyson's contention is that at this early time, the nativity narrative was not even available

---

[12] Klinghardt builds his hypothesis on the large group of scholars including Farrer, Goulder, and Goodacre who challenge the long held assumption that a document or source, which was labeled Q, along with the Gospel of Mark, influenced the Gospels of Matthew and Luke. Klinghardt's assumption is that the Gospel which Marcion had in hand, rather than Q, influenced the Gospels of Matthew and Luke.

to Marcion.[13] These nativity stories, such as Elizabeth, Zachary, and John (Luke 1:5–80); the Magnificat (Luke 1:52–54); the story of Simeon and Anna (Luke 2:21–38); the circumcision of Jesus (Luke 2:21–38), link Jesus to Judaism and are not found in the other Gospels. Tyson also hints that certain other sections of our present *Gospel of Luke* were also not in the gospel at the time of Marcion. (Tyson 2006, 38-49; 79-131)

2. Marcion and Paul's Epistles

In *Marcion: The Gospel of the Alien God.* (*Marcion: Das Evangelium vom fremden Gott*), Harnack makes this earthshaking statement: "the apostle Paul had no more devoted pupil than Marcion . . ." (Harnack 1920, 1976, 123–24). Sixty years later, the Oxford scholar, Joseph Hoffmann, in *Marcion: On the Restitution of Christianity, An Essay on the Development of Radical Paulinist Theology in the Second Century*, gives almost definitive support for Harnack's conclusions. Hoffman states: ". . . by Marcion's day the gospel of Paul was in clear danger of being forsaken altogether." Furthermore, Hoffman finds evidence for this in the fact that Paul is never mentioned in *The Epistle of Barnabas* and *The Didache*. Also, Hoffman points out that Justin has "negligible use . . . of the Pauline epistles." Because of this, Hoffman stipulates that ". . . Marcion made the reestablishment of Paul's teaching the basis of his theological reform," and thus, "he was early identified as a claimant to the authority of the Apostle"

---

[13] This contention is implicitly supported by reputable scripture scholars, such as Raymond E. Brown (*The Birth of the Messiah*, New York, Doubleday, 1993, 239–43) and Joseph Fitzmyer (*The Gospel according to Luke I–IX*, Garden City, New York, 1981, 57). Brown believes that Luke's Gospel and Acts were both written after 70 and probably in the 80s when Luke, according to tradition, lived in Greece (Brown: 236–37). The infancy narrative, Brown believes, was "prefixed to the Gospel after the Book of Acts was completed" (Brown: 240). Early accounts of Luke, then, would not have contained the nativity accounts (even though Brown admits that no such copy of Luke, as far as he knows, has survived to this day). Marcion was born in the year 85 at approximately the same time as the writing of the Gospel and probably before the writing of Acts, and certainly before the writing of the infancy narrative. According to Brown, then, the infancy accounts were not yet finished at Marcion's birth. It is a real possibility that Marcion's text of Luke did not include the infancy accounts.

However, Brown does not believe, as Tyson does, that the nativity accounts were written specifically to refute Marcion. Brown, in footnote 18, page 241, goes along with the common historical opinion of the time: "Marcion seemingly omitted the infancy material from his form of the Gospel of Luke, but that was probably because of the OT atmosphere which he would find objectionable." He does not specifically mention the possibility that the infancy accounts were not even in Marcion's copy of Luke, but his time frames make it quite possible. Regarding the writing of the Gospel of Luke and Acts, Fitzmeyer gives us a date of ca 80–85 for the writing of the Gospel of Luke and Acts, give or take 10 years. After that, Luke wrote the Infancy Accounts.

(Hoffman 1984, 101). Robert W. Wall in "The Function of the Pastoral Letters within the Pauline Canon of the New Testament: A Canonical Approach," likewise supports Harnack's views:

> The first known collector of Paul's letters is Marcion (160 CE). Given the prior history of the Pauline corpus to this point, Marcion's Pauline collection was likely an edited collocation of one popular already in wide circulation. Marcion collected and used Paul, however, with clear theological intent, since his theology was predicated on Pauline theology. Often in sharp contrast to emergent catholic Christianity, which did not pay undo attention to Paul, Marcion's innovation was to vest an extant Pauline collection with normative authority for Christian formation: that is, the Pauline corpus was no longer "scripture" (as in 2 Peter) but "canon." (Wall 2004, 31–32)

This move was to push the Catholic Church in the direction of a Christian Bible of its own, perhaps sooner than would have been the case otherwise.

Wall further stipulates that the 10 epistles that Marcion accepted as Pauline were the same as the epistles found in the Beatty Manuscript (P^{46}), which is one of the oldest manuscripts that is available to date (Wall 2004, 31–32). About the manuscript p^{46} T. C. Skeat, scholar in residence of the British Museum, and home of the Beatty manuscripts, wrote to Bruce Metzger in 1988 stating:

> We would have to accept that it is, by a very wide margin, the oldest surviving Christian manuscript and the oldest surviving example of a papyrus codex. Moreover, p^{46} uses an extensive and well-developed system of nomina sacra [holy name, sacred ascription, designation, or normative authority as with Wall above], which it is difficult to believe can have existed, not merely in A.D. 80, but, presumably, in one of its ancestors. (Metzger 1992, 264)

John Clabeaux, in a *Catholic Biblical Quarterly* monograph, states quite rightly and from excellent research that Marcion brought the "Pauline corpus" to Rome from Sinope. But then, Clabeaux makes the statement:

CHRISTIANITY: ENDANGERED OR EXTINCT?

"His journey to Rome was hardly the first time nor the only time that this text was brought to that city." (Clabeaux 1989, 148) "Hardly," however, is not good research. All the evidence that we have pointed out above in The Shepherd, Barnabas, and Justin does not support the existence of Paul's Epistles in Rome. It is most likely that it is to Marcion's credit that we have the Pauline corpus at all. We speculate that some day in a cave in Turkey or elsewhere somebody may find an urn containing a Marcionite manuscript that will shed much more light on the formation of the New Testament text. Furthermore, with Wall, Tyson, Williams, Klinghardt, Thomassen, and other recent commentators, we are left with the thought that Marcion was more orthodox than his adversaries ever recognized.

Of all Paul's epistles, Marcion found *The Epistle to the Galatians* as the most instructive. As a good student of the scriptures, Marcion had looked for clues and keys in the text of Paul to aid his understanding of the Gospel. According to Harnack, Marcion found "two guiding stars" in Galatians to help him move more correctly through the labyrinth of inchoate traditions: The first star was that there was only one Gospel and that was the Gospel of Jesus Christ. The second star was that he believed that the other Christian writers proclaimed a Jewish Gospel, which Paul simply had to oppose. He believed that Paul thought that the church was held captive by the false belief that the Father of Jesus Christ was identical with the Creator of the world and the judgmental and wrathful God of the Old Testament (Harnack, 1921, 1990, 24). Such passages as Galatians 3:10–14 led Marcion to such conclusions:

> 10 For all who rely on the works of the law are under a curse; for it is written, "Cursed is everyone who does not observe and obey all the things written in the book of the law." Now it is evident that no one is justified before God by the law; for "The one who is righteous will live by faith." But the law does not rest on faith; on the contrary, "Whoever does the works of the law will live by them." Christ redeemed us from the curse of the law by becoming a curse for us—for it is written, "Cursed is everyone who hangs on a tree"— in order that in Christ Jesus the blessing of Abraham might come to the Gentiles, so that we might receive the promise of the Spirit through faith.

MARCION'S PLACE IN A VIOLENT WORLD

Marcion was not the only one who was enthralled by the implications of Paul's use of law and Gospel. Since the Reformation, a multitude of theologians and exegetes, including Luther, have debated the implications of Paul's use of law and faith in the Gospel. We have cited above only one passage of Paul to indicate the intricacies of Paul's thought which Marcion and others pondered and emulated. Galatians reads: "Christ redeemed us from the curse of the law." This was the word in which Marcion believed and trusted. The law was, of course, the law of the Old Testament. Marcion soared and took the relationship with the law and the Old Testament to new levels. He taught that not only the Old Testament law, but the whole Old Testament had been superseded by the Gospel. F. F. Bruce, in *The Canon of Scripture*, states:

> The gospel, he believed, was an entirely new teaching brought to earth by Christ. The law and the prophets made no sort of preparation for it, and if some passages in Paul's correspondence suggested that they did, those passages must have been interpolated by others—by the kind of Judaizers against whom Paul polemicized in Galatians and other letters. (Bruce, 1988, 135)

3. MARCION AND THE OLD TESTAMENT

There is considerable evidence, archaeological and textual, contrary to Tertullian's claims, that Sinope was not a barbaric region, and that it was highly civilized (Hellenized). A large settlement of Jews dwelt in Sinope dating as far back as 178 BCE. Furthermore, Epiphanius reported that a person by the name of Aquila, a Jew who converted to Christianity and then back to Judaism, translated the Hebrew/Aramaic of the Old Testament to a much more literal Greek translation than the Greek of the Septuagint (Hoffman 1984, 4). More than likely, this was the Old Testament that Marcion studied.

From all the evidence from Marcion's detractors, it is certain that Marcion had access to the Old Testament. If Marcion had a problem, it certainly was not lack of knowledge of the Old Testament text. For Marcion, the God of the Old Testament, the Creator-God, was harsh, cruel, and incompetent. He inflicted women with the agonies of childbirth. He favored bandits and terrorists, men like King David. That God was, in the words of Harnack, "the petty and fickle, impatient and jealous, warlike and wild Creator-God" (Harnack 1924, 1990, 69). Michael Allen Williams affirms the words of Harnack: "Marcion seems to have spotted passage after passage in which some embarrassing or problematic behavior, weakness, or humanlike emotion is ascribed to the creator God of the Jews" (Williams 1996, 24).

The fathers who accused Marcion of infidelity to the scriptures were those who themselves would explain away the Old Testament by allegory or by imposing lengthy Platonic rationalizations on the text. Marcion was faithful to the literal text. Furthermore, in future centuries, church fathers such as Eusebius, Ambrose, and Augustine, through allegorical use of the Old Testament, implied that the church needed the Roman Empire. Marcion firmly believed that the Roman Empire needed the true Christian Church of Jesus. Marcion faced the Old Testament squarely, literally, and he refused to allegorize it away. One could say that many, if not most, of the texts that bothered Marcion bother people of the modern age.

Bernhard Anderson of Princeton, one of the preeminent Old Testament scholars of the last century, in *The Old Testament and Christian Faith: A Theological Discussion*, wrote:

> Before we hastily pick up stones to cast at this "heretic," let it be said that the questions raised by many Christians today about the Old Testament betray a sympathy for Marcion, whose attractive teachings gained a considerable popular following in the second century and even later. The God of the Old Testament, we still hear today, is a God of wrath, the stern, severe Judge whose judgments fill men with terror; on the other hand, the God of the New Testament is a God of love, the kind and merciful Father who treats his children with patience and forgiveness. Or, it is said, the God of the Old Testament is understood anthropomorphically as a kind of glorified human being; the New Testament, however, abandons such theological naïveté and affirms that "God is a Spirit." The God of the Old Testament is a warlike Being who satisfies Israel's nationalistic pride by slaughtering his enemies; the God of the New Testament, by contrast, is not bound by

nationalistic limitations but is concerned for the universal brotherhood of man. (Anderson 1963, 3)

Anderson stipulates that in the early second century there were probably many churches that did not possess copies of the "Old Testament" scriptures (Anderson 1969, 2). Jesus was everything to the Christians of the age, as he was to Marcion.

Marcion and the Alien God of the New Testament

Harvard Professor Thomassen firmly asserts that Marcion's theology should not be easily discarded. Rather than brushing aside Marcion with other so-called heretics, Thomassen believes that Marcion's theology has value. In his mind, Marcion believed the following:

> The god revealed by Jesus Christ is distinct from, and infinitely more elevated than the creator and ruler of the world worshipped by the old religions. The god of the Christians, as described in the Gospels and in the letters of Paul, must not be confused with the aggressive and vindictive deity of the Jewish scriptures. (Thomassen 2004, 242)

From Harnack's in-depth study, Marcion expressed certain beliefs strongly. Harnack says that Marcion did so when he spoke about Paul and the relationship of the Christian church to God, to the Old Testament, and to Greek philosophy. In those areas, Marcion felt he needed to make an impact because he was convinced that the church was sliding into error. Harnack tells us:

> The point of departure for Marcion's criticism cannot be mistaken. It was provided in the Pauline contrast of law and gospel: malicious, petty, and cruel, punitive correctness on the one side, and on the other side, merciful love . . . It must have been a bright day for him . . . when he came to see that Christ represented and proclaimed an entirely new God; further, that religion is simply nothing other than devout belief in this redeemer-God who transforms man; that the totality of world events down to the present

time is the evil and contradictory drama of a deity who possesses no higher value than does the obtuse and loathsome world itself, whose creator and ruler this deity is. (Harnack 1921, 1990, 21)

In Marcion's mind, Jesus was not the final chapter of the Old Testament, nor was he the minion of the Roman Empire. Rather, Jesus stood alone. He felt that theologically and politically, the church needed to break some Old Testament ties if it was to be like Christ who was most like God. Furthermore, it would be impossible to carry Christ's message into the Roman world if the connection between Christianity and the Jews was too strong. Marcion opted for a church that was plain and transparent, and completely freed from the bondage to the Old Testament. The God of the New Testament was a God hitherto unknown. In fact, Marcion and the Marcionites chose to call the New Testament God the Alien on earth. He was totally "other." This was a turnaround for the Christians of the age. Harnack states: "All Christians at that time believed that they were aliens on earth. Marcion corrected this belief: it is God who is the alien, who is leading them out of their homeland of oppression and misery into a completely new paternal house, one that had not even been imagined previously (Harnack 1921, 1990, 3)."

Confronted by the overwhelming violence within the Roman Empire, it is easy to understand that Marcion felt that Jesus was an alien among them.[14] Marcion went on to state that before Christ came, human beings could never know the God of the New Testament. This Alien God was, by nature, unknowable and was revealed only in the witness and words of Jesus. Because of the accusation that Marcion had an "unknown" God, his adversaries accused him also of being a dualist. In fact, Marcion was not a dualist. He did not believe in two gods (Harnack 1924, 1990, 14). He was the one who was concerned that many other Christians were dualists. He simply believed that the "God" which others thought a deity, the God of the Old Testament, was not a God at all in comparison to Jesus, and could not aid in connecting God with humanity, any more than the best human thinking or human reasoning could ever know the God brought to us by

---

[14] We will return to this issue of an alien God in another chapter of these volumes when we deal with the Bogomils. There, we will find that the reaction and theological development of the Bogomils were not only caused by the violence of the Roman Empire, but also by the violence and oppression of the church. This violence will continue throughout the history of the church.

Jesus. For Marcion, Jesus was completely other until he decided to reveal himself. Furthermore, the God of the Old Testament with all its wars and violence resembled too much the gods of the Romans. No, Marcion was not a dualist. His God of the Old Testament was too much a part of the earth, too much a part of the mind of man to be a real God.

As we have sorted through the scholars' assessments of Marcion, we have to acknowledge again that the only real light into Marcion is Tertullian who said,

> But I would have attacked Marcion's own *Antitheses* in closer and fuller combat, if a more elaborate demolition of them were required in maintaining for the Creator the character of a good God and a Judge, after the examples of both points, which we have shown to be so worthy of God. (*Against Marcion*, II, xxix, CCEL)

This means that he actually had a copy of Antitheses. As biased as Tertullian's analysis was, we have gleaned what Marcion may actually have believed:[15]

- 1. Christ's love for humans was even greater because he redeemed those, who were not his own.
- 2. Humans created the Old Testament God.
- 3. Christ was love and grace.
- 4. Christ only work in our regard was self-revelation or redemption of humanity.
- 5. Jesus was so great that the Old Testament God was nothing in comparison.
- 6. Jesus' teaching in Luke 16:13, "No one can serve two masters..." meant that no one could serve both the God of the Old

---

[15] Some of his stinging remarks about Marcion are mentioned in the previous chapter. Other rhetorical remarks in his five books on Marcion make stimulating reading, but are also distortions of equal magnitude: "To a man who has diseased eyes, even one lamp looks like two" [in reference to Tertullian's contention that Marcion believed in two gods] (*Against Marcion* 1.2, *ANF* 3.CCEL); "Marcion, how can you say that you are freed from his [the Creator God's] kingdom, when his flies are crawling around on your face? (*Against Marcion* 1:24 *ANF* 3. CCEL); "You can more easily find in this world a man like Marcion, who has no heart and no brains, than a man without a body, like Marcion's Christ [in regard to Tertullian's contention that Marcion was a Gnostic and did not believe that Jesus had a human body] (*Against Marcion* 4.1, *ANF* 3. CCEL).

Testament and the God of Jesus. Therefore the religion of Jesus was totally set apart from the religions of the Jews and the pagans.

Conclusion

We conclude that Marcion, along with most Christians, saw the Christian God as our Redeemer and Savior. But Marcion believed that Jesus, the Christ, is not our Creator and not our judge. He is not wrathful. He does not punish. He is not the cause of our misery and pain. Furthermore, human beings do not return to their Creator through redemption, as we know it, with all its trappings. Rather, they are simply beckoned by Jesus into his own glorious foreign land, which becomes their homeland. Such thoughts sound reasonable to the average Christian, who is not theologically embedded. However, changes of thought do occur in even theological settings. In church history, many "dogmas" have been accepted as orthodox for a period of time and for certain theological schools, then the church/churches have moved on to reformulate their thinking, so that the older "orthodox" view that was considered "common opinion" may now even be considered "heretical." A case in point is *limbo* or the nature of purgatory in Catholic theology. As we stated, some of the Christology of most of the early church fathers would today be considered heresy. If a person has trouble with second-century Marcion's simple view of the last days, this person has to know that it is the common view of most average Christians even today; it is certainly not time for anybody to start throwing stones.

Ken Smits, a Roman Catholic priest and liturgist of merit, said in a homily printed *Recap*:

> Doctrine is a limited agenda. This tends to engage only the religious professionals, and it operates in a very conceptual approach to faith. . . . Common Baptism will always be there, and will always draw us toward a common table . . . (Smits 2008, 1)

Similarly young 18-year-old Dietrich Bonhoeffer was in Italy at Easter in 1924. He was enthralled by the Catholic liturgy. Even individual confession was fascinating to him—without question. The Catholic people were truly devout. Bonhoeffer attended almost every liturgical function

MARCION'S PLACE IN A VIOLENT WORLD

from Palm Sunday right up to Easter at St. Peter's Basilica and in other basilicas in the city. Afterward, in Bologna, he made friends with a student for the priesthood, who enlightened him more on the Catholic faith. He became deeply fond of Catholicism and found his jaunt in Italy to be a truly religious experience. In his doctoral thesis entitled *Sanctorum Communio* (*The Communion of Saints*) he summarized his experience:

> I find I am once again much less sympathetic to Catholicism. Catholic Dogma veils every ideal thing in Catholicism, without knowing that this is what it is doing. There is a huge difference between confession and dogmatic teachings about confession, unfortunately also between "church" and the "church in dogmatics. (Bonhoeffer, (1927, 2010, 89 ff.)

Down through the ages, the church of the elite took over. Dogma overpowered the unity of the Christian faithful in the church, and eventually the logos of God became not Jesus, but the Bible. Gradually, the church splintered into thousands of disparate groups. Tiny diversions of thought held by Marcion were not the dogmas held by Tertullian. Tiny diversions of thought held by Tertullian were not the dogmas held by Pope Victor. Tiny diversions of thought held by Luther were not the dogmas held by Leo X. And so we have journeyed—until the bumps in the road caused by the diversions and the dogmas make us nauseated. Indeed, the storm that brewed around Marcion was unwarranted. Furthermore, we will repeat: Marcion did not make the storm. He was its victim. And his statement at the beginning of *Antithesis* is still good news today: "O wonder beyond wonders, rapture, power and amazement is it, that one can say nothing at all about the Gospel, nor even conceive of it, nor compare it with anything"(*Antithesis* 1, 1).

3

The Spirit Blows Anew, Pentecost for Women as well as Men

Then from the plains between the mountains in central Asia the Holy Spirit blew in a land long pillaged by pagans. This was a new Pentecost. But unlike the reporting of the moving of the Spirit in Acts 2, women stood in the forefront as the receivers of the Spirit. From what we know, these participants in the new, similar Pentecost were much different from their Marcionite neighbors to the north, both in doctrine and manner, but they shared one thing in common: they were both rejected by the male Greek philosopher-theologians who were taking over the Church.

Comparison of the Women in the First and Second Pentecost

In all 4 Gospels, women are prominent in the life of Jesus and in the Resurrection accounts (Matthew 28:1–10; Mark 16:1–10; Luke 24:1–12; John 20:1–18). But by the time Pentecost rolled around, the book of Acts gives them at best bit parts. For example, in Acts 1, when Jesus ascends into heaven, women are not reported as being present. After he ascends, angelic beings (men in white) appear and say to the apostles, "Men of Galilee [ανδρει Γαλιλαιοι specifically male as versus ανθροπος, humans], "why do you stand here looking into the sky? This same Jesus, who has been taken from you into heaven, will come back in the same way you have seen him go into heaven." (Acts 1:11) In Acts 1:14, after the specific naming of the apostles (vs. 13), the text reads almost apologetically: "They all joined together constantly in prayer, along with the women and Mary the mother of Jesus . . ." After that, Mary, the mother of Jesus, the other Mary, Martha, Mary Magdalene, and the rest of the women disciples who followed Jesus from Galilee to Jerusalem (Matthew 27:55; Mark 15:41; Luke 23:49) are lost to us in the reporting of Acts.[16] Later, the Pentecost text in Acts confirms this: ". . . each one heard them speaking his own language" (2:6), and again people asked one another: "Are not all of these men who are speaking Galileans?" (2:7)

Again Elisabeth Schüssler Fiorenza proclaims the grim reality of church history: in the general forum of Christianity, early in the history of the Christian church, women's voices were already silenced by the male leadership. But the evidence from Asia Minor is that women's voices were not so easily silenced, and that women still stood in the forefront as the receivers of the Spirit and in the leadership of the Church.

Setting for the New Group's Beginnings

Somewhere between the year 147 and 175 CE, this second Pentecost took place in the towns of Pepouza and Tymion located in Phrygia in central Asia Minor. Phrygia was flat, fertile farmland, tilled by peasants. The Tembris River ran through it, fingering into marshy streams, terminating in wetlands. There the plain ended abruptly on the north, the east, and the south at the feet of mountains and high hills. These hills and peaks enclosed the community. Winters were severe and demanding, further isolating the people.[17]

Phrygia is fifteen miles from ancient Philadelphia, one of the churches addressed by John of *The Apocalypse*. Most of the churches addressed by

---

[16] See Introduction, p. 7.
[17] In his article, "The Discovery of Pepouza and Tymion," *Journal of Early Christian Studies*, 11.1 (2003), pp. 87–93, William Tabbernee states: "Tymion can now be identified as having been situated near the modern village of Susuzoren . . . eighteen kilometers south of Usak . . ." (p. 89) . . . there was . . . "a church in a cave . . ." [a spectacular, rock-cut monastery] in the Ulubey Canyon . . . in the district of Karahalli, thirty kilometers south of Usak (p. 91). Approximately five kilometers south . . . is a mountain [really a very high hill of 1,141 m] called Omercali. From its summit, we discovered that, looking north toward the area where the monastery is located, we not only had a magnificent view of the whole Pepouza site [5 kilometers northeast] but could see all the way to the site of Tymion [12kilometers further due north]" (p. 91).

CHRISTIANITY: ENDANGERED OR EXTINCT?

John were in Asia Minor, but he mentions neither Pepouza nor Tymion in Phrygia. Also, Paul traveled on a path from Ephesus to Hierapolis, but we have no reason to believe he entered the Tembris Valley. Nonetheless, Montanists called Pepouza and Tymion, "Jerusalem." The territory was a special religious site for them.

Asia Minor, Center of Early Christianity

By the end of the third century, according to W. H. C. Frend, the majority of Christians were not in Rome, not in Greece, but in Asia Minor, in and around Phrygia (Frend 1984, 20, 521–37). Credit is given to Bartholomew, Thaddeus, perhaps John of the Apocalypse, and other disciples; not Paul or Peter for the fact that the Gospel reached Phrygia to a people so open to the Spirit.[18] Because of the rugged terrain surrounding Phrygia, and because of its isolation, Christians could have easily sat back and waited for the Second Coming of Jesus or for martyrdom whichever came first. This was not the case with them. Between 160 and 175, within 20 years of Marcion and within 100 miles of Sinope, Marcion's hometown, this group of Christians, led by three prophets, two women, Priscilla and Maximilla, and one man, Montanus, followed Christ with missionary zeal. The evolving hierarchy of the church reacted to the group with hostility. Typically, it refrained from calling them Christian at all, but it labeled them "the Montanists" calling them by the name of the male leader of the group.[19]

Life in Early Montanist Communities

In the mystical, prophetic communities of Montanists, Christians lived in harmony in the faith and love of Jesus. Here, women and men were equal to one another, and bishops and presbyters worked side by side with their brothers and sisters in Christ.[20] They modeled the spirit of the words of Ignatius of Antioch who only decades before prophesied: "The last times have come upon us. Let us therefore be of a reverent spirit and fear the long-suffering God. Let us stand in awe of the wrath to come and show regard for the grace which is presently displayed" (Ignatius of

---

[18] By the time of the great persecution (306), there was a town in Phrygia which was "inhabited totally by Christians" (Eusebius, *Church History* 8 .11.1 *NPNF, 2nd Series* 1).

[19] Montanist is what we will call the group throughout this volume. However, we agree with Christine Trevett that Montanus may have been an incidental leader of the group (Trevett, pp. 159f.).

[20] The Didache, the Epistle of Aristides, the Epistle of Barnabas, Trevett, and Milavec support this.

THE SPIRIT BLOWS ANEW, PENTECOST FOR WOMEN

Antioch: *Ephesians* 11.1–2, *ANF.* CCEL). Ignatius continued:

> Seeing, then, that all things have an end, these two things are simultaneously set before us—death and life; and everyone shall go unto his own place. For as there are two kinds of coins, the one of God and the other of the world, and each of these has its special character stamped upon it, so the unbelieving are of this world, and the believing, in love, bear the image of God the Father given them by Jesus Christ. If we are not ready to die into his passion, his life is not in us. (Ignatius of Antioch, Ephesians 1.3, *ANF.*CCEL)

Ignatius's thoughts are typical of writings from Asia Minor in the last part of the first century and the first part of the second century. They could have come from *Revelation, The Epistle of Barnabas, The Shepherd of Hermas,* the *Epistula Apostolorum* [*Epistle of the Apostles*], or any other Christian document of that place and age. Priscilla, Maximilla, or Montanus could have also spoken them (Barnes 1971, 185). Even though historians can only guess the incidentals concerning the how or the why, Asia Minor became the center of Christianity, full-bloomed and beautiful in the first, second, and third centuries. Priscilla, Maximilla, and Montanus were examples of the Christianity that flowered there.

The Spirit of Millenarianism and Montanism

The blossoming Christianity in Phrygia grew out of chaos and pain. Roman soldiers ran through Phrygia. Blood flowed. Martyrdom was a real possibility. Out of such situations some sociologists and anthropologists would say millenarian movements arise. These movements believe that the end of the world as they were experiencing it with all its pain and suffering was at an end and Christ was returning. Out of this history comes a voice of a Montanist woman, either Quintilla or Priscilla, stating that she had a strange dream.[21] Christ came "in the form of a woman . . . dressed in a bright robe and cast wisdom in me, and revealed to me that this place is holy, and that Jerusalem will descend from heaven here" (Aune 1996, 315). And because of such oracles, historians have thought that the

---

[21] This is one of the 16 genuine oracles of the Montanists, which Kurt Aland isolated. We will deal with them in more detail later on.

CHRISTIANITY: ENDANGERED OR EXTINCT?

Montanists were millenarians.

The historian, Christine Trevett, is wary about comparing the Montanists with later phenomenon such as the millenarian movement of the Middle Ages (Trevett 1996, 15). This is especially true because the very word "millenarian" carries within it the suggestion of a thousand years after Christ, the time when some people in the Middle Ages believed that the Second Coming of Christ would take place. Montanism began in the second century. But it is clear that in these early days the Montanists and other Christians believed that Christ would come soon. They had the same spirit as the later millenarians.

"Millenarianism" has meant various things dependent on the needs of the times and the various people and ages in which the term was used. The sociologist Norman Cohn in his book *The Pursuit of the Millennium: Revolutionary Millenarians and Mystical Anarchists of the Middle Ages* states that millennium referred:

> ... to the belief held by some Christians, on the authority of The Book of Revelation (XX, 4–6), that, after his Second Coming, Christ would establish a messianic kingdom on earth and would reign over it for a thousand years before the Last Judgment. (Cohn 1970, 13)

In this very literal, pristine interpretation of millenarianism, Christ would reign with the resurrected martyrs. Later, other Christians adjusted their view of the end times. They believed martyrs were the suffering faithful. In their death they were immediately with Christ in heaven. For the suffering faithful on earth, Christ was to come to earth and establish his reign during their lifetime. Their expectation was that this was to happen at any moment, especially during the Easter vigil. (Cohn 1970, 13-14)

Later Christians believed that Christ was coming after one thousand years. Thus, the year 1000 became a key year on the calendars of some Christians. In recent years, the word "millenarian" has been used in an even more liberal sense. Anthropologists, sociologists, and historians use it as a convenient label for talking about anyone who believes that the Second Coming of Jesus will be soon—even in the lifetime of the believer. For the most part, this is how it will be employed in this book.

The Montanists were not millenarians in the strict sense. They did,

THE SPIRIT BLOWS ANEW, PENTECOST FOR WOMEN

however, believe that Christ would come soon. Cohn delineates five characteristics of millenarian movement:

a) collective, in the sense that the Coming of Christ is to be enjoyed by the faithful as a group;
b) terrestrial, in the sense that it is to be realized on this earth and not in some otherworldly heaven;
c) imminent, in the sense that it is to come both soon and suddenly;
d) total, in the sense that it is utterly to transform life on earth, so that the new dispensation will be no mere improvement on the present but perfection itself;
e) miraculous, in the sense that it is to be accomplished by, or with the help of, supernatural agencies. (Cohn 1996, 15)

D. H. Williams underscores Cohn's analysis, in his article, "The Origins of the Montanist Movement: A Sociological Analysis": "Disaster is prominent in the genesis of millenarian movements. . . Millenarian expectations flare up as a reaction to . . . hardships and suffering . . ." (D. H. Williams 1989, 337) In William's opinion, backwoods areas and rural regions were more susceptible to millenarian expectations than urban areas, as were more politically passive people. Such people felt that they had no power in society, and they looked elsewhere for relief. According to Williams, all of these elements came together in Asia Minor during the time of Priscilla, Maximilla, and Montanus. (D. H. Williams 1989, 336)

Marcus Aurelius and Disaster

While Christians faced constant societal problems, in the last half of the second century disaster stormed down on all of Phrygia. Williams points out the facts of the matter. Marcus Aurelius ascended the throne of the Roman Empire in 161 CE (337). The Roman governor of Cappadocia, Severianus, invaded Armenia and was utterly defeated. It took 5 years for the Romans to eventually achieve victory. The returning, victorious Roman legions brought the plague with them, and it spread throughout the empire.[22] Half the population of the Mediterranean world died. In

---

[22] Not only did Asia Minor have the war and the plague to deal with, but Marcus Aurelius then taxed them to pay for the war.

the same year, Williams continues, the northern frontier of the empire collapsed, and Germans and Slav immigrants pushed southward, overrunning thinly manned defenses. On top of these realities, the imperial treasury of Rome was empty. Panic struck! (Williams 1989, 336–51).

The conditions that we described that Marcion and his followers faced were almost the same as those faced by the Montanists. Because it is so appropriate we repeat Tertullian's description: "If the Tiber floods to the walls, if the Nile floods not the fields, if the sky gives no rain, if the earth shakes, if there is famine or pestilence, immediately comes the cry 'The Christians to the Lion!'" (*Apology*, 40, 48 *ANF* 3. CCEL) In his comprehensive article, "*The Epistula Apostolorum*: An Asian Tract from the Time of Polycarp," Charles Hill asserts that Asia Minor suffered more extensively than any other place from disasters of any kind (Hill 1990, 20f.). Because the Christians were an illegal sect that did not worship the gods, they were in the pagan superstitions the causes of the gods anger and therefore, as Tertullian said, thrown to the lions.

Stephen Friesen, in a recent work entitled *Imperial Cults and the Apocalypse of John: Reading Revelation in the Ruins*, picked up on the epic work of Mircea Eliade, historian and phenomenologist. Friesen challenges the accusation of unreality in the apocalyptic literature, especially in the *Apocalypse of John*. He asserts that Apocalypticism is not an abnormal human response, even in our own age, but rather a normal response to overwhelming human suffering. Rephrasing Eliade's work, Friesen wrote:

> We should wish to know, for example, how it would be possible to tolerate, and to justify, the sufferings and annihilation of so many peoples who suffer and are annihilated for the simple reason . . . that they are neighbors of empires in a state of permanent expansion . . . And in our day, when historical pressure no longer allows any escape, how can man tolerate the catastrophes and horrors of history—from collective deportations and massacres to atomic bombings—if beyond them he can glimpse no sign, no transhistorical meaning . . . if they are only the blind play of economic, social, or political forces, or, even worse, only the result of the "liberties" that a minority takes and exercises directly on the stage of universal history? (Friesen 2001, 7–8)

THE SPIRIT BLOWS ANEW, PENTECOST FOR WOMEN

This traumatic frame of life produced and continues to produce prophetic figures.

David E. Aune, in Prophecy, in *Early Christianity and the Ancient Mediterranean World* spends more than 200 pages writing about the prophets of early Christianity: "Prophets and their revelations played an integral role," Aune asserts, "within early Christianity until the beginning of the second century A.D." (Aune 1989, 189) Many of these prophets received their revelations in the state of ecstasy. Even the Apocalypse of John, Aune asserts, shows classical signs of prophecy. He also believes that these revelations were most likely received in a state of ecstasy. Among the first- and second-century works that Aune classifies as prophecy are: *The Odes of Solomon, The Shepherd of Hermas*, the works of Ammia of Philadelphia (ca 100–150 CE), the writings of Quadratus during the reign of Hadrian (117–138), the writings of Polycarp of Smyrna (ca 100–150), the writings of Melito of Sardis who died ca 190, the writings of Cerinthus (late first century and early second century), and, finally, *The Epistula Apostolorum*. (Aune 1983, 247–48)

Bruce J. Malina, in his *On the Genre and Message of Revelation: Star Visions and Sky Journeys*, states that during all ages people have had "visions involving celestial entities and celestial phenomena," and "many report having ascended into the sky…" Erika Bourguignon, who compiled a sample of 488 societies in all parts of the world at various levels of technological complexity, found that 90 percent of these societies evidence "alternative states of consciousness." Her conclusion: "Societies which do not utilize these states clearly are historical exceptions which need to be explained, rather than the vast majority of societies that do use these states" (Malina 1995, 2).

To our knowledge, none of the prophets Aune mentions were labeled heretics. Prophets were expected to be part of the church. Paul says so emphatically in 1 Corinthians 14:1: "Follow the way of love and eagerly desire gifts of the Spirit, especially prophecy." Paul, in fact, knew a person who entered an ecstatic state. Many believe that Paul was talking about himself: "I know a man in Christ who, fourteen years ago, whether he was in or outside his body I cannot say, only God can say—a man who was snatched up to the third heaven. I know that this man . . . was snatched up to Paradise to hear words which cannot be uttered, words which no man may speak" (2 Corinthians 12:2–4, NEB).

CHRISTIANITY: ENDANGERED OR EXTINCT?

J. R. Harrison, in his excellent article "In the Quest of the Third Heaven," indicated that Paul and his apocalyptic imitators "did have experiences with spiritual beings, but these spiritual beings were sent by Christ and were his creations, as opposed to having independent existence" (Harrison 2004, 24–55). Paul called such experiences "extraordinary revelations (τη υπερβολη αποχαλυπσεον) " (2 Corinthians 12:7, NEB). It is a curious reality that in spite of the fact that Paul and many other Christian prophets and ecstatics felt the acceptance of the early church, the Christian Montanist prophets were rejected. Aune puts it this way: ". . . institutionalization banished prophets [such as the Montanists] from their roles as leaders and marginalized the revelatory significance of their proclamations" (Aune 1983, 189). These banishments were instituted by distinct personalities, and these personalities were male aristocrats trained in philosophy. They used their philosopher's reasoning and the prestige of their philosopher's cloak to gain control of Christianity and distort and suppress other modes of thought.

Justinian's Persecution of the Montanists

We must not be too hasty in our reporting of history. There were some more profound changes happening in the Jesus Movement that are not readily apparent. In the period of the pre-Christian Empire, Roman philosophers freely exchanged ideas, and there was not really much consternation over their discussions. Furthermore, during and after the Christian Empire, within most branches of Christianity, apocalypticism and mysticism have been accepted as valid experiences. In reality, apocalypticism and mysticism had nothing to do with the reaction to the Montanists. What we are dealing with is, in Foucault's terms, "the development of the web-like network of power" and, specifically, with how that "network of power" was developing in the Jesus Movement. As with Marcion, there is no reason to question whether the Montanist were sincere followers of Jesus, and in fact there is every reason to accept that they would have passed all orthodox views. But we find in three centuries that the dogmatism of the church fathers develops into what it truly is, and that is violence.[23]

Nothing expresses the pathos of the successors of these prophets better than a description given by Tabbernee at the beginning of his monumental

---

[23] This is further development of Michel Foucault's thought see pp. iv-v; 31-33 this volume.

book *Montanist Inscriptions and Testimonia*. According to Tabbernee, when Emperor Justinian I was persecuting the Montanists around 530 CE, the troops of John, the bishop of Ephesus, discovered and defiled an archeological gem:

> They discovered a great marble shrine on which was inscribed: "Of Montanus and the women." When the reliquary was opened, they found the skeletons of Montanus, Maximilla, and Priscilla, with golden plates upon their mouths. The bones of the founders of Montanism, along with their "abominable books," were burned . . . and the building purified to allow it to be used by the official church. (Tabbernee 1997, 1–2)

This description was a horror story. If it was true it was symbolic of the destruction of the Montanist movement. The Montanists and all of history had lost the bones and the books of their founders.

Another bit of shocking news related to this event is that the bishop of Ephesus, successor of the apostles of Jesus, inheritor of the Jesus Movement, actually had military troops. Let us place all this in the perspective of the history of Justinian.[24] Before he became emperor (527–565 CE), Justinian had been schooled in political science, philosophy, military strategy, and Eastern-Nicene theology. He prided himself on being a foremost theologian. Nonetheless, despite his knowledge of theology, he justified and codified the type of violent repression perpetrated by John, the bishop of Ephesus and his troops. Even more shocking, *The Catholic Encyclopedia* does not recognize Justinian's activity as reprehensible. It states:

> The thirty-eight years of Justinian's reign are the most brilliant period of the later empire. Full of enthusiasm for the memories of Rome, he set himself, and achieved, the task of reviving their glory. The many-sided activity of this wonderful man may be summed up under the headings: military triumphs, legal work, ecclesiastical polity, and architectural activity. Dominating all is the policy of restoring the empire, great, powerful, and united. Of

---

[24] To summarize history a bit, the campaign against the Montanists by Roman emperors was not initiated by Justinian. It was certainly in effect at the time of Marcus Aurelius, Constantine in 325, Theodosius I in 379–395, and Theodosius II in 408–450.

CHRISTIANITY: ENDANGERED OR EXTINCT?

these many features of his reign, each of them was epoch-making ... (*The Catholic Encyclopedia*. advent.org)

Western Catholics had only one problem with Justinian, and it was not his use of violent repression. The problem they had with him was a theological one: he was a Monophysite. He believed that Jesus had only one essential divine being, whereas the Council of Chalcedon (451 CE) stated that Jesus was at the same time truly human and truly divine. The Eastern Catholics, the Orthodox, had no problem at all with Justinian. They actually canonized him (and Constantine, as well) as a saint. However, Justinian was a brutal ruler who reigned for a long time as emperor. His moral code was skewered, even though he thought himself a great theologian and undoubtedly saw himself as a deeply religious man whose goal was religious unity. He had no qualms about murdering a person who disagreed with his own religious beliefs. In his *Christianity and Paganism in the Fourth through the Eighth Centuries*, Ramsay MacMullen, likewise confirms this assessment of the emperor:

> A brutally energetic, or energetically brutal, ruler enjoying a very long reign, he pursued the goal of religious uniformity as no one before him. "He did not see it as murder if the victims did not share his own beliefs." Those who disagreed with him were likely to be mutilated if he didn't behead or crucify them ... (MacMullen 1997, 27)

Justinian promulgated from Constantinople laws against the Montanists somewhere between 529 and 534. This more than likely means that the Montanists were still very active in that time frame. The following are the laws that were enacted against the Montanists:

- "With regard to the unholy Montanists we ordain that none of their so-called patriarchs, koinonoi, bishops, presbyters, deacons, or other clergy—if indeed it is quite proper to call them by these names—should be permitted to reside in this fortunate city ... " (Justinian 1.5.20.3)
- "We do not permit them, in general, to transact business within the sacred boundaries, so that the orthodox faith's pure mysteries

may not be heard by people who are both polluted and unworthy to hear every clean and pure sound . . ." (Justinian, 1.5.20.4).
- "The privilege of trading within earshot of the orthodox mysteries should belong only to "those honoring the right faith" (Ibid. 1.5.20 praef. 1–2): orthodox pearls were not to be cast before Montanist swine." (Justinian, 1.5.20.3–4)

As a result of these laws, the Montanists remaining in the sixth century lived under intense pressure. They could not transact business or own property, and their clergy could not reside in Rome.

Christine Trevett writes: "Though Montanism in its many forms took a long time to die, we do not know of any single event which made it extinct" (Trevett 1996, 223). These Christians were simply hounded to death. To the relief of clergy and politicians, the intense Christianity started by women was apparently lost to the Christian church.[25]

Who Were These "Montanists"?

As we stated above, the Montanists would not have considered themselves Montanists but rather Christians evangelized by the apostles or by some early Christians. The dominant Christian philosopher or theologians in Rome may not even have known them, like many other groups of Christians in distant lands. The contact with these men could have come from female missionaries who made it to Rome, or it might have come by Christian slaves or support staff who accompanied Marcus Aurelius on his return to Rome. Whatever the case might have been, "the church fathers" hung the label Montanist around the necks of these women prophets, a message of stigma and condemnation separating them from the rest of the Christian population. This must have been baffling to the members of the Montanist congregations who considered themselves integral and upstanding members of the Church of Christ. This designation did not conform to reality either, for the Montanists were, indeed, intense followers of Jesus and brothers and sisters of Christians everywhere.

---

[25] There are indications that the Montanists may have survived these persecutions and continued to evangelize and establish themselves even into the twelfth century. Sadly, Justinian's violence towards Montanists was not the first violence of Christians on Christians and it would not be the last, but it is the first and only record of the violence towards the Montanists.

CHRISTIANITY: ENDANGERED OR EXTINCT?

Tertullian, a staunch Catholic who also became a Montanist, wrote about the attacks on the Montanists by the "psychics," as he called the non-Montanist Catholics, especially their clergy, bishops, and popes of the time.[26] The main reason they attacked Montanus, Priscilla, and Maximilla is not because of dogmatic reasons:

> ...[T]he new prophets do not preach about another God, nor do they deny that Jesus is God (1 John 4:3), nor do they overturn the rules of faith and hope. Rather, it is apparent that they attack them because the Montanists teach that Christians should fast more than they wed. (Tertullian, *De Ieiunio* [*Concerning Fasting*] I. 3)

Tertullian, of course, was using some sarcasm and rhetoric here. He and the Montanists were against second marriages, even after a spouse died. Furthermore, they did much fasting "to keep in check the desires of the flesh."

Tertullian was terribly frustrated. He had given up a good life as a Roman jurist to become a Catholic Christian and he was dedicated to the Church. He found in the Montanists, Montanus, Priscilla, and Maximilla, kindred spirits with the rigors of discipleship that he believed all Catholics should have. But Tertullian's orthodoxy was supported not only by his own words, but confirmed by the testimony of the great Saints Cyprian, and Jerome. In *Concerning Fasting against the Psychics,* Tertullian lays out his frustration with his non-Montanist Catholic clerics. He states:

> The Psychics accuse us [the Montanist Catholics] of having two spiritual disciplines which oppose their own addictions to food and sex. The first is fasting which reins in the appetites. For sometimes we eat no meals, at other times we eat late meals, and at other times we eat only dry meals. The second allows only one marriage in a lifetime. It is really disgusting to have to fight with them [the Psychics] on such matters. I am ashamed that I have to deal with such altercations. Even the defense which I must

---

[26] It is interesting to note that Tertullian is one of the chief sources of Catholic information about Marcion, but when he becomes a Montanist he becomes a heretic.

THE SPIRIT BLOWS ANEW, PENTECOST FOR WOMEN

raise is in itself shameful. How can I protect chastity and sobriety without lowering the good name of my adversaries? Nonetheless I must again mention their name: they are the Psychics who dispense such exterior and interior niceties. They fight against the Paraclete by rejecting the new prophets. (Tertullian *De Ieiunio* [*On Fasting*], I. 3)

By rejecting the Montanist Christians, Christianity took another step toward intolerance, which was foreign to Jesus' own vision for his church.

Prophesies of the Montanists and Other Discoveries

In 1960, through a methodical study of ancient inscriptions and other texts, Kurt Aland isolated genuine quotes from the Montanists. David Aune included these quotes, which he had translated into English from German, in his comprehensive *Prophecy in Early Christianity and the Ancient Mediterranean*. The following are 16 simple sayings as Aune transmits them:

1. [Montanus says:] "I am the Father and I am the Son and I am the Paraclete."
2. [Montanus says:] "I am the Father, and the Son, and the Paraclete."
3. [Montanus says:] "I the Lord, the Almighty God, remain among men."
4. [Montanus says:] "Neither angel, nor ambassador, but I, the Lord God the Father, have come."
5. [Montanus says:] "Behold, man is like a lyre, and I rush thereon like a plectrum. Man sleeps and I awake. Behold, the Lord is he who arouses the hearts of men, and gives a heart to men."
6. [Montanus says:] "Why do you call the more excellent man saved? For the righteous man shall shine a hundred times more than the sun, but the little ones who are saved among you will shine a hundred times more than the moon."
7. [The Paraclete in the new prophets says:] "The Church can forgive sins, but I will not do it, lest they sin again."
8. [The Spirit says:] "You will be publicly displayed before God. Let it not perplex you! Righteousness brings you into the midst. What

perplexes you about winning glory! Opportunity is given, when you are seen by men."
9. [The Spirit speaks:] "Desire not to die in bed, nor in the delivery of children, nor by enervating fevers, but in martyrdom, that He may be glorified who has suffered for you."
10. [The Paraclete says through the prophetess Prisca:] "They are flesh and they hate flesh."
11. [The holy prophetess Prisca proclaims:] "A holy minister must understand how to minister holiness. For if the heart gives purification, they will also see visions, and if they lower their faces, then they will perceive saving voices, as clear as they were obscure."
12. [Quintilla or Priscilla says:] "In the form of a woman arrayed in shining garments, came Christ to me and set wisdom upon me and revealed to me that this place is holy and that Jerusalem will come down hither from heaven."
13. [Maximilla says:] "After me there will be no longer a prophet, but the consummation."
14. [Maximilla says:] "Listen not to me, but listen to Christ."
15. [Maximilla says:] "The Lord has sent me as adherent, preacher, and interpreter of this covenant and this promise; he has compelled me, willingly or unwillingly, to learn the knowledge of God."
16. [The Spirit says through Maximilla:] "I am chased like a wolf from the sheep; I am not a wolf; I am word and spirit and power." (Aune 1983, 1996,. 313–316).

Aland's isolation of these words as authentic was a remarkable feat. But the words are remarkable in themselves for a number of reasons:

1. The words are written in the true prophetic tradition. In other words, they are not words emanating from Greek philosophy, nor are they words of ordinary conversation. They flow, as the Montanist Christians would insist, from the Father, Son, and Spirit. The phrasing indicates Trinitarian thought, even though, as far as orthodoxy is concerned, the Trinity is not spelled out until the year 325 at the Council of Nicaea.[27]

---
[27] According to the *Catholic Encyclopedia*, even Hippolytus did not have well-defined Trinitarian views.

2. Many of the words, maybe all of them, were uttered under ecstatic states. By ecstatic, we do not mean irrational (pp. 103-107 of this volume).
3. As Christine Trevett states, they include introductory formulas in the tradition of the great prophets, such as "I, the Lord have spoken ..." (Trevett, 1996, 82–84; see also Amos, Isaiah, Jeremiah, etc.).
4. These are only partial revelations. Most of the revelation in each case is missing. Most likely, the main body of the sayings was treacherously destroyed. Nonetheless, each terse statement is meaningful in itself, and each can be prayed over with benefit.
5. Evidence we have from these words, and from other sources, supports the fact that the Montanists were orthodox Christians. Sheila E. McGinn-Moorer drives home this point in her paper, "The 'Montanist Oracles and Prophetic Theology":

> All told, these few oracles demonstrate the doctrinal orthodoxy of the New Prophecy—a point which is by now a matter of consensus among Montanist scholars. The powerful sense of the immanent presence of God among Christians, especially via the prophetic word, is perhaps the most central element of the constructive theology of these oracles. This belief in divine immanence, in turn, provides a solid foundation for several aspects of Montanist prophetic theology. The proximity of God to Christians prompts the importance of holiness of life among them. This is expressed in the prophetic exhortations to chastity and abstaining from wine, the rigorous Montanist attitude toward forgiveness of sins, and the high value placed on martyrdom for the greater glory of God. (McGinn-Moorer 1997, 128–35).

6. The Montanists, with women leaders, challenged the elite church authorities. Elsa Gibson found strong evidence of this in graffiti written on the walls in Phrygia. This has been supported by other archeological findings found in Asia Minor. Here we will summarize her conclusions as they are found in

CHRISTIANITY: ENDANGERED OR EXTINCT?

the introduction to her *Montanus, Priscilla, and Maximilla. The "Christians for Christians" Inscriptions of Phrygia*:

> The New Prophecy believed in the outpouring of the Spirit and the appearance of a new, authoritative prophecy, which brought fresh disciplinary demands to the churches. Women were prominent as leaders and the Prophets clashed with catholic representatives on matters such as the nature of prophecy, the exercise of authority, the interpretation of Christian writings and the significance of the phenomenon for salvation-history. (Gibson 1978, 5–8)

While in church history it was not unusual that poor laypeople (both men and women) should prophesy, this does not mean that elite people in the church would always be happy about it. In so doing, these prophets sometimes trampled on the lawn of learned religious theologians and church authorities, men who had spent much of their lives studying philosophy and church matters; who insisted that their territory remain tidy, unruffled.

7. There is no gender hierarchical distinction among the prophets. Six of the prophecies are designated as originating from Montanus and seven from the women. The source of three prophecies can not be determined.
8. While lay prophecy was accepted in Catholicism, women prophets in leadership were rejected. As far as we know, only the prophetic Montanists were declared heretics. In light of the prophecies themselves and in light of Tabbernee's total research, he does not hesitate to say that Maximilla and Priscilla soon "provided the primary prophetic content," overshadowing Montanus (Tabbernee 1996, 19). These women, in the tradition of Mary, Martha, and Mary Magdalene, sat at the feet of Jesus—they were the disciples and apostles of Jesus (Luke 10:38–41).

Trevett describes it best:

The ideal of Montanist Christian womanhood embraced the public sphere as well as the private sphere and in ways anathema to the Catholics . . . A suitably charismatic woman was called upon to respond to the Spirit's leadings in the congregation and even (like Priscilla and Maximilla or the prophetess known to Firmilian) to be an itinerant evangelist and prophet. She might flout society's conventions in the cause of total discipleship—leaving her husband. The Montanist woman was called on to accept willingly the public declaration of her faith in times of trial. There was to be no shunning of the public gaze out of modesty or appeal to domestic and female obligations...but if the extant oracles preserve the truth, the Montanists were anxious that women, no less than men, should be wholly disciples: disciplined and fervent, continent and Spirit-filled, uncompromising and seen. They did not fear to defend their stance, debating scripture and appealing to revelations. There is nothing to suggest that they relied on men to be their advocates. (Trevett 1996, 176)

Elsewhere, Tabbernee indicates that the Montanists considered themselves to be an important part of the official church, not separate in any way, and that the members of the church considered them sisters and brothers. He points to evidence in Jerome (Epistle 41. 3) that they had a patriarch before the rest of the Christian church used the term in any official documents (Tabbernee 1997, 122). They also had bishops, presbyters, deacons, and missioners whom they supported by raising funds. In short, they resembled the church in its evolving form. The Montanists, from all indications, were models of the church and its structure rather than an aberration. They were constantly and painfully present and painfully helpful to the church.[28]

Today, thanks to Tabbernee, Heine, Aland, Trevett, and other

---

[28] Tabbernee asks the question, "...[H]ow should the first phase of the movement be defined?" (1997, pp. 23–24) He answers, "There is no consensus about this question." He then goes on to summarize and footnote the best scholarship of the past. They have been called an anti-Gnostic phenomenon, a type of Gnosticism, an attempt to preserve the primitive "charismatic" nature of Christian ministry, a reaction to the official church's compromise with secular society, a reaction to the authority and teachings of the official church itself, the patriarchalization of mainstream Christianity different from the way in which Montanism empowered women, a peculiar form of Jewish Christianity, an exaggerated expression of apocalyptic Christianity influenced especially by Johannine literature, a millenarian movement, a product of the socioreligious crisis resulting from the persecution of the church, an expression of rural, rather than urban, Christianity, and a classic example of the enthusiastic sect type of the church destined to reappear throughout history.

CHRISTIANITY: ENDANGERED OR EXTINCT?

historians and archaeologists, we know more than scholars of the past about the Montanists. Perhaps recent and future studies will give us more knowledge about them.[29] Tabbernee tells us about their growth:

> The New Prophecy established its headquarters at or near the small neighboring Phrygian villages of Pepouza and Tymion" (Apollonarius, ap. Eusebius, 5.18.2)...From there Montanism spread to other parts of Phrygia and to various other provinces in Asia Minor. It also spread rapidly to places which Asiatics had close contacts. (Tabbernee 2001, 20)

---

[29] In fact, shortly after Tabbernee published his works, archaeologists found the ruins of an ancient Christian cathedral in Phrygia, which Tabbernee has identified as a Montanist cathedral. We expect that more information will be shortly coming (Tabbernee, "Portals of the Montanist New Jerusalem: The Discovery of Pepouza and Tymion," *Journal of Early Christian Studies*, 11).

4

The Spirit Blows in Africa, Tertullian and the Carthage Community

Christine Trevett writes that the spread of Montanism was obvious and earthshaking, reaching points west and east. She likewise asserts that there were sizeable crowds at their gatherings. (Trevett 1996, 50) The Montanists were just one of the true communities of Jesus, but they spread from Asia Minor to Carthage, in Africa, and from Gaul to Thrace (Tabbernee 1997, 355). Trevett picks up on Kurt Aland's warning to historians that they should be wary of the "hereticmongers" (such as Constantine, Justinian, Hippolytus, Epiphanius, etc.) in documenting the spread of the Montanist form of the Jesus Movement. Of his warning, Trevett states:

> Kurt Aland is rightly cautious about tracing its spread, for scholars have been over-reliant on lists of heresies as evidence of Montanism's existence in a given area. Montanism soon acquired a fixed place in such lists. And while in the East the laws against heretics seem to suggest that Montanism continued as a reality down to the fifth century and beyond, one has to suspect that in many places writers habitually condemned Montanists without ever having encountered one. Yet . . . the impact of the Prophecy

was considerable and . . . it moved within a decade to being more than a local Phrygian affair. (Trevett 1996, 53–54)

The Vigor of the Carthage Montanist Community

We are certain that the community not only existed, but also thrived, in Carthage, a large metropolitan area in North Africa. The vigorous activity of well-trained Montanist missionaries is the only reason that their presence was found with such vitality in this far point of the Empire. The fact is that we know more about the Carthage Montanist community than any other because this community included the recognized intellectual and spiritual giant, Tertullian (ca 160–ca 230), and the great martyrs, Saint Perpetua and Saint Felicitas. It was especially Tertullian's ready pen, which tells our age about many of the details of that community.

In the previous chapter, we saw some strong indications that Montanism was a dynamic, Christ-like force within the Jesus movement. Questions immediately come to our mind—questions we would like to ask Tertullian. This chapter will undoubtedly answer some of them because Tertullian was not a bashful disciple of Jesus. While Carthage had its own special character, the writings of Tertullian indicated that a basic connection in values and customs did exist between the Montanist mother church in Asia Minor and this mission. The Montanist missionaries in Carthage must have been remarkable human beings, with deep, and solid religious convictions.

Persecutions in the city were a sporadic, but constant reality which Christians had to face. In March 203, Felicitas, Perpetua, and others were brutally martyred. These Christians came from all social levels of society: Felicitas was a slave, and Perpetua was from a respectable, even rich, family. At least these two members of the group and maybe all of the rest of them were Montanists. The question raised by Trevett (1996, 1) and many students of Montanism, even Soyres, who wrote over a century ago (1878), is this: "Was the 'spirit' which Tertullian preached, and for which Perpetua died, the spirit of the father of lies, or was it the Spirit of God?" (Trevett: 1996, 131ff.) These knowledgeable historians write that in this early era, Montanism was more than a branch of the tree which was withering and dying from persecution. Tertullian heartily agreed.

THE SPIRIT BLOWS

Tertullian's Intimate Account of the Vibrant Carthage Montanist Community

Tertullian tells us about the intimate lives of the followers of Jesus of Nazareth in the Carthage Christian community:

- We are a body knit together by a common religious commitment, by one discipline, and by a common bond of hope.
- Wrestling with him, we assemble together as a united force to offer prayer to God in supplications. This type of violence God delights in . . .
- We pray for the emperor, for his ministers and for all in authority, for the welfare of the world, for peace, and for the delay of the final consummation.
- We do not swear by the genius of the Caesars, we only prayed and hoped for their safety.
- We assemble to read our sacred writings if current events indicate that we should take warning or that we need to reminisce.
- We exhort one another at these gatherings, rebuke one another and administer censures, if they be necessary.
- Tried elders preside at our assemblies, and they constantly tell us that honor cannot be purchased—it is earned.
- We do have a "treasure-chest." On the designated day of the month, a person can put in a small donation if the person is able and willing to do so. There is no pressure; all is voluntary. These gifts are piety's deposit fund . . . to support and bury poor people, to supply the needs of orphans and prisoners, to aid anyone who might be shipwrecked, suffering in the mines, or banished to the islands.
- One in mind and soul, we do not hesitate to share our earthly goods with one another. All things are common among us except our wives and husbands.
- The feast we regularly share with one another is called in Greek an agape meal. Before reclining, we taste first of prayer to God. We then eat enough to satisfy our cravings of hunger; we drink enough to satisfy our thirst. Afterwards, we light candles, and we entertain one another: each one stands before the others and sings a song to God, using Holy Scripture or a poem of their

liking, or we tell a story or sing a song of our own creation. The meeting closes with a prayer (The above statements are found in *Apologeticum*, XXXIX).

- We marry only once, even if our spouse dies. (See *De monogamia* [*On Monogamy*], *De ieiunio* [*On Fasting*], *De exhortatione castitatis* [*Exhortation to Chastity*], *Ad uxorem* [*To Wife*]).
- "The Psychics" [the Catholics, especially the Catholic clergy, bishops and pope][30] accuse us of keeping fasts, prolonging them into the evening, observing xerophagies [eating food unmoistened by the juice of meats and succulent fruits, avoiding drinking or cooking with wine, and abstaining from the bath during the fasts] (De ieiunio [On Fasting], I, 3).
- Outside of these things, "we live like everyone else in the world. We join with the others at the forum, in the streets, in the bath, at the inns, at the weekly market, and at other places of commerce. We sail with you, share our burdens with you and till the ground with you . . . In the various arts, we make public property of our works for the benefit of all. How it is that we seem to be useless pieces of humanity to you, living with you and by you as we do, is difficult for me to understand" (Apologeticum [*Apology*], XLII).
- We do not commit crimes. If we are in prison, it is simply because we are Christian (Apologeticum [*Apology*], XLV).
- Furthermore, we treat our ordinary neighbors with the same respect that we show the emperor . . .
- We are forbidden to wish anyone ill, to do ill to anyone, to speak or even to think ill of anyone . . . If we are committed, then, to love our enemies, then whom else is there to hate? If injured, we are forbidden to retaliate . . . (Apologeticum, [*Apology*] XXXVI–XXXVII).
- We witness to Christ from the jails, and many of us are called to give their lives as witnesses for him. The community feels a responsibility to minister to the prisoners' needs until the day they die. We denounce "the madness of the circus, the immodesty of the theatre, the atrocities of the arena, and the vulgar uselessness

---

[30] The name utilized by Tertullian for the Catholics. It is a reference to their utilization of their human mind to claim special divine knowledge. How could human beings know so much? They must be "psychic."

of the wrestling ground." (*Apologeticum*, XXXVIII)

Tertullian's description of the life of the Montanist is clear and straight forward. He describes a manner of living that was Christ-like down to the last detail. In a previous chapter, we cited Tertullian of Carthage as using his rhetoric to attack Marcion and the Marcionites. A kinder, gentler Tertullian wrote the above description of the Montanist community. Obviously, he had had a conversion.

Summary of Tertullian's Life

Quintus Septimus Florens Tertullianus (Tertullian) was born in Carthage around 160 CE. He was, according to many, the son of a Roman centurion. Certainly, he was one of the Roman elite. Tertullian's father secured for him the best classical education. He became an intelligent, master rhetorician. He appreciated the art of argumentation. Tertullian not only used the canned lists of historical events taught to every rhetorician, but he dug deeply into history and the classics. He was well trained in philosophy, in Greek, and in Latin.

Tertullian, Christian, Catholic, and Montanist

When Tertullian became 40 years of age, he became a Christian. In his work *Apologeticum*, he wrote to the pagans: "At one time, I joined you in ridiculing the Christians. I am of your stock and nature. I grew to become a Christian, I was not born one" (*Apologeticum*, xviii). After his conversion, even though some church members thought him "strange," most loved having him as a brother. He used his knowledge, insights, and writing abilities to defend the Christian faith against many philosophers and others in secular society. In Christianity, he found a foundation for his life, which no philosophy could give him. He found Jesus. Furthermore, no one in the recorded fathers of the church, with the exception of Jerome, knew scripture as well as he did. He married. We do not know the name of the woman he married.

Tertullian took considerable risks in becoming a Christian. His own writings and the martyr's journal, *The Passion of Perpetua and Felicitas*,[31] show that Christians in Carthage were rejected and persecuted

---

[31] Some scholars believe that *The Passion of Perpetua* was written by Tertullian, but we contend that it is not his style, and that he would have had to go through a personality transformation to write it.

CHRISTIANITY: ENDANGERED OR EXTINCT?

by the community at large. Around the year 206, Tertullian joined the Montanists. In the nineteenth century, John De Soyres believed that the two Montanist Christian martyrs, Perpetua and Felicitas, had some influence on Tertullian's decision to join that group (De Soyres 1868, 43). In the last few years, scholars such as Tabbernee (1997, 55–58) and Alex Butler (2001, passim) also believe that Perpetua's and Felicitas' presence was important for Tertullian's conversion.

Today, the Catholic Church venerates the women, but not Tertullian, as saints of the church. While Tertullian was influenced by others to join the Montanists, he was, nonetheless, always his own person. If he believed the Montanists had something special to add to Christianity, he had to have solid reasons, his own reasons, for joining the group. He is one of the brightest, if not the brightest, of all the early church fathers. He was also a firm believer in the Catholic hierarchy. He was not a man who could be led astray by some fly-by-night sect. Furthermore, Tertullian did not see his joining the Montanists as a separatist event. As Trevett says so well, "Tertullian the Montanist was Tertullian the Montanist Catholic" (Trevett 1996, 69).

The Christian-Montanist life of Tertullian was exemplary. He was never considered a saint or a doctor of the church because the Catholic Church eventually considered his Montanist affiliations heretical. Indeed, Tertullian, even in his lifetime, knew that he and the Montanists were viewed with suspicion by the Catholic Church bishops. With consternation, he wrote in *On Fasting* [*De Ieiunio*]:

> I wonder about the Psychics [Catholics]. They are enthralled by extravagance. They marry more often than we do and they waste their lives with gluttony. It is clear that they hate fasts . . . They reproach us with practicing novelties, which they consider either forbidden or even heresy. Do they speak thus by some human presumption, or do they consider themselves some sort of pseudo-prophets? Either way they consider their attitude toward us as some spiritual indictment. I cannot but hear it as anything but an announcement of an anathema against us. (Tertullian, *De ieiunio*, I, 3)

Why does the Catholic faith even today question Tertullian's integrity? When his teachings and life are examined in the light of the teachings of Jesus, we find that he was a religious and saintly Christian man. In addition to his own example, and his beautiful description of the life of the Montanists, he wrote these words to Scapula, a man who persecuted the Christians:

> We are not in any panic or alarm about the persecutions we suffer at the hands of the ignorant. For when we became Christian we fully accepted the terms of the Christian covenant . . . We are sending this tract to you not because of any alarm concerning our own welfare, but because of our concern for you, for all our enemies, and certainly for our friends. Our religion commands us to love even our enemies and to pray for those who persecute us. It aims at a new perfection which is higher than the commonplace goodness of the world. For all love those who love them; it is distinctly Christian to love those that hate them. Therefore we mourn your ignorance, and we have mercy on your human error. (Tertullian, *Ad scapulam*, I, 4)

The words are distinctly Christian, and they reiterate the words of Jesus himself. Tertullian goes on using indisputable logic:

> . . . [O]ne person's religion neither harms nor helps another. It is assuredly no part of religion to force itself upon another. For religion is a free-will offering. Free will and not force should govern the willing mind. You will render no real service to your gods by compelling us to sacrifice to them.(Tertullian, *Ad scapulam*, II, 1)

Tertullian the Unifier

For all his rhetoric, Tertullian was, paradoxically, a unifier by nature. Even as a Montanist, Tertullian had nothing against philosophers. He united his own philosophy into his theology and into his reading of the Bible. When he became a Montanist, no one in his age doubted that he was also a Catholic. He believed in the apostolic lineage of the bishops. He claimed in *The Prescription of Heretics* (*De Praescriptione Haereticorum* 36), that the "seats" of the apostles are in those churches of apostolic foundation. Also in *Against Marcion* (*Adversus Marcionem*, iv, 5, 1–2), he mentions that certain churches could claim authentic apostolic succession. At the same time, he abhorred the practice of bishops keeping lists proving their lineage to an apostle, and then putting them on their mantles like trophies. He expected them to "prove it" by their example. Faithfulness to the Gospel message was much more convincing to him than mere "physical pedigree." With all sincerity, he often saw the Montanist prophetesses as carrying the message of the Gospel more authentically than many of the bishops. Finally, even with his wholehearted Christian faith, which he proudly and publicly proclaimed, he managed to walk free around Carthage while many of his fellow Christians and dear friends died in the arena.

Tertullian's Defense of the Montanists

Tertullian has tremendous value for us who are attempting to piece together the thrusts and dedications of the early Montanist. He forces us to halt before joining in the chorus of later condemnations which rained down on the Montanists throughout history. The *Apologeticum* is a work of a special kind. Tertullian formed the work by reworking two of his previous volumes, the *Adversus haereticorum*, (*Against Heretics* I and II). He set them up in the framework of the forensic work of a defense lawyer. He wrote the work to the governors of the Roman states. It is an impassioned plea defending himself and his Christian brothers and sisters. Tertullian knew that there was little likelihood that the governors would pay attention to his work. In spite of that, he knew that the case had to be made for Christians and the injustice of the Roman court system in regard to them. He saw his Christian brothers and sisters, his friends in Carthage, imprisoned and cruelly tortured and killed. He made the case in the hope that someone, somewhere, would read and attend to his words.

At times, the work is also intimate, giving us a close insight into the life of the early Christians. In place of the impassioned plea usually given by a defense lawyer to the judges for justice and fairness, Tertullian opened with an onslaught on those judges and on the rulers of the Roman Empire who were martyring his friends. It was a bitter, painful condemnation for the lack of justice in the past and a plea for a change in the future:

> Rulers of the Roman Empire, you are seated on your lofty thrones
> for the administration of justice in all but the highest position in

the state. Under the gaze of every eye, you are obviously unwilling to openly inquire into and sift before the world the truth regarding the charges made against the Christians. You have rather inflicted extreme pain on our people in specific recent private judgments. You are now afraid of or ashamed to change your manner of judging by doing what is right and just, by exercising your authority correctly according to the law and making careful, public inquiry into the charges against the Christians. Hopefully, you will allow truth to reach your ears by the secret pathway of this harmless book which I have written. (Tertullian, *Apologeticum* I)

Then Tertullian pleaded with the governors to realize the injustice of the ruling Trajan gave to Pliny the Younger, which stated that Christians ought not to be sought out, but if they were brought before him, they should be punished.[32] Tertullian asked the governors to consider the matter carefully:

When the charges similar to those made against Christians are made against others charged with crimes, they are permitted to make a defense, even hiring defense lawyers to help show their innocence. They have every opportunity to answer questions and bring up information that will acquit them. Everyone else has the right to a defense. It is against the law to condemn anybody without hearing their defense. Christians alone are forbidden to say anything to the judge to prove their innocence. All that is needed is what public gossip and public hatred demand. Their name [Christian] alone is proof sufficient of their guilt. No examination of the charge is necessary. (Tertullian, *Apologeticum* II).

Indeed, the common rumors on the street were spine-chilling. These rumors said that Christian Montanists gathered together to murder and eat children in their feasts and commit incest afterward. The truth of the matter was that the Christian Montanists simply refused to offer incense or worship to the gods or to the emperor. Tertullian was incensed. Nothing could be further from the truth. He argued that it was not possible for Montanists to

---

[32] See Chapter 2, this volume, p. 30

kill anybody, not even their enemies. As to the charge that the Montanists were killing their children, he protested, "We may not destroy even the fetus in the womb." The Montanists' morality was beyond question. He stated: "Perseveringly and steadfastly we protect the chastity of our members. We allow no adulteries or sex outside of marriage. We certainly do not allow incestuous sex" (*Apologeticum* IX).

Then Tertullian went to the crux of matter. He wrote to the Romans:

> 'You [meaning the Christians, Montanists or not] do not worship the gods,' you say, 'and you do not offer sacrifices to the emperors . . .' This is the chief charge against us. Indeed, it is the only charge against us. So let us dig into the matter and give it a good hearing . . . We do not worship your gods because we know that they do not exist. This, therefore, is what you ought to do: call on us to demonstrate their non-existence. We would be happy to do so. We will come before you and prove that your gods are not divine, and that they have no claim to adoration. After all, you must agree with us that any obligation to give supreme homage demands a reason for giving it. Then, if it becomes clear that your gods are divine, and we Christians still refuse to do so, then by all means, punish us. (*Apologeticum*, X)

Tertullian then gave examples—showing the human stock of various Roman gods (Chapter X–XI). He wrote that Christians believe in the one God (Chapter XVII), who spoke through the prophets (XVIII), and gave us the scriptures (Chapter XX). Finally, he wrote that Christians believed in Christ, the Son of God who came "to renew and illuminate man's nature" (Chapter XX), who was "born—but not so humanly born as to make Him ashamed to call Himself the Son of his Father." He used an analogy to bring home his point:

> When the ray is shot from the sun, it is still part of the parent mass; the sun will still be in the ray, because it is a ray of the sun; there is no division of substance, but merely an extension of it. Thus Christ is Spirit of Spirit, and God of God, as light from light is kindled . . . This ray of God, then, as it was always foretold in ancient times, descended into a virgin, and became flesh in

her womb. Thus he is both God and man united. This God-man grew to manhood, spoke, taught, worked, and is the Christ whom we worship. (*Apologeticum*, XX)

Tertullian is not the voice of a heretical sect, but the voice and defense of a more authentic Christianity. In fact, if there is any group that Christians would want to emulate, it is this group of Montanists.

Tertullian the Rhetorician

We have already seen the ugly work the rhetorician Tertullian did on Marcion, a man he never knew. Certainly, his five-volume work, *Contra Marcionem*, was not his best effort. Perhaps it was the work of a younger Tertullian. It fits with something Jerome called "his impetuous nature," which, at times, reached the point of being gossipy. It was part of the human weakness of the man, an aspect of his personality, which Tertullian undoubtedly had to work on all his life.

Tertullian's Use of Scripture

While Tertullian's use of rhetoric reflected poorly in his use in relationship to Marcion, as a Montanist his use of rhetoric was more humane. He always was a good rhetorician, and most frequently writing to fellow Christians he masterfully weaved excellent interpretation of scripture with good rhetoric. Tertullian not only knew scriptures well, but he used it liberally in his writings—except when he was writing to pagans. Professor Geoffrey Dunn states that at one time or another, Tertullian used all of the books of the Bible except Ruth, Obadiah, 1 Chronicles, Esther, 2 Maccabees, 2 John, and 3 John (Dunn 2004, 19). Most of the books not used might not have been in the canon of scripture or the books known and/accepted as scripture at the time. He also used *The Book of Enoch* insisting that it was part of the canonical scripture, because a quote from *Enoch* is found in *The Epistle of Jude*. He claimed in his *De Cultu Feminarum* (*On the Apparel of Women*) 1, 3, 1, that Noah could have rewritten the Book of Enoch from memory.

As a general rule, he also insisted that one passage of scripture had to be read in the light of all the rest of scripture (Dunn 2004, 22). Tertullian remained the practical rhetorician. He was trained to use whatever method of using scriptures that would win the argument for him. Even though he wrote that discussing the proper interpretation of scripture with heretics was unprofitable, he found himself constantly itching to do so. Sometimes he argued from an allegorical or typological position. For Tertullian, the bottom line was winning the argument. But he was not interested in winning it for his own personal glory. He was clearly only interested in correcting what he thought were erroneous opinions (Dunn 2004, 35). He wrote with passion and with definite intent.

Tertullian's Relationship with Women

One of the charges against the Montanists was that they destroyed the family—they took up heretical views and ran away from their families to spread their views. However, Tertullian, as chief apologist for the Montanists by his life and words, laid those charges to rest. He married a Christian woman, and he wrote two letters to her, which Montanists cherished. At the end of his second letter to her, he gives a beautiful picture of a Christian marriage, which reflected the mutual respect Montanists had for the unity of woman and man:

> Especially beautiful is the couple, who is married in the Church of God. Each is equal to the other not only in their shared union with their God, but also in the troubles which they share—their falling into difficulties, even persecution—and their working their way out of them. Neither one avoids the other. Neither is harsh to the other. Freely they visit and provide for the needs of the sick. Cheerfully they give alms together, supporting one another so that each can give without uneasiness. Daily each bears with the other without hindrance. Neither holds any secrets from the other. Each praises the other in their successes, and they encourage and support one another in their failures. They sing psalms and hymns together, competing with one another concerning who can sing more beautifully to God. Hearing and seeing all these things, Christ rejoices. He sends his peace to them. The Evangelist gives them much to think about regarding the life Jesus has given them. He says that when the two of them are united, Jesus is in their midst, and there can be no evil present there. Reflect on all these things when you

need to do so. Reflect also on the little, loving things that you notice other Christian couples doing for one another. For Christians are not permitted to marry in any but this loving and sharing way. If, at times, Christian couples fail to act thus, they are certainly on the wrong path (*Ad Uxorem* [To Wife], II, VII, 7–9 CSEL).

Tertullian also had a close relationship with Felicitas and Perpetua as well. He also held in high esteem the woman prophet who prophesied in his church and Prisca, of the mother Montanist Catholic Church (De Soyres 1868, 43; Tabbernee 1997, 55–58; Butler 2001, passim). His relationships with them reflect the basic and caring attitudes toward women which Jesus himself maintained. However, he was against women baptizing and becoming bishops (see *Adversus valentinianos* [*Against the Valentinians*]32; *De baptismo* [On Baptism]17). In *Tertullian's Theology of Divine Power*, Roy Kearsley suggests, and we think correctly, that the legacy of tradition and his desire for unity accounts for his position on women in the clergy (Kearsley 1998, 159).

Tertullian firmly believed in Christian women prophets. He thought that Montanist women prophets had more right to call themselves the followers of the apostles than did many of the bishops of the time. Tertullian, then, was not antifeminist. He made statements in his *On the Apparel of Women* [*De Cultu Feminarum*] which a superficial reader could take as antifeminist. But if we look at the statements, take out the rhetoric, and place them in the context of his other writings, they are not statements against the feminine gender at all, but they are statements much in accord with Montanist thought and mores against running after the changing fashions of the age. In *On the Mantle* (*De Pallium*) Tertullian, in the same rhetorical fashion as he uses in *On the Apparel of Women*, excoriates the men of Carthage for donning immodest mantles.

The Catholic Church and the Montanists

Because Catholicism has considered Montanism heresy, one can understand why within Catholicism there is the desire to separate Tertullian's writings as into Catholic, when he was "orthodox" and Montanist when he was a "heretic."[33] The presumption is that at some point Tertullian un-

---

[33] For example see Cleveland Coxe's "Introductory Note", *ANF* 3, p. 11.

derwent a "conversion" or "diversion" into Montanism. In Tertullian's age and in Tertullian's mind, the Montanist Tertullian was also the Catholic Tertullian. This is clear when he painfully takes on the Psychics, the Catholics, in *On Fasting* (*De Ieiunio*). He says clearly that he does not want to criticize them, because he does not want to put them in a bad light, but he feels that he has to do so in order to be truthful.

Tertullian's References

Tertullian has impressive references. His credentials show his unifying influence. They also show the deep respect other theologians and Christians had for the man. This man, though he struggled against being a meddler and a gossiper, deserves to be among the ranks of the saints and the doctors of the Catholic Church. Cyprian (ca 195–258 CE), bishop of Carthage, saint and doctor of the church, who was martyred in 258 CE, was a student of Tertullian. He never questioned his teacher. Certainly if Tertullian had been a heretic, of all people, Cyprian would have lamented the fact.

Yet Cyprian had some of the strictest standards for church inclusion. He wrote: "Who is separated from the Church and is joined to an adulteress, is separated from the promises of the Church; nor can he who forsakes the Church of Christ attain the rewards of Christ" (*On the Unity of the Church* 6, *ANF* 5, 425. CCEL). If Cyprian considered Tertullian separated from the church or if Tertullian were excommunicated from the church in his day, Cyprian would have certainly mentioned it, and he certainly would have lamented it.

At the end of the third century Eusebius, who reported Anonymous' and Apollinarius' cases against the Montanists, described Tertullian as "a man well versed in the laws of the Romans, and in other respects of high repute, and one of those especially distinguished in Rome" (Eusebius: *Church History*, II. 2. 5). In book V. v. 5, he wrote: "Tertullian is a trustworthy witness . . ."

Some 70 years after Eusebius and a hundred years after Cyprian, the highly respected scholar Jerome (ca 347–420), who translated the scriptures from Greek and Hebrew into Latin, complimented Tertullian.

This presbyter (Tertullian) is now regarded as chief of the Latin writers after Victor and Apollonius. He was from the city of Carthage in the province of Africa, where his father was a proconsul and a centurion. Tertullian was a man with an impetuous temperament. He was well-known in the reign of the emperor Severus and Antoninus Caracalla. He wrote many books, which I need not name because they are well-known. I have met a certain Paul, an old man of Concordia, a town of Italy, who, while he was a very young man, had been secretary to Blessed Cyprian, who, at that time, was already old. He said that he had seen how Cyprian never passed a day without reading Tertullian, and that he frequently said to Paul, "Give me the master," meaning, of course, Tertullian. (Jerome, *Lives of Illustrious Men*, LIII *NPNF* 2nd Series, 3.353. CCEL)

All of his fellow contemporary theologians respected Tertullian. Later, Latin-writing theologians went to him for their theological language. They, too, respected the man. Geoffrey D. Dunn, in his book *Tertullian*, states that terms that were used in later Orthodox theology such as *sacramentum* (sacrament), *trinitas* (Trinity), *persona* (Person), *substantia* (substance), and *satisfactio* (satisfaction) were either Tertullian's formulation or his perpetuation. (Dunn, 2004, p. 10)

Conclusion

Outside of his writings and a few other Christian writings, quality Latin literature was sparse during his period. Tertullian's excellent Latin writings alone would have given him prominence. One of the great scholars of the first part of the last century, T. R. Glover, who translated Tertullian's *De Spectaculis* (On Shows) made this profound observation:

Tertullian... may be said to have made Christian Latinity; it came from his hands rough-hewn, needing to be shaped and polished by later workers, but destined never to lose the general character which he had impressed upon it. He did more; he laid the foundation of Latin Christianity. (Glover 1931, ix, xviii)

CHRISTIANITY: ENDANGERED OR EXTINCT?

Tertullian found in Montanism a movement that was totally consistent and essential to Christianity. After years of research into archaeology and ancient texts, Tabbernee describes the movement which Tertullian more than likely found:

> The basic self-understanding of the movement as a prophetic renewal movement informed by the Holy Spirit must not be overlooked... This new revelation did not produce new doctrine, but it did usher in a new age in which 'spiritual Christians' would finally be able to attain the 'spiritual lifestyle,' which, they believed, God had intended for humanity from the beginning. (Tabbernee 1997, 24)

5

The Torrents of Condemnation Come Cascading Down

The Synod of Laodicea and the Council of Constantinople

The agents of the Catholic Church in the third to the fourth century were in the process of centralizing the church. In that process, they placed the value system of Jesus into the Greek philosophical framework, which was familiar to them. Many Christians had difficulty with the changes. They wondered if even Jesus or his apostles would have agreed with the "new," centralized church, and the values added and subtracted by the new pillars of the church, the Greek philosophers. Those who resisted the changes, and even some who did not, were called "heretics." Christian though they were from head to toe, these so-called heretics had neither the power nor in some cases the will to counteract the sweeping new system, imposed on them by presbyters, bishops, and popes-people with strange titles not found in Jesus' Gospel message. The growing hierarchy of the Catholic Church called them "heretics" nonetheless and treated them with disdain. The period of diversity in the church now was beginning to fade into history.

The church of the time considered itself the good wine in new wine skins. They had no doubts that the Montanists and other "heretics" were the dregs. But who, in fact, were the true wine, and who the dregs? Who truly were the sheep, and who were the wolves? (Matthew 10:16)

One of the first recorded and codified ecclesiastical condemnations of

CHRISTIANITY: ENDANGERED OR EXTINCT?

"heretics" came at the Synod of Laodicia (a heretic mongering Council) in 343. In one breath, the synod drove the Montanists, Novatians, and Photinians out of the church, but not with equal venom. The Novatians and Photinians could return to the church by merely "anathematizing every heresy," and then be "anointed with holy chrism" (Canon VII, *NPNF* 2, 127). The requirement for the Montanists' return was much worse:

> Persons converted from the heresy of those who are called Phrygians [Montanists] even should they be among those reputed by them as clergymen, and even should they be called the very highest in rank, are with all care to be instructed and baptized by the Bishops and Presbyters of the Church." (*NPNF* 2nd Series, 2, 128, CCEL)

Within this instruction (indoctrination), the Montanist "converts to Catholicism" had to make believe that they knew nothing at all about Jesus, and that they had never been baptized. Even though they showed every indication that they were already devoted Christians, they had to be "reeducated" by the presbyters and bishops. Then they were to be baptized once more.

Montanist Christians, of course, would have had difficulty with such a charade. Unhappily, the 7th Canon of the Council of Constantinople in 381 also agreed with the Synod of Laodicea. In their decrees, neither the Synod of Laodicea nor the Council of Constantinople gave any reason for the severe condemnations of fellow Christians, let alone the requirement for rebaptism of the Montanists.[34] Furthermore, the church never baptized an already baptized Christian. Baptism was, and remains, the one ledge of unity to which Christians throughout the world have always clung. The church, no matter what group of Christians did the baptizing, has always considered a baptized Christian a baptized Christian. The church condemned the

---

[34] *The Catholic Encyclopedia* in its section on "Baptism" states: "The Montanists baptized in the name of the Father and the Son and Montanus and Priscilla (St. Basil, Ep. I, *Ad Amphil.*). As a consequence, the Council of Laodicea ordered their rebaptism." That Basil had anything to do with the Council of Laodicea is unlikely because he was approximately 13 years old when the council took place. For many other reasons, the weird statement that the Montanists omitted the Holy Spirit and added Montanus and Priscilla in the Holy Spirit's stead is beyond belief. Tertullian, for one, would not have stood for it. Furthermore, the statement reeks of the hearsay, innuendo, defamation, and calumny, which were rampant in the church concerning the group.

Donatists in the fourth and fifth century for rebaptizing Catholics.

Also, much later, various groups of disparate Christian sects killed the Anabaptists of the sixteenth and seventeenth century partially for rebaptizing Christians. The church picked up the notion of heresy and sometimes utilized it when heresy was either not present, or when heresy could have been avoided with some diplomacy and care. The history of abuse that the Montanists faced is described by Trevett:

> The Montanists readily accepted the slanders thrown at them [Montanus, Priscilla, Maximilla, and the rest of their group] and others. Those who followed after them were vilified by rumour and in writing about their teachings . . . There is little evidence of evenhandedness in the Asian accounts . . . These Asian sources are the products of some decades after the beginnings of Prophecy, and, of course they reflect hardened attitudes against it. Matters had deteriorated to the level of personal abuse. Perhaps the debate could have been on a higher and more objective level . . . [if] the degrading writings of Melito and Apolinarius [were not used]... We owe Eusebius's use of these "low specimens" only to an accident of finding them in Pamphilius's library. We do not know. Perhaps, too, some of the rumours were true. (Trevett 1996, 48)

Witness of Tertullian to the Slanders of the Church

Tertullian documented the slanders of the church against the Montanists in approximately the year 202 CE:

> For the bishop of Rome [either Zephrinus or Victor] had already recognized Montanus, Prisca, and Maximilla as prophets, and because of that recognition, he had bestowed his peace on the churches of Asia and Phrygia. Then he [Praxeas] stirred up false accusations about these prophets and their churches. Defending the authority of the bishops' accession to their sees, he compelled the Bishop of Rome to revoke the letter of peace, which had already been sent, and to withdraw his support of its contents. By this Praxeas did a twofold service for the devil at Rome: he drove away prophecy, and he brought in heresy; he put to flight

the Paraclete, and he crucified the Father.³⁵ (Tertullian, *Against Praxeas* 1, 5, *ANF* 3)

Consistent with Tertullian's comment, in the beginning of the third century, the bishop of Rome began to isolate the Montanists who lived in Rome. The group remained there, but in an ambiguous position. They were clearly disowned, but they were not formally condemned. In the nineteenth century, John De Soyres brought a new assessment of the Montanists. He asserted that the problems with the Montanists began when a group of Montanists in Rome ran into conflict with the established churchmen and politicians in that city (De Soyres, 1868, 43–44). But the question remains—Why? So we continue to run down the ages to find veritable heresies or misdeeds of the Montanists. None have materialized.

Emperor Constantine and the Montanists

In 325–326 Emperor Constantine established himself as Christian spokesman. He certainly was not a clergyman, certainly not even yet a baptized Christian. He was, however the most powerful person in the Empire. With his power he initiated the systematic and official persecution of "heretics." The "spiritual elite" and their clergy supported Constantine. Eusebius, in his *Life of Constantine*, wrote that Constantine took on all his "heretics" in one decree:

> VICTOR CONSTANTINUS, MAXIMUS AUGUSTUS, to the heretics: Understand now, by this present statute, ye Novatians, Valentinians, Marcionites, Paulians, and ye who are called Cataphrygians (Montanists) . . . ye haters and enemies of the truth . . . Why then do I still bear with such abounding evil; especially since this protracted clemency is the cause that some who were sound are become tainted with this pestilent disease? Why not at once strike, as it were, at the root of so great a mischief by a public manifestation of displeasure? (*Life of Constantine* III, LXIV, NPNF, second series, CCEL)

---

³⁵ This is essentially Praxeas's heresy—that the Father and the Son are identical.

THE TORRENTS OF CONDEMNATION

If the truth be told, Constantine personally knew about no faults of any of his heretics, nor did he know anybody who had any contact with these heretics. He simply accepted the rumor that they were separatists and, thus, possibly revolutionary groups. Each emperor after him, with the exception of Constantius I, Julian the Apostate, and Jovian, followed Constantine's example, and used the imperial forces to persecute dissenting Christians of all types. Yet the decrees of these politicians were not always in line with church teachings, and in the case of the Montanists, every indication demonstrates that they clearly were not.

Objections to the Early Montanists by Their Peers

Detailed opposition to the Montanists came from only a few contemporaries: Hippolytus (ca 236 CE), who became the bishop of Pontus, Italy; Eusebius of Caesarea (ca 260–ca 340), and Epiphanius (ca 315–403).

1. HIPPOLYTUS

As is true of many early Christian personalities, biographical information about Hippolytus is sparse. Of the Montanist detractors, only Hippolytus lived during the early Montanist era. During the time of these prophets, he was just a child. When he wrote he was bishop of Pontus, which is an immense distance from Phrygia. We believe that he had no intimate knowledge of these prophets and relied on hearsay evidence.

Hippolytus was a well-educated, Platonic philosopher who wrote in flawless Greek. After death, he became a saint of the church. Saint of the church though he might have been, Hippolytus's résumé is smudged. Even *The Catholic Encyclopedia* portrays him as a factious man at odds with the pope. It also states that Hippolytus believed that the Father was completely different from the Son, the Logos. From Pontus, Italy, Hippolytus wrote the following about the Montanists: "They [the Montanists] err because they are enthralled by [two] wretched women, Priscilla and Maximilla, whom they suppose to be prophetesses. They assert that the Spirit descends upon them. They also believe that Montanus preceded these women as a prophet." (*The Catholic Encyclopedia*. advent.org)

Without knowing Priscilla and Maximilla, he calls them "wretched women." It is these women who were the culprits who led people astray, not Montanus. He continued: "They own an infinite number of books,

CHRISTIANITY: ENDANGERED OR EXTINCT?

which aid their delusions." He admits that the Montanists, or at least some of them, were literate, for they had their own literature, or books, on hand. This was supported, as we reported in chapter 3,[36] by the fact that Bishop John of Ephesus burned their books. Hippolytus then goes on to say:

> They do not judge their own statements by the criteria of right reason. Nor do they listen to those who are competent to make decisions. Rather, they are swept onwards by the reliance, which they place on these imposters. And they allege that they have learned something more through them than from the law, from the prophets, and even from the Gospels. They praise these wretched women above the apostles and above every gift of grace, so that some of them even presume that they have something superior to Christ Himself. They introduce novelties of fasts, and feasts, and meals of parched food and repasts of radishes, alleging that they have been taught to do so by the women . . . We therefore are of the opinion that the statements made concerning these heretics are sufficient after we have briefly emphasized that the majority of their books are silly, and their attempts at reasoning weak and worthy of no consideration. It is not necessary for those who possess a sound mind to pay attention either to their volumes or their arguments. (Hippolytus, *Refutation of All Heresies*, VIII, XII *ANF* 2 CCEL)

Without citing any of their books or giving any further data, he states that the Montanists are "silly," "their attempts at reasoning weak and worthy of no consideration." Hippolytus, here, is the one who is difficult to understand. Would not a person with a sound mind pay attention to their volumes or their arguments? Would not such a person wish to make his or her own decisions regarding the group rather than taking Hippolytus' word for it? Once more, we have stumbled on another classic example of the rhetoric of the Roman Empire. Rhetoric, not intelligent content, held sway in Hippolytus' writings.

---

[36] See p.67

THE TORRENTS OF CONDEMNATION

2. Eusebius of Caesarea

The church historian Eusebius of Caesarea, around 300 CE, gave the next contemporary witness against Montanism. But even this evidence is second hand. Eusebius asserts that his authority is Apolinarius of Hierapolis. (It is interesting to note that the only source about Apollinarius is Eusebius.) Eusebius tells us that Apollinarius stated:

> There was said to be a certain village called Ardabau in that part of Mysia, which borders upon Phrygia. There . . . a recent convert, Montanus by name, through his unquenchable desire for leadership, gave the adversary opportunity to rail against him. And he became beside himself, and being suddenly in a sort of frenzy and ecstasy, he raved, and began to babble and utter strange things, prophesying in a manner contrary to the constant custom of the Church handed down by tradition from the beginning. Some of those who heard his spurious utterances at that time were indignant, and they rebuked him as one that was possessed, and that was under the control of a demon . . . But others, imagining themselves possessed of the Holy Spirit and of a prophetic gift, were elated and not a little puffed up . . . And he stirred up besides two women, and filled them with the false spirit, so that they talked wildly and unreasonably and strangely, like the person already mentioned . . . But those of the Phrygians that were deceived were few in number . . . For the faithful in Asia met often in many places . . . to consider this matter . . . and rejected the heresy, and thus these persons were expelled from the Church and debarred from communion. (*Church History*, V. XVI, 7, *NPNF* 2ⁿᵈ, Series, CCEL)

Again, we see no statement about any concrete heresy or any wrongdoing on the part of the Montanists, only strong accusations that the Montanists erred. Eusebius was concerned about Montanus's so-called "unquenchable desire for leadership." Most of the Montanists' prophecies were not attributed to Montanus, but to the Montanist women. In fact, according to Christine Trevett, Montanus may not have been the leader of the group. Citing the work of a German scholar, Ann Jensen, Trevett writes:

CHRISTIANITY: ENDANGERED OR EXTINCT?

> It was a posteriori assumptions in the Church which created the term 'Montanism,' for Catholicism thought in terms of heresies with a nameable and male head . . . Montanus was a supporter or helper, the advocate of Priscilla and Maximilla and not their Paraclete or inspiration at all, and they were not his spiritual dependents. Indeed, the early witnesses show that the main prophetic activity was by women. It was they who were refuted and exorcised. (Trevett 96, 159)

Montanus certainly did not have an unquenchable desire for leadership. Even the charge is suspect of Roman elitism. Elite societies tended to suspect that the poor and oppressed were envious of their power and wealth (see de Ste. Croix 1981, 240–50). By the time Eusebius wrote his *Church History*, the church paid mere lip-service to the servant model of Jesus. The institutional mold of bishops and hierarchy had taken hold. The charismatic nature of the Montanists was, by then, seen as threatening to the church. Rather than accepting the Montanists as a blessing, church functionaries saw these visionaries as a threat and projected onto them their own desire for power.

Recent historians also take some exception to the statement of Eusebius, given above, that the Montanists were few in number. Evidence supports that this Christian group developed in the pre-Constantine era, and its numbers were considerable in relationship to the total amount of Christians living in the area (Tabbernee 1997, 350ff.; Frend 1997, 31; Trevett, 1996, 91ff.). Furthermore, there is no evidence of any gatherings in Asia at the time of the early leaders of the Montanists at which the Montanists were supposedly excommunicated. Eusebius is the only one who mentions any such events, and we have every reason to suspect that Eusebius is being very creative in his reporting of history.

Eusebius also mentions that Montanus spoke in states of ecstasy—states that were "contrary to the constant custom of the church handed down by tradition from the beginning." This is a strange statement coming from this historian of the early Christian era. St. Paul never thought that ecstasy was contrary to church tradition. The prophets of the first century never thought so. If, in fact, no accepted prophets lived at the time of Eusebius, the church was correspondingly deficient. If all that was left of merit was the rhetorician, the functionary, the Greek philosopher, and the growing church elite, certainly the church had lost much of itself. In another place in his writings, Eusebius trumped up the charge that the Montanists extorted money from their followers (*Church History* V. xviii, 8). Tabbernee and Tertullian affirmed that the Montanists did collect offerings to support their extensive missionary efforts. Many fathers of the church, including Eusebius, might not have understood the reasons for such collections. They came from the elite class and were able to support themselves in their own endeavors, but the people from Phrygia were poor and could not do so.

Another farfetched accusation that Eusebius recorded in another part of his writings was that Maximilla and Priscilla "taught the dissolution of marriage" (V, xviii, 2 CCEL). He said, "When the women were filled with the Spirit, they abandoned their husbands" (V, xviii, 3 CCEL). In reality, these prophetesses did nothing different than their male apostolic counterparts. They left their families temporarily, sometimes for a long period of time, to proclaim the Gospel message. Jesus advocated that they do so: "I tell you the truth. No one who has left home or wife or brothers or parents or children for the sake of the kingdom of God will fail to receive many times as much in this age and, in the age to come, eternal life" (Matthew 19:29).

The Montanist women were accused of many other farfetched activities: dying their hair, staining their eyelids, delighting in adornments, playing dice, committing usury, and committing suicide by hanging themselves. On top of all these, they were considered to be possessed by evil spirits. All of these charges were nothing but rhetorical overkill. The Montanists were, if anything, morally strict.

3. Epiphanius of Salamis

The next evidence against the Montanists comes from Epiphanius of Salamis (ca 315–403). Most Christians have never heard of him. In the last century, many church historians never even mentioned him. But the church considers him a doctor and a saint. *The Catholic Encyclopedia* states that he was a brilliant orator, but that "his confrontational approach got in the way of persuading his opponents." "Confrontational" is a weak word to describe the man. "Combative" and even "destructive" are better descriptions of Epiphanius of Salamis.

Epiphanius admitted that he had only "heard about" some of the heresies of which he wrote, and that he did not know these heresies in any other way (Epiphanius, 40, 22). Unfortunately, in his text on the Montanists, he never explains if he personally knew any Montanists who were "heretics," or if he merely "heard about" them.

Epiphanius wrote about 200 years after Montanus, Priscilla, and Maximilla lived and died. He is valuable because he lived most of his life in Asia and Cyprus, close to Pepouza. Indeed, he was undoubtedly acquainted with Montanist writings and teachings. Adversary of the Montanists though he was, he is one of the sources of Aland's and Heine's quotes. In other words, Epiphanius, in spite of himself, has aided historians to understand the group. Nonetheless, while Montanists still lived in the empire at his time, it is possible that he did not know any of them.

Epiphanius's Statements against the Montanists

Epiphanius writes his attack against the Montanists in what he called The *Panarion or The Medicine Box*, "Medicine to heal the disease of heresy." Of the eighty heresies that Epiphanius tries "to heal", he writes the most verbiage "refuting" the Montanists, some fifteen chapters in Book IV. As perturbed as he was with the Montanist, he states in the beginning that the problem with the Montanists was not that they had un-orthodox theological beliefs. He states:

> These Phrygians, too, as we call them, accept every scripture of the Old and the New Testaments and affirm the Resurrection of the dead as well. But they boast of having Montanus for a prophet, and Priscilla and Maximilla for prophetesses, and have lost their wits by paying heed to them. They agree with the holy Catholic Church about the Father, the Son, and the Holy Spirit (*Panarion*, IV, 1:1–3; 3, 11).

Epiphanius called the Montanists, "these" Phrygians. In context, it placed the Montanists at a distance from himself. It was a derogatory statement. It meant "these hillbillies" or "these lowlifes." Certainly, they were not one of "his own." But at the same time, he had to admit that the Montanists "accept every Scripture of the Old and New Testament," and

THE TORRENTS OF CONDEMNATION

that they "affirm the resurrection of the dead." He also admitted that they "agree with the holy Catholic Church about the Father, the Son and the Holy Spirit." In all this, he proclaimed their orthodoxy. He left very little, if anything, out that could be conceived as heresy. If this were the case, why did the councils find the Montanists so heretical that the Montanists needed to be rebaptized?

After he praised the Montanists, Epiphanius did an about-face:

- But when the Phrygians profess to prophesy, it is plain that they are not sound of mind and rational. Their words are ambiguous and odd, with nothing right about them (*Panarion*, IV, 3, 1).
- Montanus, for instance, says, "Lo, the man is as a lyre, and I fly over him as a pick. The man sleeps, while I watch. Lo, it is the Lord that distracts the hearts of men, and that gives the heart to man" (*Panarion*, IV, 3, 1).
- Now, what rational person who receives the "profitable" message with understanding and cares for his salvation can fail to despise a false religion like this, and what rational person can fail to despise the speech of someone who boasts of being a prophet but cannot talk like a prophet? (*Panarion*, IV, 4, 1)
- For the Holy Spirit never spoke in him. Such expressions as "I fly," and "strike," and "watch," and "The Lord distracts men's hearts," are the utterances of an ecstatic. They are not the words of a rational man, but of someone of a different stamp than those prophets who spoke in words from the Spirit . . . (*Panarion*, IV, 4,3)
- Their stupidity is exposed in two ways: a prophet always spoke with composure and understanding, and delivered his oracles by the Holy Spirit's inspiration (*Panarion*, IV, 2,2)
- The Phrygians mix falsehood with truth and rob those who care for intelligent accuracy. (*Panarion*, IV,4,4)
- They collect heaps of texts to make a false case for their imposter, and they prove their lies from them . . .(*Panarion*: IV, 1:1–3; 3, 11).

In this section 4, 4 Epiphanius reveals a fantastic fact. He states: "...they collect heaps of texts to make a false case for their imposture, and to prove their lies from them say that certain scriptures bear a resemblance to it."

CHRISTIANITY: ENDANGERED OR EXTINCT?

What is amazing in this statement is that it reveals that at least some of the Montanists were literate, and were using the scriptures to defend their arguments and their behavior. When less than ten percent of the Roman Empire were literate, this is simply an amazing revelation about the Montanists and undermines Epiphanius's claims that they were irrational.

Epiphanius's Statements Related to the Statements of Others

Epiphanius's problem with the Montanists was not that they had female visionaries and ecstatics, but "after the time of the holy apostles . . . they had visions and ecstasies at all" (2:2). For him, the Old and New Testament prophets were prophets of a more "rational" ilk. Eusebius had raised this same objection 70 years earlier: "But the false prophet falls into an ecstasy, in which he is without shame or fear. Beginning with purposed ignorance, he passes on, as has been stated, to involuntary madness of soul" (CH V, xvii, 2). But Epiphanius goes further than Eusebius. He calls the visions and ecstasies of the Montanists not mere "madness of the soul," but "stupidity" (2:3). He then writes many chapters defending the rationality of the revelations of the biblical prophets and the apostles. For example, he asserts: "Look here, the Holy Spirit and the spirits of error are perfectly recognizable! Everything the prophets have said, they also said rationally and with understanding; and the things they said have come true and are still coming true" (2:5). Here Epiphanius is led by the thinking of Hippolytus. "Rationality" is the basis for Hippolytus's attack on the Montanists' "false" prophets. Epiphanius's incessant stress on the rationality of the biblical prophets and apostles, and the "irrationality" of the Montanists reveals Epiphanius's philosophical background.

Even though he gave Platonism a passing nod as one of his recognized heresies in his *Panarion* (Migne, 42, 293: Lib. I, Tome 1: IV, VI), he shows Platonic bias in his attack on the Montanists. Epiphanius's words concerning the prophecies of Montanus could have come straight out of the writings of Plato, who wrote:

> But the region above the heaven (the area of idea-reason-God) was never worthily sung by an earthly poet (in mantic [ecstatic] style). Nor will it ever be . . . For the colorless, formless, and intangible, truly existing essence, with which true knowledge is concerned,

holds this region and is visible only to the mind (not to mindless mantics [ecstatics]), the pilot of the soul. Now divine intelligence is nurtured in mind and pure knowledge. The intelligence of every soul which is capable of receiving it rejoices in seeing reality. (Plato, *Phaedrus*, 247b–c, *Great Books of the Western World* 7)

Epiphanius, in fact, was consumed with "rationality" rather than the Spirit of God. For Plato and Epiphanius, ecstatics were "mindless." Epiphanius clearly did not know or understand these prophets or the genre in which they spoke. In true rhetorical style, he mocked their language, which was part of the prophetic idiom, saying that, by using such words, the Montanists "gave heed to seducing spirits and doctrines of devils . . ." He carefully made a distinction between "prophet" and "ecstatic," implying that a true prophet could not be an ecstatic. Thus, he flew in the face of many prophets of the Old and New Testament.

Contrary to all that Epiphanius wrote, the Christian movement of Jesus was not based on the human mind working with Greek philosophy, but on the power and presence of the Spirit of Jesus working in the midst of his believers. The first three centuries, in fact, were saturated with prophetic messages, which were not based on what the Greek philosopher would call human "rationality", but on the power of God revealed in Jesus. Even the hint of "ecstasy" within the scriptures forced Epiphanius into lengthy, hairsplitting explanations and denials. After he spent only a few sentences (3:3–10) indicating that Moses, Isaiah, Ezekiel, and Daniel all received their revelations rationally, he spent the next three chapters (3:11–7:1) dealing with one verse, attempting to explain away Genesis 2:21a, which reads: "God sent an 'ecstasy' upon Adam, and he slept." Epiphanius asserted that:

> ...[E}ven in sleep the soul does not abandon its function of governance or thought. It often imagines and sees itself as though it were awake and walking around; it does work, crosses the sea, addresses crowds—and sees itself in more situations, and more striking ones, in its dreams. (*Panarion*, IV, 5, 5-7)

Epiphanius even tries to explain away Peter's vision as recorded in Acts 10:9–16. In this vision, which Peter has on a rooftop in Caesarea, he sees all sorts of unclean animals coming down on a sheet. The Greek word that is used in the text to described Peter's state of mind is εκστασις (transliterated: ekstasis, from which English, ecstasy is derived). εκστασις means being in a state of trance, being beside oneself, in a state of confusion, the Greeks would hardly call this a "rational state of mind". Consequently, Epiphanius argues that the word does not mean what it meant, and he than changes the whole narration of the event.

As Epiphanius narrates Peter's rooftop experience, he states: He [Peter] became hungry and wanted something to eat, and while the meal was being prepared, he fell into a trance (εκστασις)." Epiphanius is quick to correct the text and states that "ecstasy" (εκστασις) here does not mean that Peter was irrational.

His explanation is: "Rather, he saw things other than men usually see in the everyday world. He saw heaven opened and something like a large sheet being let down to earth by its four corners. It contained all kinds of four-footed animals, as well as reptiles and birds."

Observe, Epiphanius states, that St. Peter was rational, and not mindless. For when he heard the words, "Get up, Peter. Kill and eat," he did not obey like a person of unsound mind, but he told the Lord, "Surely not, Lord!" Peter replied. "I have never eaten anything impure or unclean."

Epiphanius failed to mention that, on the rooftop, the incident did not make any sense to Peter. It was only when he arrived at the home of the Gentile Cornelius that he realized the meaning of the vision, and then he said: "I now realize how true it is that God does not show favoritism but accepts from every nation the one who fears him and does what is right" (Acts 10:34–35 NIV).

While Epiphanius spent much time and effort explaining that "the folly of ecstasy" excluded human rationality, he completely ignored the Pentecost event (Acts 2), which was a super-ecstatic event filled with apparent "folly". This is how the event is narrated:

> When the day of Pentecost came, they were all together in one place. Suddenly a sound like the blowing of a violent wind came from heaven and filled the whole house where they were sitting. They saw what seemed to be tongues of fire that separated and came to rest on each of them. All of them were filled with the

THE TORRENTS OF CONDEMNATION

Holy Spirit and began to speak in other tongues as the Spirit enabled them". (Acts 2:1–4)

Something incredible happened which was indescribable to their human minds. So those present described it as tongues of fire descending on them, and a violent wind blew from heaven. Now is this really what happened? It is improbable, but what else could they say? They had to say something. The apostles then went out and spoke in languages not their own nor did they understand the language. Those who witnessed the event did not see it as clear and rational. Many said that the disciples were "drunk."

Epiphanius also overlooked Paul's statement in 2 Corinthians 5:13: "If we are 'out of our mind,' as some say (εχεστημεν), it is for God; if we are in our right mind, it is for you." Indeed, if we are ever caught up out of ourselves (εχεστημεν), God is the reason; and when we are brought back to our senses, it is for your sakes." He overlooked as well 2 Corinthians 12:2–4: "I know a man in Christ who fourteen years ago was caught up to the third heaven. Whether it was in the body or out of the body I do not know—God knows. And I know that this man—whether in the body or apart from the body I do not know, but God knows—was caught up to paradise and heard inexpressible things, things that no one is permitted to tell." In the context of 12:1–10, it appears that Paul himself was that man. It is clear in verse 7 that Paul did receive "extraordinary revelations."

Another major objection of Epiphanius was that some of the prophecies which came from Montanus, Priscilla, and Maximilla were spoken in the "I" form, that is, as though, they were spoken by God himself: "I am neither angel nor ambassador, but I, God and Father, who am come . . ." David Aune points out that such speech was common among the first- and second-century Christian prophets. As a prime example of this he points to the book of Revelation. This book frequently has revelations delivered from God or Jesus in the first person singular. The Lord God spoke, "I am the Alpha and the Omega," says the Lord God, "who is, and who was, and who is to come, the Almighty" (Chapter 1:8). "I," Jesus, am the one who speaks to the seven churches (Chapter 2–3). In other places in the book of Revelation, "I," Jesus is the one who is speaking (Chapter 4:1). John has Jesus saying, "Yes, I am coming soon!" (Chapter 22) John wanted to be clear: it is not he, but Jesus speaking. So, too, Montanus wants us to know that it was not Montanus speaking, but God himself.

Aune also cites another early work, the *Odes of Solomon*, as an example of Christian prophecy. Aune states, "Although the Odes do not easily surrender their secrets, it appears that they are best regarded as a distinctive type of prophetic hymnbook which, while it has connections with other types of early Christian prophetic speech, nevertheless remains unique." They are a good example of the "I" type of prophecy ("I" here meaning Jesus) Ode 42:

> I stretched out my hands and came near my Lord. It is my sign, stretching my hands as on a tree... I became useless to those who did not take hold of me. I hide from those who do not love me, but am with them who love me. My persecutors died. They sought me because I am alive. I rose up and am with them and speak through their mouths...

Aune goes on to discuss a whole range of Christian literature, originating within orthodox and non-heretical Christianity, which had the same "I" framework as the Montanists. This includes *The Odes to of Solomon*, *The Shepherd of Hermas*, *The Didache*, and *The Apocalypse of Peter*. In reality, if the Montanists were heretics, a whole host of others also qualified. As far as we can determine, Peter, Paul, and John of the Apocalypse would have been the most likely candidates.

Attacks on the Montanists by Others of the Age

As Trevett asserts, the defamation of Montanism became common among Christians ironically enough without reason, and perhaps through thoughtless hearsay (Trevett 1996, 48, passim). As the elite, rich, and powerful increased in numbers within the church, they monopolized the Jesus Movement. As a consequence, they oppressed anything within the church that they could not control. Thus, it became acceptable to speak untruths and spread hearsay about others like manure across the Christian fields. For example, the well-educated St. Jerome (347–420 CE), highly respected by the elite, fingered Montanus as one of the castrated priests of Cybele, the mother of the gods. Before his conversion, Montanus might have been a priest of Cybele (B. Sherrat, in *Pentecostal*, vol. 1, no. 27). Today, we do not know for sure. But even *The Catholic Encyclopedia* says that it is more probable that Jerome, who was never much concerned about the Montanists, was wrong. He had heard about the similarities between the trances and gyrations of the priests of Cybele and those of Montanus and the Montanists. He then made an assumption, which was completely unwarranted, and he spread the rumor. Jerome, too, was human and not above human error.

Appraisal of Attacks

Hippolytus, Eusebius and Epiphanius are symbols of the evolution or, better yet, the devolution or dilution of the Jesus Movement. Hippolytus represents the male dominance over the Jesus Movement and the suppression of any form of feminine leadership. Anonymous and Apolinarius, in the writings of Eusebius, represent the suppression of dissent and the ascension and dominance of the episcopate. Epiphanius represents the triumph of Greek philosophy, intellectualism, and theological dogmatism over the Spirit working in the poor communities of the church. The dilution of the Christian movement had much to do with the ascendance of a bitter struggle and a transfer of power within the church. Sadly, the church of Christ became an elite and rich church.

The Montanists were one of the prime victims of this power struggle. Christine Trevett tells us: "There is every cause to think that the Prophets saw their task as renewal in the Church . . . but inevitably their increased insistence on the voice of the Spirit . . . was bound to be seen as a threat to Catholic clerical authority" (Trevett 1996, 39). The anxiety which the Montanists and their prophesies caused the clergy is expressed by W. H. C. Frend. He says tersely: "The orthodox clergy ran scared" (Frend 1984, 255).

Women in a Male-Dominated Church

As we have reported, the elite Christian male, philosopher/theologians within the Jesus Movement found that the Montanists were heretical for the following reasons: the Montanists made the judgment that the Catholic Church was not holy enough; that there were ecstatic prophecies, of which most were found with God speaking in the first person, and the last was that women led the community. We have, likewise, pointed out that the first two reasons were abundantly found within the early church without any accompanying accusation of heresy. This leaves only one issue for the condemnation of the Montanists and that was the fact that women were in the leadership roles.

Such a community may have produced *The Gospel of Mark*, which many Scholars believe was the first gospel. This is one of the central points in Marla Selvidge's seminal work *Women, Cult, and Miracle Recital: A Redactional Critical Investigation on Mark 5:24–34*. Selvidge indicates that, "the leaders of the traditional religion, the apostles, are also targets of criticism, mockery and condemnations by the writer . . . (Mark 2:11, 10:25, 10:42, 12:38. Selvidge 1990, 33)." Mark, she asserts, describes the apostles as "seeking their own personal self-gratification," and that they were exclusive and ethnocentric (Selvidge 1990, 43). It is women that are described by *The Gospel of Mark* as being true followers of Jesus; role models of what Jesus taught, and thus excellent servants (Selvidge 1990, 99-107).

From what we know, the Montanist women were similar to the woman who anointed Jesus' feet. They were, in another way, similar to the gentle, persistent, protest movement started by the community of Mark. Like the woman who anointed Jesus' feet, the Montanists were perceived as a group of ignorant peasants led by women whom the church wished to forget. Like the Gospel of Mark, the group certainly did gently protest, and they gave the established clergy fits. Montanus prophesied pointedly, but gently: "Why do you call the more excellent man saved? For the righteous man shall shine a hundred times more than the sun, but the little ones who are saved among you will shine a hundred times more than the moon." Is the "more excellent man" the ruling elite? Is the "righteous man" the believer in the prophecy movement?

However, the situation of women in the church up to today continues to be dire. Kenan Osborne in *Christian Sacraments in a Postmodern World* states:

> By and large during the last two millennia, women have not been allowed to participate in the theological academy. Three women have been declared Doctors of the Church, but they are exceptions. Because of this, theology has been understood by males, argued by males, written by males, and adopted by males. Moreover, these men have been basically from a dominant class

as well, whether the aristocracy or a highly educated class . . . Women . . . are considered second-class Christians and, at times, even second-class humans (Osborne 1999, 32).

The very fact that women have been excluded from the leadership in the Church has had some disastrous effects that are becoming more and more apparent in the present age.

None of the early councils of the church ruled against the ordination of women. It took until 419, the Council of Carthage, before the Catholic Church ruled that women should not be ordained. Could this mean that women were ordained before this time; or does it mean that women were leaning on their bishops to ordain them? These questions we can only wonder about. We do not know. Certainly, the suppression of the Montanists marked the end of the era, the only era in church history when women exerted leadership roles in the church.

Women, Bishops, Πρεσβυτεροι, and the Uncomfortable in the Church

Osborne challenges the fact that bishops had any early history in the church saying:

Historical data does not substantiate the standard presentation that "bishops" succeed the apostles. During the entire second century, there is major historical data that indicates that Πρεσβυτεροι [elder, Senior member, presbyter], not επισκοποι, [bishop, episcopoi as in Episcopal Church] were considered the successors of the apostles. Nowhere in the gospels is there any indication that the apostles were ordained, nor, with the exception of Luke, are the twelve and the apostles seen as identical. Theologians have continually raised the issue whether the phrase "bishops are the successors of the apostles" can really be held up as a doctrine of the church. (Osborne 1999, 46)

Thomassen agrees. There is no indication in any early writings, not even those of the staunch Clement in the year 190 CE, that would give us reason to believe that any distinction in rank existed between presbuteroi and episkopoi. He states: ". . . bishops appear to be simply presbyters whose special duties included caring for the poor." (Thomassen 2004, 246)

Montanists Perceived as Fanatics

Officialdom eventually wiped out most of the writings and every vestige of the Montanists. They did so literally by burning their writings. They then wiped out the Montanists verbally by presenting them as fanatics. The label "fanatic" is a difficult defamation to deal with. Should it ever be used in intelligent company? What can a person say in his or her defense? "No, I am not"? That tends to be unconvincing once popular society sticks the label onto a person or group. "I have lots of ardor and vigor, but it does not add up to fanaticism." That, too, does not convince people. The sticky label on a person's back grabs onto a leg or arm as well and demobilizes the person. Releasing the label is tantamount to proving a negative. Philosophically and theologically, it is impossible to do. Even though they bore the label "fanatics," the only Montanist who was ever recorded as harshly criticizing the hierarchy, bishops, or pope was Tertullian. Furthermore, no one in the church ever accused the Montanists of being opposed to essential church dogma: the Trinity, the resurrection, salvation, the divinity of Jesus, the humanity of Jesus, or any other dogma. Also, interestingly enough, key contemporaries of Montanus—Polycarp, Irenaeus, and Justin Martyr—were relatively silent when it came to condemning the Montanists. Tertullian, in his turn, who roundly denounced Marcion, actually ended up a Montanist. Felicitas and Perpetua were also Montanists, and they have been accepted as church martyrs and saints.

Montanists, True Followers or Divisive Element?

The key questions here are, as the later Tertullian would say, "Who had the power of Jesus? Who were the true witnesses to Jesus?" Was it the bishops, who increasingly sat in their castles with masses of servants encircling them? Or was it the Montanists, who, from all that we know, struggled daily to follow in Jesus' footsteps? The established church of Jesus was becoming an exclusive, elite, and man-centered club. This elite club fingered the Montanists as a divisive group because their very existence was threatening to the growing hierarchy, so they persecuted the Montanists. Even if their manner was different than other Christians of their age, did that make them divisive? No! It was the "church fathers" that were truly divisive.

Paul said that not all Christians received the gift of prophesy. But certainly those who did would have a different manner about them. They could be prophets, even ecstatic prophets, and be united to the church at the same time. Paul would swear to it. The Montanists were a pious group with a prophetic manner. Yes, they were different from others. They were especially different than the elite clergy and political leaders. So were Amos, Micah, Isaiah, and Jesus different from the authorities of their age. They, like the Montanists, prophesied to keep the church in touch with God. In truth, was not the church, not the Montanists, the divisive element? The Montanists sought inclusion and recognition as true prophets. The church clergy excluded them.

We have substantially documented the reasons that these clergy excluded these Montanists, and called them heretics. None of their reasons were based on any possible reality, although the Church would vehemently defend the reasons. They objected to them as being ecstatics, but ecstatics have been accepted in all ages of the Church. They complained that they were divisive, but there were no signs of disagreements. There were obviously many other reasons in these clergies' minds, but the only reason that holds any weight was that women were church leaders. The end of the Montanists marked the end of any acknowledged, realistic leadership of women in the history of the Jesus movement.

Despite the fact that the Montanists were so persecuted, the evidence is that they lasted as a group into the sixth century. Women prophets, even groups of women prophets, and men prophets as well, would resurrect prophesy as a spiritual art, an art which would continue to be respected in certain groups throughout the ages of the Church.

The Scourge of Greek Philosophy in the Church

After looking carefully at Marcion and the Marcionites, and Montanus and the Montanists, the question can be legitimately asked: "What was happening to the church at large?" The stability and rationality of Greek philosophy led the established church astray. Church fathers in the Greek philosophical mode destroyed saintly people. Increasingly, they pounced upon every vestige of supposed and suspected "division"

CHRISTIANITY: ENDANGERED OR EXTINCT?

or "heresy". Leaders of the Christian community were unable to allow, let alone deal with, dissent or differences in any form. Then politicians slipped themselves into the mix with their own agendas. Montanus and the Montanists, true Christians in the Jesus tradition, were declared heretics—even though they certainly were not. No faith-based reasons existed for the dominant church's hostility toward these groups.

Robert A. Markus, in his appropriately titled book *The End of Ancient Christianity* describes the state of the church:

> Christians had already gone a long way in appropriating the culture and life-styles of their pagan contemporaries before the time of Constantine. The emperor's conversion to their religion did nothing to reverse this trend. In the third century the thunder of Tertullian and Novatian seems to have fallen on deaf ears; around the middle of the fourth, there were no Tertullians or Novatians to recall Christians to a more intransigent standard. (Markus 1990, 102)

6

The Storm Intensifies: Arius, Athanasius, and the Age of Arrogance

The storm endangering the church continued and intensified. Between the fourth and sixth centuries, the church fathers stirred the winds within and around them to hurricane force. The intensity of the winds that raged all but destroyed the way of Jesus. Caught in the high winds of swagger and belligerence toward one another, the fathers held 14 or more church synods and councils, and produced seven or more creeds. The violence that this generated was especially incredible and lamentable considering that Jesus who was claimed as Lord and master by all sides in the dispute had taught them not only to love one another, but also to love even their enemy.

Alexander, Athanasius, and Arius caused the storm, and it revolved around the meaning of one word and two verses in the Bible. The word was "begotten" (μονογενη) as it is found in two passages of John's Gospel, verses 1:14 and 3:16. In *The New English Bible* John 1:14 reads: "And the word became flesh and dwelt among us and we beheld his glory, glory of the only begotten of the Father." John 3:16 reads: "For God so loved the world that he gave his only begotten son, that whosoever should believe in him should not perish but have everlasting life." The question was simply this: What does "begotten" mean when speaking of the Father and the

Son in the Trinity? Arius said "begotten" meant that the Son of God was created by the Father at one point in the eons before time, and the Son was then endowed with all that the Father possessed. The Son of God was thus able to suffer and die—for he was created. Alexander and Athanasius insisted: No! God the Father and God the Son are realities sharing one Godhead. Both are coequal in all respects. Both share in eternal majesty. This is a simple dispute, is it not? It is the type of difference of opinion two student theologians might share over a cup of coffee, have a good laugh about it, and then go back to their rooms to study for an exam or continue writing their thesis. It was, in fact, theological Trivial Pursuit. Yet, certainly, these men were dead serious. It was now theological Trivial Pursuit with a vengeance.

Athanasius and Arius fought over "begotten" as though their whole reputation, their whole lives, depended on it. The church said Athanasius was correct. But in spite of the amount of jargon thrown around, both were fumbling badly—neither was able to clearly frame his message. We gain some realization about what Edmund Burke, the British statesman of the eighteenth century, was insinuating when he said: "A very great part of the mischiefs that vex this world arise from words." This we know for sure: Athanasius and Arius were venturing into the unknowable and indefinable, the great mystery of God, which humans in this life will never fully understand. Was it even blasphemous?[37]

The classical story of Sherlock Holmes and Watson reminds us about how easily humans can miss essential realities: Holmes and Watson are camping together. In the middle of the night Holmes gives Watson a nudge. "Watson, look into the sky. What do you see?" "I see millions of stars," says Watson. "And what do you conclude from this, Watson?" Watson tries to wake up and make a meaningful statement: "Well, astronomically, there are millions of galaxies, billions of stars, and potentially billions of planets out there. Meteorologically, we will have a beautiful day tomorrow. Theologically, God is all-powerful, and we are small and

---

[37] Certainly some believe "theological trivial pursuit" are dismissive words in what became such an important controversy. For Athanasius's followers and the church which supported them, either Jesus was fully God, or he was incapable of redeeming mankind. All of them looked at Arius through the eyes of Athanasius. Because of scholars like Groh and Greg, we now know that the essence of Arianism, the one aspect of Jesus which Arius was anxious to defend, was Jesus' ability to redeem humankind. That is why Arius insisted that the begotten Son of God, who became man in Jesus, was a creature of God.

insignificant. What does it tell you, Holmes?" "Watson, you idiot, someone has stolen our tent!" Both sides are like Watson here. While both men strove to show their great intellectual and theological excellence, the tent, the way of Jesus, was stolen from them.

Enter Arius

Arius, who was the center of the storm, was born around 256 CE in Cyrenica in present-day Libya. Cyrenica was west of Egypt. It was primarily a desert community, making life difficult. But Cyrene, its most important city, was one of the main port cities on the Mediterranean Sea. According to Michael Grant, Cyrene was also once "one of the major intellectual centers of the world." Emperor Trajan destroyed it in 115. His successor Hadrian tried to restore the ruins, but in its weakened state, African tribes attacked it, and it never regained its previous prestige (Grant 1997, 102). Most likely, Arius was raised and educated in Cyrene. At a bare minimum, he received his early education there. We know very little about his life because he was the loser and his works were destroyed.

Arius was neither Greek nor Roman. From the little that remains of the historical record, we know that he was not a part of the Alexandrian establishment. He was born into a pagan family, probably of the poor, rural Berber tribe that lived in North Africa. Undoubtedly, through hard work, he became a presbyter in the church and a teacher of the New Testament. He was obviously respected by many.

Enter Athanasius

We know more about Athanasius. He was "the victor" in the struggle. The Catholic Church acknowledges him as defender of the truth, and as such, he became recognized as one of the great lights in church history. Athanasius was born into a Christian family sometime around 296 CE. He was, then, considerably younger than Arius. Of his childhood, *The Catholic Encyclopedia* states:

> It is impossible to speak more than conjecturally of his family. Of the claim that it was both prominent and well-to-do, we can only observe that the tradition to that effect is not contradicted by such scanty details as can be gleaned from the saint's writings. Those

writings undoubtedly betray evidences of the sort of education that was given, for the most part, only to children and youths of a better class. It began with grammar, went on to rhetoric, and received its final touches under some one of the more fashionable lecturers in the philosophic schools.

The Tumultuous Era of Arius and Athanasius

These theological pugilists were born in tumultuous times, which undoubtedly have influenced their belligerence. From 193 until 283, 32 emperors ruled the empire. One was killed in battle, and one was captured. The Romans, once undefeatable on the battlefield, lost battles not only to the Goths, but to the Persians and the Sassanids as well. The borders of the empire had become porous, and marauding bandits were increasingly successful at sacking villages and disrupting supply lines into the empire. Inflation also was rampant. In general, the Roman Empire bordered on anarchy.

Persecution of Diocletian

In 284, Diocletian, the most competent emperor that Rome had seen in three centuries, took the throne. His father was a scribe and most likely a slave in the service of a Roman senator. Diocletian was from the lowest segments of society. But he was, as was his father before him, well educated. Afterward, he developed into a brilliant administrator. Of Diocletian, Michael Grant states: ". . . he was the most remarkable imperial organizer since Augustus (31 BC–AD 14)" (Grant 1997, 204). Diocletian brought stability out of anarchy. He stabilized the economy and opened up the agricultural supply lines. He eventually divided the empire into four sections with a person appointed as Caesar or emperor over each: Constantinius (Constantine's father), Maxentius, Licinius, and Diocletian himself. The emperor eventually came to believe that his efforts at stabilization demanded one further step from him. He was convinced that Christians were a threat to the unity and stability of the empire. He had put up with them for 14 years, and he had had enough of them. On February 23rd in the year 303, he signed a decree outlawing the Christian sect (Frend 1977, 477).

Frend states that two of the emperors in this last period of the empire, Diocletian and Maxentius, came from the least Christianized areas and, thus, could not be expected "to sympathize with this new cult." Diocletian came from the mountains of Dalmatia (Bosnia) (Frend 1965, 440). Frend clarifies Diocletian's fears: "When the frontiers were at last secured, Christianity would be judged according to whether it was regarded as a unifying or a disrupting element in the Empire. In key productive and defensible provinces, especially on its eastern frontiers, Christianity was immensely strong" (Frend 1965, 441). Frend then places Diocletian's attitude in perspective for us: "If one were to look at a map of the Roman Empire on the eve of the Great Persecution, and indicate the degree of Christianization by darker or lighter colouring according to density, western Asia Minor, Syria, the Nile valley and Cyrenica, Roman North Africa and the city of Rome would show up as the most christianized areas (Frend 1965, 441)."

Recently, Rodney Stark, using sociological, archeological, and statistical data, demonstrates that the estimates concerning the population of Christians in the empire were much greater than the 2–5 percent which others had estimated. He states that by 313 CE, the date of Constantine's conversion, and only 30 years from the beginning of Diocletian's reign, 16.5 percent of the Greco-Roman population and 18 percent of the Egyptian population were Christian. He likewise concluded that, by that time, the Christian population of Egypt had been above the 10 percent mark for at least 30 years, back to the beginning of Diocletian's reign (Stark 1997: 13).

Because of their ever-increasing numbers, Christians had indeed become a threat to the unity of pagan society and its established Roman traditions. Frend asserted, "By the year [303 CE] Christianity had taken a firm hold and was well established in North Africa. There was little desire among the majority of converts to compromise with Rome" (Frend 1971, 3). Professor A. H. M. Jones insists that Christianity had made "significant inroads," even among the African rural majority. It was more than likely that in North Africa after 300 CE, Christianity dominated the rural areas, including Cyrenica—the birthplace of Arius.

The persecution of Diocletian was a venture into inhumanity. Eusebius of Caesarea (ca 260–ca 340), in his *Church History*, gives some bone-chilling descriptions of the persecutions and imprisonments. He himself experienced it. While he might have exaggerated as he was prone to do, he knew that the Romans tolerated no dissent and used gruesome means to

CHRISTIANITY: ENDANGERED OR EXTINCT?

suppress it. According to Eusebius, a great number were martyred. Many others relented and sacrificed to the imperial gods. Even some bishops and presbyters were too weak, humanly speaking, and burned their scriptures in front of the fanatical crowds. Later, their apostasies created major problems for the church, especially among the more "rigorist" North African Christians.

Constantine and the Changing Times of Christianity

As to the great increase of the number of Christians, Frend wrote: "The great movement of Christian expansion eventually ensured the defeat of persecution" (Frend 1965, 463). While this is indeed true, it might be even more accurate to say that Christian expansion ensured the success of Constantine, who was politically savvy enough to bring an end to Christian persecution. After Constantinius died, there developed a power struggle between the co-emperors. Succeeding his father, Constantine rose to the occasion. Constantine's story is well known. On October 28, 312, at the Milvian Bridge on the Tiber River on his way to do battle with his co-emperor Maxentius, he had a vision of the cross and heard a voice say, "*In hoc signo vinces*" ("In this sign conquer"). He then painted the cross on the shields of his soldiers, and he defeated and killed Maxentius. Legend has it that he threw Maxentius into the Tiber where he drowned. He legalized Christianity in 313. Later, in 320, he killed Licinius and became sole emperor.

After his victory at the Milvian Bridge, even Constantine could not believe his eyes. As he led his legions into local communities throughout the empire, throngs of Christians rose up to support him. Amazingly, Christians who refused to fight in the Roman army now joined him in battle. Many Christians saw this as a miraculous victory. After all, the emperor was now on their side. Persecution had ended. They could worship as they pleased, and they were encouraged to do so. Others saw it as a devastating blow to the way of Jesus. The event changed the whole complexion of Christianity from an embattled minority to an oppressive majority, and solidified it into a hierarchical community. It was no longer a peace-promoting society, but it became a domineering and militant one.

The rest of this chapter and the remaining chapters of this book will show that Christians persecuted dissenters from "true Christian doctrine," just as they had once been persecuted. What happened with this change of events is that the pre-Constantine power struggle that began within Christianity in the first and second century now became more intense. While many other struggles continued within its now oppressive domain, the struggle between Arius and Athanasius now took center stage and was the most historically recorded.

The War of Words

Of course, church history books record that the conflict was between the "faithful Saint Athanasius" and the "apostate Arius." Using recent textual and archaeological finds, scholars now glean precious tidbits as they read between the lines of that history. They have found a more balanced analysis of the conflict between the two sides in the Arian strife. Insights drawn from sociological analyses dealing with patronage, class, honor, and shame in the Roman Empire are particularly applicable in the Arian dispute.

From these analyses we learn that the struggle was a conflict between the North African rural, poor, on the one hand, and the settled, aristocratic, and more genteel Christians of Alexandria on the other. The "ecclesiastical" victory of Athanasius had more to do with the class of people to which Arius and Athanasius belonged than their theological thought and preached word. Furthermore, placing Arius's and Athanasius's discourses under Michel Foucault and Elisabeth Schüssler Fiorenza's perspectives, it is not just words that contribute to a possible understanding of their thought. Fiorenza insists "context is as important as text" (Schüssler-Fiorenza 1998, 216). As Foucault states, it is "the intention of the author, the form of his mind, the rigour of his thought, the themes that obsess him, the project that traverses his existence and gives it meaning" (Foucault 1972, 28–29). Descriptively, Arius and Athanasius were like two dominant rams during the mating season, butting up against each other for prime position in the empire. They each had their own flock that embraced them, but they wanted more influence and undoubtedly more power.

Migration of Rural North African Christians into Alexandria

The population of Berber North Africans in Alexandria was increasing considerably at the time. This was most likely due to the fact that rural elements in society needed the city's protection from persecution, roving bandits, and, in general, an increasingly hostile environment. Their survival was at stake. But the migration was a threat to the elite of the city. The elite population of Alexandria did not know how to control the migration. No law, no wall, no tribune could keep them out.

In previous centuries, Christianity reached across class and cultural lines. But things had now changed. The waves of cultural honor and shame, class rank and power submerged the church. Frend describes the environment that set up the struggle:

> .... [T]he influx of rural Christians, inspired by strong motives of rejection of Greco-Roman culture, took place just at the moment when the Church represented by its urban congregations was coming to terms with that culture. In all the provinces...there was latent tension between the ideas of the new rural Christians and those of the settled and long-established congregations. (Frend 1965, 463)

In *Arius: Heresy and Tradition*, Rowan Williams states that before 306, sixty constructed church buildings graced the landscape of Alexandria. These churches, of course, belonged to the well-established elite Christians who had the resources to build them.[38] Also, these elite Christians had a long history of education. They had their own famous Christian school with its great philosopher-theologians, Clement and Origen.

Williams gives an excellent description of Christianity in Alexandria before Constantine:

> The plurality of churches in Alexandria suggests that the beginnings of Christianity in the city were piecemeal...no single congregation under its Catholic bishop . . . The presbyters . . . were not docile diocesan clergy but members of a collegiate body. It is not entirely surprising that we should come across disputes between bishop and presbyters over the respective limits of their authority. (Williams 2001, 44–45)

---

[38] This is not to say that there were churches in Alexandria built for the immigrants from North Africa. They did have churches in Cyrene, Carthage, Numidia, and Mauritania. The North Africans in Alexandria more than likely worshipped in their own homes and community buildings (Williams 2001. 44–45).

ARIUS, ATHANASIUS, AND THE AGE OF ARROGANCE

Consistent with Williams's observations of the North African Christian bodies before 312 CE, churches had their own sometimes-independent presbyter or elder. Two of these known groups were followers of Melitius and Donatus who insisted that the deacons, presbyters, and bishops, who had sacrificed to the gods or burned scriptures during the Diocletian persecution, could not be reinstated in their positions. These North Africans believed that the Alexandrian elite were too willing to compromise Christian truth and too lenient in their life practices.

Constantinian Changes in Church Structures

Richard Vaggione, in *Eunomius of Cyzicus and the Nicene Revolution*, stipulates that within a quarter century after Constantine's conversion, the bishop of Alexandria was one of the most powerful persons in the empire. He had at least 100 bishops under his charge. Vaggione asserts that the emperor recognized the main bishop as "a king." Consequently, the emperor enhanced the bishop's life: "The generous gifts of Constantine and later emperors provided Church leaders at Alexandria with abundant opportunities for personal enrichment—and embezzlement was sometimes part of that enrichment!" (Vaggione 2000, 32–34)

The elite considered that the bishopric and the power in the church was theirs by right, and they considered that the North Africans were by education and by status "country bumpkins." The establishment expected the migrants to honor the wise tradition of the fathers of the city. They certainly expected them to honor and not question the established bishop.

The Rise of Athanasius

From all indications, Athanasius was part of the Alexandrian establishment. To support this, a legend has come down to us about Athanasius as a young boy. Whether the story tells us about "the historical Athanasius" is not the point—it was, we know, a story, which was cherished by the established Christian of Alexandria:

> It was the custom of the Alexandrians to celebrate with great pomp at an annual festival in honor of one of their bishops named Peter, who had suffered martyrdom. Alexander, who then presided over the church, engaged in the celebration of this festival,

and after having completed the worship, he remained on the spot, awaiting the arrival of some guests whom he expected to breakfast. In the meantime he chanced to cast his eyes towards the sea, and perceived some children playing on the shore, and amusing themselves by imitating the bishop and the ceremonies of the Church . . . (*The Ecclesiastical History of Salaminius Sozomenus* [ca 375–447 CE] II. xvii *NPNF* 2nd Series 2, CCEL)

Athanasius was the child playing the role of bishop. This whole picture is descriptive of the society: 1) "the Alexandrians" were celebrating "with great pomp"; 2) the boys were obviously imitating the bishop; 3) the bishop was waiting for his important guests who we can suppose would have a leisurely breakfast with the "very important bishop". Clearly, we are speaking of an elite Christian society, and clearly, at an early age Athanasius was on a fast track to a place among the powerful elite of the Church (Frend 1965, 440). And so it happened: After receiving a first-class education in rhetoric, Athanasius became secretary to the bishop of Alexandria. It was typical of the patronage system of the Roman Empire.

Essential Arianism

Into this world came the low-class Berber presbyter. For Arius, God the Father was the most perfect, everlasting, and all-powerful God. Jesus was the "only begotten Son of God." Jesus, the Son of God, was the revealer of the will of God and the savior of humanity. Was this so evil? Was it heresy? Only God the Father was "unbegotten." The Son was "begotten," and therefore, capable of suffering and redeeming humanity. Because God the Father was perfect, he could not become a creature, a human being. Therefore, he had to beget a Son who could redeem. Arius and the Arians would have agreed with Athanasius that God the Father could not suffer and was indivisible. But they were uncomfortable speaking such language. These terms were derived not from Jesus, but from Greek philosophy, along with other similar terms such as *infinite, all-knowing, all-powerful,* and *all-present.* Arius and his followers could not understand how the all-knowing, all-powerful, all-present, undividable God, who could not suffer, could die on the cross to save humankind. The answer, Arius found, was the term "begotten" found in John. This meant that God created Jesus for the purpose of redeeming humankind, and thus, he was different from the Father in one respect—he had an origin; he was not "un-originated."

Essential Athanasianism

In opposition to Arius's views stands the triumphal theology of Athanasius. Athanasius is deemed the "Father of Orthodoxy" according to *The Catholic Encyclopedia*. *The Catholic Encyclopedia* also states: "Athanasius was the greatest champion of Catholic belief on the subject of the Incarnation that the Church has ever known . . ."

As such, Athanasius was canonized a saint of the church. Athanasius's views are best set forth in his *Defense of Nicaea*. Even Arius agreed with the first part. It goes as follows: "For God creates, and to create is also ascribed to men; and God has being, and men are said to be, having received from God this gift also. Yet does God create as men do? or is His being as man's being? " (Vaggione 2000, 32–34).

Athanasius's reasoning is burdensome. We get the impression that we are being dragged down in a whirlpool and are suffocating. It does not seem to be a fitting statement from one of the great minds of "orthodoxy":

> Within him [God], all exist according to his own goodness and power, yet without him, nothing exists. Men, then, do not create as God creates, because man's being is not like God's being. So men's generation is in one way, and the Son is from the Father in another . . . He is Father of One Only Son . . . "This is My beloved Son, in whom I am well pleased." (*The Catholic Encyclopedia*)

With this also Arius agreed. However, Arius did not agree with Athanasius on the conclusion of his statement which follows: "And He . . . is the Father's Word, from which may be understood that he is not capable of suffering and feeling as we suffer and feel . . . and he has a unity which does not consist of parts. He is the very nature of the Father Himself. His human word is not even begotten with feeling or passion or parts . . ." (Vaggione 2000, 32–34). Arius's refusal to believe this last part was more than Athanasius could take. He called Arius's disagreement with him a crime deserving punishment (*Concerning the Creed* [*De Decritis*] I: 2). There is logic to Arius's arguments, far more logic than the Athanasians have given him credit. But no matter which side of the argument Christians have taken, Arius's or Athanasius's, the very raising of the question concerning "begotten" in the Gospel of John brings up a raft of questions. Is this not an argument in futility? Can anyone really know what happened in the inner life of God? Can anyone even begin to comprehend the meaning of "begotten"? Can anyone really say that "Such and so" is certainly what God is? Can anyone really pin God down like this? Is not the internal life of God a mystery beyond our comprehension?

Today in an age that is becoming increasingly aware of the fact that human beings can only know a little about the inner workings, motivations, and meaning of the human heart, the inner workings of a blade of grass, and the inner workings and meaning of the world (or worlds) around us, can anyone really presume to begin to understand the inner meaning and workings of God? The feeling grows among thinking human beings that Athanasius and Arius should have kept spiritual silence, and we would be better for it. In his letter to Bishop Alexander and Arius, Constantine shows similar frustration:

> I understand, then, that the origin of the present controversy is this. When you, Alexander, demanded of the presbyters an opinion regarding a certain passage in the Divine law, or better, I should say, when you asked them a completely unprofitable question, then you, Arius, inconsiderately insisted on bringing into the discussion something that ought never to have been brought up at all, or as I see it, should have been buried in profound silence. Hence it was that a dissension arose between you, fellowship was withdrawn, and the holy people were divided into various parties and no longer preserved the unity of the one body. (Eusebius of Caesarea, *Life of Constantine*, II, LXIV–LXXII, *NFPF*, 2nd Series, 1, 515-516. CCEL)

The Genesis of the Dispute

Rowan Williams recounts a letter written by Alexander to the bishop of Constantinople. In this letter, Alexander complains about ". . . the greed and ambition of Arius and some of his fellow presbyters: through the espousal of alien doctrines about Christ, Arius, Achillas, and their

ARIUS, ATHANASIUS, AND THE AGE OF ARROGANCE

followers have produced a virtual state of schism in Alexandria." Alexander was projecting. He was constantly afraid of loosing power and his wealth to the poor, as were many wealthy persons. He locked horns with Arius, and was afraid that he could easily as not loose the combat. As for Arius, he was eager to lock horns with Alexander in the public forum. But the lean mice and rats that, ill-advised, took up residence in Arius's hut had as little to eat as Arius did.[39] In reality, greed and ambition, or as we would say, power and money, is certainly often the undercurrent of theological disputes, but Arius never had power or money in Alexandria—it does not seem to be an issue with him. He was a poor man among a poor cultural group. The fact that Alexander mentioned power and money is significant as a projection on his part. They incriminate only Alexander. At the same time, they show how emotional the battle between the two camps had become (Williams 1986, 37).

Greed and ambition on the part of Arius did not cause the doctrinal problems. They had no necessary connection to "alien doctrines about Christ." If "greed and ambition of Arius and some of his fellow presbyters" was a problem, neither history nor specifically the Council of Nicaea in 325 mentions such vices. The only "greed and ambition" mentioned in the mandates of the council is canon number 17 of the disciplinary section. Here the council condemns any clergyman who lets out money at extreme interest (even 50 percent). Certainly Arius was not guilty of this or the council would have mentioned him by name.

Outside of canon 17, the council simply mentions the controversy between "believers" and "heretics." In entrenched battles, whether between individuals, nations, or members of the church hierarchy, power and wealth are the preeminent reason for problems in the world. In Christian circles, however, these less-than-honorable motives must always be disguised in theological jargon and hidden under the holy chasuble and stole. In other words, a church official may accuse his enemies of seeking power and wealth, but he himself must always present himself as having "the best interest of Christ and his kingdom" at heart.

R. P. C. Hansen, after a lengthy discussion of Arius's views, reports

---

[39] While we are expressing this humorously, our humor is an attempt to show that the conditions of the poor in Alexandria were very similar to those in Rome which were discussed with Marcion in Chapter 1, pp.4-8, and will be again discuss with Ambrose in Chapter 7, pp.141-146

that Arius's opponents called him the teacher from Satan. Historians have no reason to believe these words. There are no indications that Arius was evil. In the historical records, there are no indications that during the persecution he offered incense to the gods. Nor are there any indications that he burned the scriptures. In fact, there is no indication that he did anything evil at all. Certainly, if he had done so, his enemies would have mentioned it.

The dispute was clearly one over doctrine. There is no evidence of evil behavior. Hanson, one of the foremost scholars on Arius and Athanasius and the Arian struggle which erupted between the years 315–317, tells us about Arius: "He was eclectic in his philosophy…[H]is most startling doctrines, that of the creation of the Son out of nonexistence, has no parallel in Greek philosophy. . . He was in his way attempting to discover or construct a rational Christian doctrine of God . ..At the same time, he was not a member of the elite "in-group" which was taking over the church. (Hanson 1988. 133-137)"

The basis of Arius's theology had to be the Bible for he was a teacher of scriptures (Hanson 1988, 133–37). Furthermore, Arius was a competent biblical theologian in his time and place. In an article in *The Harvard Theological Review*, Kevin Madigan stipulates that for too long in history scholars have accepted Athanasius's accusation that Arius quoted scripture out of context. According to Madigan it was just the opposite. He demonstrates that the Arians were generally on much-stronger ground than Athanasius when expounding on the biblical text (Madigan 2003, 96:3.255).

Council of Nicaea

To resolve the dispute between Athanasius, Bishop Alexander, and Arius and bring unity in the Catholic Church and most importantly the Empire, Constantine in 325 called for a universal council of all bishops to meet in Nicaea. Nicaea was directly across the Straits of Bosporus from Constantinople, the seat of the empire. For many of the bishops, this was immensely inconvenient, but for Constantine the location was perfect. He could control both the empire and happenings at the council at the same time.

It is so diabolical that now the emperor, the head of the Roman state,

ARIUS, ATHANASIUS, AND THE AGE OF ARROGANCE

which just fourteen years earlier had been persecuting Christians, was calling more than 250 Christian bishops together in the imperial palace in Nicaea and was providing abundant financial rewards for them. It does not seem to bother the Catholic Church that Emperor Constantine was not even baptized, and, even more, that his hands were dripping with blood and would continue to drip with blood long after his "conversion" with the killing of his wife, his son, fellow emperors, and others. In the history of the Catholic Church, the Council of Nicaea is one of the most sacred events in history. At the Council most of the Nicene Creed was written. This is the lengthy creed that is recited in most liturgical churches several times a year and is the accepted definition of the Trinity by most of Christendom. *The Catholic Encyclopedia* accurately described the council as a "gala event." This would certainly fit the description given by Eusebius, Bishop of Caesarea, who attended the council. Despite his blandishments, we get a glimpse of the attitude of the hierarchy of the Catholic Church at the time. In his *The Life of Constantine*, he says:

> And now, all rising at the signal which indicated the Emperor's entrance, at last he himself proceeded through the midst of the assembly like some heavenly messenger of God, clothed in raiment which glittered as it were with rays of light, reflecting the glowing radiance of a purple robe, and adorned with the brilliant splendor of gold and precious stones. Such was the external appearance of his person; and with regard to his mind it was evident that he was distinguished by piety and godly fear. This was indicated by his downcast eyes, the blush of his countenance, and his gait. For the rest of his personal excellencies, he surpassed all present in height of stature and beauty of form, as well as in majestic dignity of men, and invisible strength and vigor. All these graces united to a suavity of manner and a serenity becoming his imperial station, declared his excellence of his mental qualities to be above all praise (*Life of Constantine*, III.X, *NFPF* 2nd Series 1, 522. CCEL).

While we must question Eusebius's assessment of Constantine's spiritual and moral integrity, the details of Constantine's apparel, more than likely, were accurate and mark another transformation of Christianity from the humble origins of Jesus of Nazareth to the religion of the rich and powerful.

Athanasius clearly displays his bias by the slant he gives on the happenings at Nicaea:

> [T]he Bishops said that the Word must be described as the true powerful Image of the Father. The Word was in all things exactly like the Father, unalterable, and without division [for never did the Word not have existence, but He always exists everlastingly with the Father as his radiant light]. Eusebius [an Arian] and his associates said they accepted my words. They were clearly unable to contradict them. Even though they were silenced by my arguments, they nonetheless whispered to each other and winked their eyes at one another, as though they had some knowledge concerning which I knew nothing. They agreed externally, yet in their hearts they disagreed. Everything remained as before (*De cretis*, V.xx, CSEL).

Whether there was "winking" going on, it is not possible to know. If there was, it might have been because Athanasius would not be convinced no matter what anyone said, so everyone might just as well keep quiet in order to maintain some order and peace. Nonetheless, Athanasius assumed that the fathers of the council set forth the concept that God the Father and God the Son were of the same essence. Hansen asserts that Athanasius was stretching the truth, and that Eusebius of Caesarea and some of the other Arian bishops subscribed with the council, particularly after Constantine assured them that the council did, in fact, agree with them (Hanson 2005, 239ff.).

Obviously, Athanasius and later church historians and theologians did not think so. One thing is certain: much misunderstanding and political maneuvering was taking place. This political maneuvering was, of course, to avoid the wrath of Constantine who had at his disposal the ability to exile any of them as he exiled Secundus of Ptolemais and Theonas of Marmerike, for not signing the anathemas against Arius. Arius was also exiled.

The fact that Constantine was pleased with the rest of the bishops is shown by the fact that immediately at the conclusion of the council,

ARIUS, ATHANASIUS, AND THE AGE OF ARROGANCE

Constantine had a grand celebration. Eusebius of Caesarea described that celebration:

> About this time he completed the twentieth year of his reign. On this occasion public festivals were celebrated by the people of the provinces generally, but the emperor himself invited and feasted with those ministers of God whom he had reconciled, and thus offered as it were through them a suitable sacrifice to God. Not one of the bishops was wanting at the imperial banquet, the circumstances of which were splendid beyond description. Detachments of the body-guard and other troops surrounded the entrance of the palace with drawn swords, and through the midst of these the men of God proceeded without fear into the innermost of the imperial apartments, in which some were the emperor's own companions at table, while others reclined on couches arranged on either side. After the celebration of this brilliant festival, the emperor courteously received all his guests, and generously added to the favors he had already bestowed by personally presenting gifts to each individual according to his rank (*The Life of Constantine*. III.xv–xvi, *NPNF* 2nd Series, 523-525. CCEL).

After the celebration, the bishops were given gifts by the emperor for their participation in the council and for their endorsing its decrees. One could not have much more evidence that Constantine had bought and controlled the church. The record of the council shows it agreed on 20 canons dealing with a number of administrative items (see *NPNF* 2nd Series VII, 8–56.). It is interesting to note that the recorded text of the Council of Nicaea contains no mention of a creed. The only way that we know that a creed might have been formulated is from references by Athanasius and by Eusebius of Caesarea. Eusebius gives us the earliest text of the creed in a letter he wrote to his church immediately after the council:

> We believe in one God, Father, Almighty, maker of all things seen and unseen; And in one Lord Jesus Christ the Word of God, God from God, Light from Light, Life from Life, only-begotten Son, first-born of all creation, begotten from the Father before all ages,

through whom all things have come into being, who was incarnate for our salvation; and spent his life among men, and suffered and rose the third day and went up to the Father and will come again in glory to judge the living and the dead; And we believe in one Holy Spirit. We believe that each of these is and exists the Father truly Father and Son truly Son and Holy Spirit truly Holy Spirit, as our Lord said when he sent his disciples to preach, "Go and make disciples of all nations, baptizing them into the Name of the Father and of the Son and of the Holy Spirit.". We are deeply convinced that these things are so and that this is our belief and has long been so and that we hold by this faith until death, anathematizing all atheists and heretics. We bear witness that we have always believed this with heart and soul, ever since we have been conscious of ourselves and that we now believe and truly proclaim God Almighty and the Lord Jesus Christ... (Hanson 2005, 159)

The final formulation of the text which we recite a number of times a year or more depending on the denomination of the church in which we worship was written, not at Nicaea, but over a century later at the council of Chalcedon in 451:

We believe in one God, the Father, the Almighty, maker of heaven and earth, of all that is seen and unseen. We believe in one Lord, Jesus Christ, the only Son of God, eternally begotten of the Father, God from God, Light from Light, true God from true God, begotten, not made, one in being with the Father. Through Him all things were made. For us men and our salvation He came down from heaven: by the power of the Holy Spirit, He was born of the Virgin Mary, and became man. For our sake He was crucified under Pontius Pilate; He suffered, died, and was buried. On the third day He rose again in fulfillment of the scriptures: He ascended into heaven and is seated at the right hand of the Father. He will come again in glory to judge the living and the dead, and his kingdom will have no end. We believe in the Holy Spirit, the Lord, the giver of life, who proceeds from the Father and the Son. With the Father and the Son, He is worshiped and glorified. He has spoken through the Prophets. We believe in one, holy, catholic, and apostolic Church. We acknowledge one baptism for the forgiveness of sins. We look for the resurrection of the dead, and the life of the world to come. Amen.

The creeds do not necessitate anything beyond intellectual belief. It does not touch on commitment to the Beatitudes, the Sermon on the Mount, or any of Jesus' norms for living. This Constantine certainly must have applauded. No council or creed in that era was willing to say anything against Constantine's or the bishops' manner of living. Certainly they did not wish to touch on anything which would censure Constantine's murdering of kin and rivals. They knew better than to censure the one who gave them their paycheck, laid the sumptuous meal before them, and gave them rich gifts.

The early Christians had a different belief, a belief in the power of the living presence of the Word in their midst. Rodger Cragun states in *The Ultimate Heresy: The Doctrine of Biblical Inerrancy*:

> This, indeed, is the essence of the New Testament word of God. It is why it is living and active, and why it remains forever, because it is not just words, it is the power of God. Because in much of Christianity the word of God has become equated with dogma, "correct thinking," "correct believing" . . . The proclamation of the Gospel in the early church was not . . . the result of a single erudite, scholarly, charismatic preacher, who has labored long and hard on the text . . . The proclamation of the gospel in the early church was an event that grew out of the presence of Christ among at least two people (Cragun 1996, 48–49).

From a different perspective, and yet consistent with Cragun's thought, Kenan Osborne writes that "God does not reveal truths about himself, he reveals himself to us in time and space, and we either respond or we do not respond to his revelation. Dogma is limited to spatial, social, and historical implications (Osborne 1999)." Likewise, Louis-Marie Chauvet states: "To make an act of faith does not mean simply either to believe that God exists . . . or to believe ideas about God . . . but to believe in, which means to have trust in someone . . ."(Chauvet 1997, ix) Then these same faithful people can formulate, if they wish, that revelation into words that are meaningful in their own social environment and in their own age.

No formulation of faith in words ever has exhausted the truth. Certainly, no formulation has ever adequately expressed the revelation for every culture or language in every age and place (13–14). Osborne goes on: "To paraphrase the Athanasian Creed the Father blesses, the Word blesses, the Spirit blesses . . . God is not some 'entity,' who says from his eternal throne, 'I am blessing! I am blessing!' The God who blesses cannot be understood apart from the ones God is blessing . . . This blessing-action of God [involves the] . . . 'response' to the blessing by individualized people" (Osborne 1999, 70).

Athanasius and Arius each had an experience with the divine and each tried to express his experience within his tradition. We might assume that Athanasius was saying, "Arius, uncouth Berber priest, not properly trained in Alexandrian School of Theology, you should have more respect for the bishop of Alexandria and the glorified Christ." Arius, we might assume, was saying, "Athanasius, I do not care where you were trained; you are not speaking truth about the crucified Jesus." The whole argument was based on misunderstandings because of different cultures and language. First, Athanasius and Arius spoke different languages. Each had a different aspect of God, which he thought important, and each formulated that belief with cultural stresses. It is simply impossible for Athanasius to set up a formula of truth for Arius, and vice versa. Second, the truth of God cannot be exhausted. If God reveals to one particular community and at particular time, this is not necessarily the last word on the subject. Arius, from a community that was suffering economically, socially, and politically, identified strongly with the Jesus who suffered and died on the cross as the begotten Son of the Father. Athanasius, from a wealthy community and with prestigious ecclesiastical connections, identified with the transcendent Christ who he perceived as standing side by side with the Father in glory for all eternity.

To go back to the beginning of this chapter, for the modern reader, the loss of energy, the unbelievable struggle over one word, "begotten," is pathetic. It was pathetic back then as well, as the letter of Constantine to Arius and Alexander indicates. On the other hand, the issue was not small, even though the real issue was not the word "begotten." The real issue went much deeper into linguistic, social, and cultural issues—into issues revolving around gross misunderstandings among cultures, classes, and even ambitions. One cannot help but notice that, while Constantine castigates them both for arguing over such "a completely unprofitable question," he fails to mention that it was Alexander who sent his servants to spy on Arius. Indeed, Arius may have been doing no more than preaching on John 3:16, rather than raising a point of contention. Constantine fails to mention that it was Alexander who challenged Arius's interpretation, but then Arius was not in the elite class. The fault, of course, in Constantine's eyes, had to be in the plebian, Arius.

The Social Background for Arius' and Athanasius' Views
Both persons in the struggle had in common the fact that they came from believing communities, which had survived the horrendous Diocletian persecutions. Instead of sharing this communality in Christ, they degenerated into a dogmatic struggle for power. The seminal idea for this dogmatic struggle could be found in the scriptural word "begotten," but it is most likely doubtful whether Athanasius or Arius understood what the sacred writer meant. The truth about the infinite, creator of universes, cannot be exhausted and comprehended by humans, much less by two male theologians. So how was it a debate between two theologians over the phrase, "begotten not made", should escalate into a full fledge battle that raged for centuries? There is no way to be certain of the answer to this question, but, in the perspective of *People's History*, we believe that the answer is in power and in individual and class domination. As we stated in the beginning, we know very little we know about Arius, because he lost the battle. On the other hand, we pointed out that we know the most about Athanasius, who was from the elite class and declare the winner by Catholicism.

There is a component in this power struggle, which we believe may have been the chief instrument for winning the minds of the people. This power struggle was the means for winning the minds of the people. It was a struggle to determine who the people would accept as "the friend of God." Virginia Burrus gives an excellent summary of Brown's thought:

> In The Incarnation of the Word, the Alexandrian bishop had already used the field of Christological doctrine to . . . foster the

emergence of those ascetic "agents of the supernatural" who set the trends for fourth century fashions in holy manhood. Whereas in the third century, "the frontiers between the divine and the human had lain tantalizingly open," writes Brown, in the fourth century, "the upward ceiling of human contact with the divine has come to be drawn more firmly"; moreover, with the heavens and earth no longer perceived as porously interpenetrating realms, the human community was apparently willing to grant more power to those few exceptional "friends of God" who might be thought to keep the narrowed channels of access open (Burrus 2000, 37).

The struggle, then, was defining who truly had the keys to the kingdom of God. Who was "the holy man" who could bring one to ultimate salvation and deliver one from this world of woe? Here was true power. It was perceived that few had it, and Athanasius would do anything to get it. Herein lies the problem, which was developing in the church. It was not that there were certain holy men and women of God, but it was that certain individuals sought investment with the keys to the kingdom. Certain men, it was clear, would do anything to become the "friend of God" and would do anything to maintain that status.

7

Ambrose, the Captain of the Ship

Family Background

In this chapter we examine a man who is projected by the church to be one of the most important "friends of God," the "captain of the ship" of the church of his day. This "friend of God" is none other than Ambrose. Ambrose had been a prestigious general until, legend says, he quelled a riot in the Cathedral of Milan, and then was mysteriously called upon to be Milan's bishop. He was immediately baptized and in the span of 7 days became bishop. Within the Christian church history books he is considered among the most influential Christians. The Roman Church considers Ambrose "to be one of the most illustrious Fathers and Doctors of the Church . . ." (*The Catholic Encyclopedia.*)

The Eastern Orthodox Church considers him "one of the most eminent fathers in the fourth century." In *The Lives of the Saints* on the web page of The Orthodox Church in America, the church describes Ambrose's ministry: "Ambrose combined strict temperance, intense vigilance and work within the fulfilling of his duties as arch-pastor. St Ambrose, defending the unity of the Church, energetically opposed the spread of heresy."

Probably the best testimony to his importance comes from Augustine, bishop of Hippo, who we will discuss in the next two chapters. Augustine, who is better known by the average Christian, states in his most known work, *Confessions*, that he came to Milan (*Mediolanium*) to teach and to hear the "the most famous person in all the world" [*optimis notum orbi terrae*] (*Confessiones*, V.xiii, iii, *CSEL*). Further on, he states that "so many powerful people honored him" (*tantae potestates honorarent, Confessiones*, VI.iii.iii, CSEL). The church claims that, while he was alive, Ambrose raised a young boy from the dead, and when he died on December 7, 397, a great number of miracles were performed by calling on his name.

While there is no way to prove these miracles, Ambrose certainly left his mark on history. He established the Nicene Confession as the correct or orthodox faith throughout the empire. He was responsible for the outlawing paganism and Arianism. He brought the emperor Theodosius to his knees begging Ambrose to forgive him. How could it be possible that a religious person, a bishop of the Catholic faith, bring a mighty Roman emperor to his knees? After all, before Constantine, the emperor was considered a god. Even in the newly Christianized empire, he still could declare war and exile whom he chose and still maintain dictatorial power. But with the Christianization of the empire, there was a monumental, if not cataclysmic, change in the power paradigm of the Roman Empire, and this was the power of the bishop to bring hell or eternal damnation down on anyone.

In *The Formation of Hell: Death and Retribution in the Ancient and Early Christian Worlds* (probably the most thorough treatment of the subject), Alan E. Bernstein states that almost uniformly within this world there was belief in the afterlife (Bernstein 1993, 3). But Bernstein writes that because every community had its own cult that developed within its own locality, it was impossible in this early age to make views of afterlife "mutually consistent" (Bernstein 1993, 91). Yet, each community believed in varied concepts of the netherworld (Bernstein 1993, 21–171). Eloquently, Bernstein explains the Christian difference:

> What is unique about the formation of the Christian hell is its location within a universe whose judge, being divine, will, by definition, judge justly and, beyond that, being an innocent victim, will judge with supreme compassion. With the rise of a more institutionalized church . . . possession of faith might come to be measured in verbal formulations, and authority could define heresy,. . . (Bernstein 1993, 171)

AMBROSE, THE CAPTAIN OF THE SHIP

As later Christian writers in the symmetrical tradition filled in perceived gaps in the accounts of what happens to the wicked, they described dire fates: eternal fire, sulfur, chains, darkness, and gnashing of teeth. If these conditions could threaten misguided members of the Christian community, how much more certainly would they imperil others who had rejected the Gospel, spurned baptism, or for other reasons, remained independent of the new revelation? (Bernstein 1993, 339–40)

G. E. M. de Ste. Croix put it more succinctly: "Religion in those days was universally regarded as a matter of enormous importance, and it was generally believed by Christians that holding the 'wrong' dogma, and sometimes even practicing the 'wrong' ritual, might involve eternal damnation—a position which is far from extinct today . . ." (de Ste. Croix 1981, 452).

Explaining the difference between paganism and Christianity, de Ste. Croix goes on:

"Heretics" and "schismatics," as well as "unbelievers," were an entirely new kind of internal enemy, invented by Christianity, upon whom the wrath of "right-thinking people" could be concentrated, for in paganism the phenomena of "heresy" and "schism," as of "unbelief," were inconceivable: there was no "correct" dogma in which it was necessary to believe in order to avoid anathema in this world and damnation in the next . . . (Ste .Croix 1981, 452).

De Ste. Croix quotes Gregory of Nissan regarding the arguments of the peasants over the terms "begotten not made," but the arguments were more shibboleths rather than substance. It was the bishops who were the definers of what was "acceptable to God" and "what was not;" and "who was saved and who was not." Here was real power! Theodosius knew very well that his life on this earth could be very short, as were the lives of Valens, Julian, and Gratian. Eternity in hell would be very long and thus he capitulated to Ambrose.

It is clear that Ambrose raised damnation to its ultimate level and that he placed the keys to the kingdom of heaven and hell squarely in the hands of the bishops and clergy. Through the ages, and even sadly today, the clergy threaten eternal damnation controlling beliefs and behavior.

How did Ambrose get this power? The church would assert that Ambrose was predestined to be in this position of power. We will argue, however, that God cannot be blamed for this debacle, but rather, that it was due to his social position in life. We have considerable evidence that places Ambrose squarely within the power matrix of the empire established by Constantine.

Ambrose and the Power Matrix

Ambrose's father, Aurelius Ambrosius, was one of the more powerful men in the empire. He was the praetorian prefect, or governor of Gaul (modern France, and Spain) and Britanniae (Britain). We, however, do not know much more about him except that he died when Ambrose was a young boy. As a widow, Ambrose's mother would have been forced to marry another man, which was the custom throughout most of history in the Roman Empire. Widows, because they were "the weaker sex and incapable of managing their affairs," were expected to remarry. This meant that another man, possibly a brother of her deceased husband, would control the family's wealth and property. Ambrose's mother shrewdly avoided remarriage by establishing her estate as a convent. In this way she protected her estate from the empire's onerous taxes.

From Ambrose's writings, we can deduce that Pope Liberius and other Catholic prelates constantly visited the convent. We know that his sister Marcellina was established as a consecrated virgin, and that Pope Liberius preached at the consecration service in St. Peter's Cathedral. All this would indicate that Ambrose's mother and more than likely his deceased father were Nicene Christians, and that they raised Ambrose to be one also. The fact that Ambrose was baptized shortly before he became bishop is not an indication that he was not a Christian, and should not be seen as contradicting his Christianity. As we have seen, in those days, people were not baptized until late in life for fear that they might commit some sin that would prevent them from being saved. Another reason to assume that Ambrose was a Nicene Christian all along, according to Michele Salzman in *The Making of a Christian Aristocracy*, was that in the military, since Constantine and the Council of Nicaea, being a Nicene Christian was the best way to advance (Salzman 2002, 107ff.).

AMBROSE, THE CAPTAIN OF THE SHIP

Ambrose became the second person in charge in the Balkans under Praetor Probus. In 372, he was appointed prefect or governor of Æmilia-Liguria, which was south of Milan, the emperor's headquarters. He was indeed an important general in the militia of Rome.

As far as the Nicene Catholics were concerned, there was a major problem in Milan. Since 355, it had been in the hands of Bishop Auxentius, whom all "Catholic bishops in good standing" knew was a dreaded Arian. Hilary of Poitiers (ca 300–368), an arch-heretic hunter, had spent years attempting, but without success, to pin the label "heretic" on Auxentius's stole or chasuble (D. H. Williams 1992, 7ff.).

Finally, Auxentius died in 373, leaving the bishopric vacant.

Arian Hysteria of Ambrose's Time

The mental framework of the Catholic mind at the time was simply paranoid as far as Arians were concerned. The amount of hysteria generated against the Arians is comparable to that generated in the United States in the early twentieth century against the Communists. After Communism triumphed in the Soviet Union in 1917, most citizens of the United States were paralyzed with fear at the very mention of the word "Communist." Every union organizer was suspected of Communism, and Communism was violently repressed. In the 1950s, the McCarthy hearings held suspect anybody with "liberal" or "leftist" leanings. Even recently, when a Democratic candidate for president suggested that the wealthy should pay their share of taxes, some Republicans accused him of being a "Communist."

While the belief that Communism could even control the United States was an illusion, the threats to Constantine's rule were part and parcel of being emperor. Emperors were not noted for having longevity. Constantine knew that at any time, some group or person could rise up and kill him. Furthermore, the empire was always under threat from those that had been conquered and those that wanted to challenge the empire's dominance. He knew to the north were the Vandals, the Visigoths, the Lombards; to the east were the Persians, the Sassanid Empire; and in Africa were the Donatists who despised the empire. It was most expedient for Constantine to make sure that his new faith and new allies were united. Constantine said as much in his speech delivered before the assembled prelates at Nicaea.

CHRISTIANITY: ENDANGERED OR EXTINCT?

Eusebius of Caesarea states that Constantine said:

> I rejoice at seeing all of you all assembled together and sharing one unanimous opinion shared by all. Let no person with an evil eye ruin our prosperity; now that tyrants against God have been swept by the power of God the Saviour, let not the evil demon encompass the divine law with blasphemies by other means. For to me internal division in the Church of God is worse than any war or fierce battle . . . (*Vita Constantini* Pin, 3.12–13).

For Constantine, then, "internal division in the Church of God was worse than any war or fierce battle . . ." Constantine would, thus, perceive any differences in the church as an "evil demon encompassing the divine law with blasphemies . . ." So any division in the church was a threat to Constantine's "peace" and his "prosperity."

Nicene theology, which stated that God was Father, Son, and Holy Spirit, three realities (οὐσία) in one being, became dogma and mantra for those who were interested in controlling church and empire. Correspondingly, they generated a paranoid fear in Nicene Christians of any suspected Arian. John Meyendorff, the great orthodox scholar, put it this way:

> But, unity, universality and order, these essential elements of the pax romana, were now inseparable from the interests and responsibilities of the universal Christian Church. The Roman emperor could not care any longer for the Empire without also being concerned with the unity, universality and good order of the Church . . . (Meyendorff 1989, 33).

It is simply amazing what transpired after Constantine became a Christian. In the centuries before, the Christians could be blamed for a famine or a natural disaster simply because they did not sacrifice to the gods. Now, any diversion from the Nicene standards was thought to bring down the wrath of God and was considered a sign of heresy and treason. Constantine had raised the fear of Arianism to fever pitch, and he was promoting Nicene Christianity on the empire by force, if necessary. Even Arius, after he had been exiled, said that the creed was saying

AMBROSE, THE CAPTAIN OF THE SHIP

what he said. As we reported in the last chapter, Eusebius of Caesarea and some of the other Arian bishops subscribed to the Nicene Creed after Constantine assured them that the council did, in fact, agree with them (Hanson 2005, 239ff.). The fact that Constantine had the prelates forge what he wanted to be the universal faith did not mean everybody fell in line. Two bishops, Secundus and Theognis of Nicaea, refused to sign the Nicene accords and Constantine exiled them. Eusebius of Nicomedia signed the accord but did so fraudulently, and he was later exiled. However, ironically Eusebius of Nicomedia baptized Constantine that meant in those days, to the chagrin of Catholics, St. Constantine died an Arian.

When Ambrose walked into the cathedral after Auxentius's death, the issue at hand was not just Arianism. The issue was who controlled the Empire. The Arian Goths and Vandals were at the door of the Empire ready to take down the Empire with its Catholicism. The pagans of the Empire were by no means defeated and in hiding. Salzman asserts that the Roman Senate continued to be controlled by pagan aristocratic senators until the last part of the fourth century (Salzman 2002, 77). T. G. Elliot believes that the pagans "lapsed into silence" because they were impressed with Constantine's victory over the Goths (Elliot 1996, 233). More than likely it was a different scene altogether. Undoubtedly, they "lapsed into silence," because, even though the Nicene Creed and this newfangled religion made no sense to them, they had to put up with it out of shear fear of the emperor.

In a dictatorial society, as the Roman Empire was, it was wise to keep your mouth shut if you disagreed with the emperor or you risked death or exile. Being a Christian did not make a difference in the way Constantine ruled as an emperor. He used the same brute force methods as used by pagan emperors. Everyone knew this to be true. Constantine defeated and murdered his co-emperors, Maxentius and Licinius; he executed his wife, Fausta, and his son, Crispus, son of his first wife, Minervina. In September of 337, he probably murdered his brothers, Julius Constantius and Dalmatius. The senators saw all this. When murders like these took place around them, it was better not to stir the deep waters. Roman senators had to consider these murders as a threat. These murders were aimed at eliminating alternate power.

CHRISTIANITY: ENDANGERED OR EXTINCT?

Crumbling Empire

Before Constantine became emperor, the Roman Empire was well on its way to its demise. Constantine slowed down the process of the destruction of the empire by bringing the growing number of Christians from the shadows to being supporters of the empire. He likewise created a means to prevent the masses of poor from starving by giving the Christian bishops the financial resources to feed the poor, thus diminishing their desire to rebel. At the same time, he supported the bishops and their clergy and exempted the church from paying taxes. The fact that the church was exempt from taxes meant that after Ambrose became bishop, he was included among those who were tax exempt as was his mother when she established her convent.

The fact that Constantine did not tax the church and even supported it created huge problems for the empire. It removed considerable payrolls and tracts of land from the tax rolls. To avoid heavy taxes, ordinary people gave even more land to the church than it already had. The church used its wealth not only to aid the poor, but also to build expensive churches, cathedrals, and homes for its bishops.

The church proclaims just how commendable it was that "Saint" Ambrose gave up his money for the poor. Being bishop, however, meant that he, himself, controlled all of his tax-free money and land. Besides his money, he had his slaves, and a large retinue of servants. He lived the life of an aristocrat in the upper echelons of society. He, as most bishops, had a life of leisure from which he pontificated and ruled his diocese. Ambrose clearly did not suffer any deprivation for his almsgiving.

De Ste. Croix succinctly states: "The Later Empire, especially in the West, was rather less a specifically urban civilization, but it was if anything even more a regime in which the vast majority were exploited to the very limits for the benefit of a few" (de Ste. Croix 1988, 464). While there is no way to determine the number of slaves there were in Roman society, de Ste. Croix believes that it was as many as a third of the population. The only way to keep such a large number of people under control was through brute force.

Jeffers describes the discrepancy between the wealthy and the predominate poor. He states: "No visitor could fail to be impressed by the ever-increasing opulence of the city of Rome . . . wealth on a scale only imagined before, gathered by a growing empire from all parts of the known world . . ." (Jeffers 1991, 3–4). Many of the monuments, the cathedrals, aqueducts, fortifications, and triumphal arches are still around today in Rome. However, Jeffers goes on to point out: "Lower-class residents of urban Rome would not be so impressed by these things." The bulk of the population was slaves, slave descendants, and peasants who were forced off their land. These people were desperately degraded, and they were forced to live in squalid conditions without the aqueducts and services that the elite enjoyed. What was worse, according to Jeffers, is that the wealthy estates and the public buildings took up over half of the 16 square miles and over 90 percent of the population was forced to live in the worst of the rest of the property of Rome. (Jeffers 1991, 4)

The conditions that the masses lived in were horrendous (see Marcion, Chapter 2). Plagues wiped out immense numbers simply because the sanitary conditions were so miserable. Of course, the wealthy were not spared from the contagious diseases that emanated from the squalid conditions of the slums, simply because they were so dependent upon the slaves and servants that would come from contaminated conditions. But, outside of these "inconveniences," the aristocracy had their plush lives within their villas and they were still largely pagan until the turn of the fifth century when it was inconvenient to be a pagan. Christian aristocrats were very interested in winning over their pagan friends. The interchanges between Christian and pagan aristocrats, Salzman characterizes like this: "As they discussed wealth, 'nobility,' office, friends—deeply held ideologies—they were attentive to the ways in which they could appeal to aristocrats anxious about their social standing . . ." (Salzman 2002, 107).

One can almost picture the scene in one of the villas of a Christian, Cicelliano, and his pagan neighbor, Horatio, as they were drinking their wine and eating bread in Cicelliano's garden balcony, while slaves fanned them. Cicelliano says to Horatio: "Look, Horatio, it's to your advantage to become a Christian. For one thing, you can secure your estate from the huge taxes by declaring it a monastery. Further, you can build a cathedral, and then get baptized and in 2 weeks we will declare you a bishop, giving you much more power than you now have. Furthermore, you will look absolutely spectacular in a bishop's gown, hat, and miter. Oh yes, Horatio, and after you die, you will live with God in paradise. What more could you want?"[40]

Ammianus Marcellinus, Pagan Telling the Truth

Coming down the hill and back into the slums with their deplorable conditions, there is a totally different reality. Somehow, this reality is never recognized or described by the Roman church fathers or the historians Sozomen, Scholastica or Theodoret. On the other side of the picture, however, the pagan historian Ammianus Marcellinus (ca 325–ca 390) presents a much more accurate portrait of what was happening in the empire. David Rohrbacker states of Ammianus: "While modern readers may not find the relentless moralizing or the encyclopedic detail entirely to their liking, Ammianus' colossal ambition cannot be denied. Ammianus' diction and imagery provide a scathing portrait of a squalid and violent age" (Rohrbacker 2002, 41).

Scholars suggest that his work needs to be evaluated because of his anti-Christian bias, but the Christian bias is so much greater in the Christian historians, to the point that they destroyed anything that disagreed with their perspective. Ammianus Marcellinus was a *protectores* in the Roman Army, and this position required knowing and reporting details. The position endowed him with considerable prestige. As a *protectores*, according to Frank Trombly, Amminiaus would have had policing power that would require him to enlist troops in the pursuit deserters bringing them back to serve in the military. Within this task he had the power to force delinquent taxpayers to pay back taxes. He further would have been in charge of supplies, and making sure the horses were not overloaded. His last responsibility and the one he was best at was recording the details of the battles. To say the least Ammianus, while he was not an military officer, he was indispensable to the army. Trombly asserts that Ammianus must have accompanied Julian on his final Persian battle in 363. We must also assume that Ammianus Marcellinus was well acquainted with Emperor Julian (Trombly 1999, 17–28).

With Ammianus then we have a very knowledgeable witness to life in

---

[40] This is clearly an exaggeration, but it does get the point across concerning the rich, the church, and the Constantinian era. While reading about the saints of this era, a person must realize that realities were not as they are portrayed. Today, from twenty-first-century perspective, it is easy to uphold and praise actual voices in the Constantinian age.

AMBROSE, THE CAPTAIN OF THE SHIP

the empire. What is so amazing about Ammianus is that we can find so much about the lower classes from the vignettes of this aristocrat.

One of his vignettes involves the prefect, of Rome, Symmachus. Symmachus, according to Ammianus, became prefect in the same year that the young Gratian became emperor in the West. This would place him in the year 367. Ammianus has high praise for Symmachus. He was "a man deserving to be named among the most eminent examples of learning and moderation." Otherwise, Symmachus, like Ammianus, was a well-educated aristocrat. According to Ammianus, during the period that Symmachus ruled, "the most sacred city enjoyed peace and plenty in an unusual degree." What he means is that the aristocracy was not experiencing rebellion. For what he states immediately following belies "peace and plenty." According to Ammianus, Symmachus built "a magnificent and solid bridge." When this bridge was dedicated, it was received "amid the great joy of his ungrateful fellow-citizens" (*magna civium laetitia dedicavit ingratorum*). There seems to be an oxymoron here. How can there be "great joy" in "ungrateful fellow-citizens"?

In the very next paragraph, Ammianus states that Symmachus' "most beautiful" estate was torched by these ungrateful citizens. He states that "some vile plebian excited them to do this." (*ea re perciti quod vilis quidam plebeius finxerat.*) It is hard to imagine that one person could create this riot and conflagration unless the distress was already at a boiling point in the empire. The next vignette of Ammianus deals with a much worse official, Lampadius. According to Ammianus, Lampadius was

> . . . a man of such boundless arrogance that he grew very indignant if he were not praised even when he spat, as if he did that with more grace than anyone else. He was, nonetheless, still a man of justice, virtue, and economy. As praetor, he was celebrated for holding some splendid games and for giving abundant gifts. But he was unable to bear the tumult of the populace, which often pressed on him to have gifts distributed to the unworthy among them. So, in order to show his liberality while also showing his contempt for the multitude, he sent for a crowd of beggars from the Vatican and enriched them with great presents.

CHRISTIANITY: ENDANGERED OR EXTINCT?

While Lampadius was prefect, he was disturbed by frequent commotions, the most formidable being when a vast mob of the lowest of people collected firebrands and torches in order to burn his house near the baths of Constantine ... For when he began to construct some new buildings, he sent officers who pretended to look over various items of iron, or lead, or copper, and then seized them without paying the price for the items. This so enraged the poor since they suffered repeated losses from such practices, that it was all Lampadius could do to escape (Ammianus, XXVII.iii.5–6, 8, 10).

The above narration is crystal clear and indicative of the growing social unrest. But there are some things that need to be highlighted. Ammianus states that the Prefect Lampadius was "unable to bear the tumult of the populace," who were most likely demanding the resources to survive. So Ammianus states that Lampadius insulted the populace, the mass of the poor, by giving gifts to the even more disenfranchised, the beggars who were found in the Vatican, a name that is recognized today by the average person as the seat of the pope. However, in ancient history, the Vatican was a sacred area in Rome by the Tiber where pagans would go and offer prayers to the gods for healing, fertility, etc. Constantine built a basilica there, and it became the seat of the bishop of Rome. Beggars came there not so much because they believed their prayers would be answered, but mostly because they felt that monks and priests would be more charitable there.

Now it is important to recognize that these beggars were the lowest category in the Roman society. The next event that needs to be underscored is the fact that when Lampadius began to construct buildings, he sent his soldiers out to confiscate building materials from the poor. This was simply a common practice as de Ste. Croix so accurately described. Again, Ammianus states that the poor were so enraged that they drove the prefect from the city. This in itself has to be astounding considering the fact that Lampadius would have been one of the most powerful persons in the empire with a good supply of Roman soldiers at his disposal (*Ammianus*, XVII.iii.10).

According to Ammianus, the next prefect is a much better person. This prefect was Juventius. He was "a man of integrity" and "prudence,"

Ammianus claimed, and his "administration was tranquil and undisturbed, and the people enjoyed plenty under it." The people, again, however, who enjoyed this "tranquility" and "plenty," were more than likely the elite.

Power Struggle for the Papacy

In the very next breath, Ammianus reports that Juventius "was alarmed by fierce seditions raised by the discontented populace" (Ammianus, XXVII.iii.11). Ammianus suggests that this was not the same as the previous riots because it was a struggle between two persons who wanted to be the bishop of Rome. He wrote, "Damasus and Ursinus, being both immoderately eager to obtain the bishopric, formed parties and carried on a conflict with great intensity, the partisans of each carrying their violence to actual battle, in which men were wounded and killed." (Ammianus, XXVII.iii.) The ecclesiastical historians, Socrates, Sozomen, Jerome, and Rufinus, also report this struggle. They all indicate that it was considerably violent. The only difference is that the ecclesiastical historians all blame Ursinus for starting the conflict.

Another voice from church history presents another perspective. What is so interesting about this voice is that it puts a totally different slant on Damasus. This voice is the Anonymous historian, whose works were preserved in the Avellana Monastery in Northern Italy and now are found in the Vatican Library. Anonymous reports that when Constantius II exiled Pope Liberius in 355 for not endorsing the condemnation of Athanasius, "all the clerics and ecclesiastical officials" declared to the people that they would remain loyal to Pope Liberius. However, Anonymous lamented that Damasus, the deacon, who was in charge of the treasury, was "corrupted by ambition." He went on to state the people, the deacons, and presbyters loyal to Pope Liberius requested that Ursinus be appointed "ordinary," which would be a temporary replacement for Pope Liberius while he was in exile. Ursinus was then ordained bishop. Anonymous then described:

> When Damasus heard about the happenings in the Basilica of Julius, he bribed all the four horse charioteers and the riff-raff of the city. Armed with weapons they broke into the basilica of Julius and for three days executed an orgy of death upon the faithful. (*Collectio Avellana: Anonymous 5*)

CHRISTIANITY: ENDANGERED OR EXTINCT?

This is a pretty grim description of a papal election. Socrates, in his *Ecclesiastical History*, stated, "many lives were sacrificed in the contention" (IV.XXX, *NPNF* 2nd series, 2, 113. CCEL). Ammianus reported a "small number" of 137 were killed (Ammianus, XXVII.13). Nevertheless, it must be assumed that Damasus's forces, who were the aggressors and were triumphant, did most, if not all, of the killing. Under no circumstances can one read this as a favorable review of Pope (Saint?) Damasus. Then put all this in the following cynical assessment of Ammianus:

> I do not deny, when I consider the ostentation that reigns at Rome, that those who desire such rank and power may be justified in laboring with all possible exertion and vehemence to obtain their wishes; since after they have succeeded, they will be secure for the long run being enriched by offerings from matrons, riding in carriages, dressing splendidly, and feasting luxuriously, so their entertainments surpassed even royal banquets. (Ammianus,, XXVII.13).

Ammianus did not mean this to be a slam against Damasus. For Ammianus, the issue was not so much luxury and power, but propriety and gentility. With regard to the struggle between Damasus and Ursinus and its violence, Professor Maijastina Kahlos of the University of Helsinki states that the struggles of the fourth century were social, economic, and religious. She asserts that when it was strictly a religious conflict it was the most violent. Most of the conflicts were, however, social and economic and were struggles of the lower classes against the upper classes (Kahlos 1997, 49). Kahlos further points out that the church historian Socrates insisted that the struggle between Damasus and Ursinus was over power rather than dogma (Socr. *hist. eccl.*, 4.29, *NPNF*, 2nd Series, 2. 113. CCEL). This struggle was clearly not over dogma. Both Ursinus and Damasus were Nicene Orthodox Catholics. Certainly if dogma had been the issue, Damasus would have made that very loud and clear, and the ecclesiastical history would have been filled with tomes of condemnation.

There is not a great deal of information about Ursinus. This only makes sense because he was on the losing side. Kahlos points out that two of the priests associated with Ursinus, Faustinus and Marcellinus, "condemned Damasus for his wealth and luxury" (Kahlos 1997, 49). Even Jerome, who was a supporter of Damasus, lamented his decision to go to Rome and complained of the decadence he found there (Letter XLV, *NPNF*, 2nd Series, 6, 58-60). Read his words as he begged Marcella to leave Rome:

> Read the apocalypse of John, and consider what is sung therein of the woman arrayed in purple, and of the blasphemy written upon her brow, of the seven mountains, of the many waters, and of the end of Babylon. "Come out of her, my people," so the Lord says, "that ye be not partakers of her sins, and that ye receive not of her plagues." (Letter XLVI.12, *NPNF*, 2nd Series, 6, 64. CCEL)

We place this comment in line with Ammianus's comments on wealth, and along with Salzman's assessment that the aristocratic Romans were still predominately pagan. We can surmise that in the economic turmoil, demagogues could be produced who might exploit the situation to their own ends. Considering the facts that Ursinus' side took the heaviest losses, and his priests made the accusations, most likely Damasus represented wealthy and powerful Christians. Henry Chadwick points out that in this struggle neither contender was a presbyter or a full priest. They were both deacons, a position of great power (Chadwick 2002, 314). The deacons were in charge of the property and ever-increasing wealth of the Christianity that Constantine began funding.

Chadwick further gives the reason that there would be such a violent struggle over the installation of a bishop.:

> The laity were increasingly coming to expect their bishop to have the social influence to protect them when they were in trouble with tax men or magistrates or when they needed a favourable reference for a job, and this capacity counted more than holiness. The office of a bishop was inevitably politicized, (Chadwick 2001, 314)

It is obvious from all the information gathered above that Damasus was the favorite of the elite and the wealthy. Ursinus was the advocate for the poor and the oppressed. Likewise, as we have seen in church history, it was the poor and the oppressed who lost out. This is definitely not the way of Jesus.

The Chaos of Power

As the internal class struggle raged on within the empire, there were mounting exterior pressures. It was as if the surrounding peoples were vultures ready to descend on and pick the remains of the once-mighty empire. The Persian Empire, long foe of Rome, kept hammering on Rome's southeast flank. Emperor Julian, the Apostate, in a valiant effort to defend the empire from the Persians, was killed in battle. The Huns from Asia were forcing the Goths, Vandals, and Ostrogoths to seek land, and they made war on Rome. Emperor Valens was killed in a battle with the Visigoths. To the west, Franks were picking on the frontier.

Constantine died in 337, and the empire was divided between his three sons: Constantine II, whose domain was the west; Constans, whose domain was Africa; and Constantius whose domain was the east. Constantine II and Constans were Nicene Catholics, and Constantius favored Arianism.

Three years after Constantine's death, the eldest brother and Nicene Christian, Constantine II ordered the return of Athanasius to Alexandria. This so infuriated Constantius, the Arian brother, that he threatened Constantine II with death. As a defensive move Constantine II attacked Constantius. However, it did not go well for Constantine II; he was killed at the battle of Aquileia (340). Events did not go well for Constans either. One of his generals, Magnentius killed him in a coup (350).

Because Magnentius was not a relative within the rules of honor and shame in the empire, it did not matter that Constans was a Nicene Christian; Constansius was duty bond to avenge his brother's death. The task of revenge was carried out a year and half later. Constansius than appointed his cousin, Gallus Caesar, to replace Constans. Then Gallus carried out extensive battles in the east with considerable success. Again, Ammianus Marcellinus portrayed the Roman hierarchy as filled with intrigue and corruption. He also portrayed Gallus Caesar as a violent person who was religious and suspicious.

AMBROSE, THE CAPTAIN OF THE SHIP

Julian, the Christian Pagan

In 355, Constantius replaced Gallus with Julian. Julian was the son of Julius Constantius, a half brother of Constantine. After Constantine died more than likely Constantius II, to prevent a power struggle and with the consent of his two brothers, co-emperors and fellow Christians, had Julius Constantius killed.

Julian was five or six and the time. For his protection he was placed under the guardianship of Eusebius of Nicomedia, the Arian bishop, who had baptized Constantine. Eusebius appointed Mardonius, a monk, to be responsible for Julian's education. The monk, Mardonius, a "nominal Christian" was given charge of Julian's education. Mardonius introduced him to the Greek classics, but apparently never seriously introduced him to Jesus of Nazareth. Julian could hardly help rejecting the state religion of Christianity because of all that he saw in the blatant hypocrisy of Constantine, his sons, and the state religion, and because Constantine's sons had made him an orphan (see Frend 1984, 594-595).

Julian became Augustus, or emperor, in February of 360. He instituted a policy of tolerance for all religious views, including paganism. In fact, he gave preference to the pagan religion, reestablishing many temples. Frend gives one quote from Julian, which reveals the humanity of Julian and which raises him above almost every Christian emperor:

> Now the crowd when they see such men [rich who disregard the poor] blame the gods. However it is not the gods who are to blame for their poverty, but rather the insatiate greed of us men of property which becomes the cause of this false conception of the gods among men, and besides of unjust blame of the gods... (Frend 1984, 603).

From this quote, one gets the idea that Julian understood the basic reason why Christianity was so very successful in the days before Constantine. It was because of economic sharing and not from the power of the sword. With the legalization of Christianity, however, much of this economic sharing social concern fell by the wayside. It is true that the church was still in charge of feeding and the caring for the poor. It was no longer the domain of the ordinary Christian brothers and sisters. It was the domain of the bishops, now the elite Christians, who looked down on the poor.

CHRISTIANITY: ENDANGERED OR EXTINCT?

The elite Christians still lived in the best estates. Some like Pope Leo I and Pope Gregory turned their estates into monasteries, thus avoiding taxes, and their lifes of leisure continued unabated. While these bishops wandered through their wonderful gardens with marble statues, discussing the finer points of theology or other refined issues, they were waited upon by slaves.

Shortly after Julian became emperor he attempted to reverse the "Christianization" of the empire. However, a small matter of revenge sidetracked him. As emperor, he turned his armed forces to attack Constantius II avenging the death of his father, and to bring an end of Constantius II attempt to take control of the empire. Constantius, however, had the good fortune of dying of natural causes on November 3, 361, and therefore no battle took place. Julian, however, did not live much longer. He was killed in battle with the Persians on June 3, 363. Of course, the Christians considered this a sign of God's wrath and vindication for their cause. It is hard for us at this time to surmise "where did the true followers of Jesus disappear." Had everyone been turned off by the hypocrisy of state religion and by the fascination with trivia and nonessentials so that there were no true followers, or had they all gone underground?

Accession of Ambrose as Bishop

Into this chaos Ambrose entered Milan, Italy. Being the consular tribune of Æmilia-Liguria, he was the military governor of two of the most prestigious provinces. Liguria was the farthest northern province of Italia or the last province of Italy or the Empire proper. The high Alpine Mountains protected the northern border. To the South was the Mediterranean Sea. All the towns and ports on the sea were heavily fortified to withstand attacks. Æmilia was one of the most verdant and agriculturally productive areas in the north of Italy. It had great fortifications to protect the Roman roads that were created to allow the Roman troops to go north to protect the borders of the empire.

A myth was promoted within the Catholic faith, that after the death of Auxentius, the Arian bishop of Milan, there was a riot in Milan's cathedral. The riot was between the Arians who wished to keep the bishopric Arian and the Nicene Christians who were insisting on a Nicene bishop. Ambrose came into the cathedral to quiet the disturbance, and a cry arose from a child (a child in a riot?) in the crowd, "Ambrose for bishop." All then

AMBROSE, THE CAPTAIN OF THE SHIP

took up the chant. Ambrose was formally baptized a Christian and within 2 weeks after his baptism into the faith, he was made bishop of Milan.

There are problems with the myth. One of the problems is: What was the prefect of Æmilia-Liguria doing in Milan? D. H. Williams suggests that in reality, Emperor Valentinian had sent Ambrose to Milan to be bishop. Williams might have hit the nail squarely on its head because for the first 3 years Ambrose, like a true general, enforced Valentinian I's policy of nonintervention in religious matters: Ambrose remained quiet, maintaining his obeisance to the emperor in charge (D. H. Williams 1996, 115–16). He could not fly in the face of the very emperor who appointed him. Furthermore, this prefect of Milan, now bishop, undoubtedly had to take some time to learn at least a cursory amount of theology. Another problem with the myth revolves around the tranquility of Ambrose's entrance into the cathedral.

We are told that he walked into the cathedral and quieted the uproar. It is clearly ridiculous. Think about the reality of the situation: the Emperor Gratian was intent on moving his throne from Rome to Milan so that he could defend the empire's borders. Most likely, Ambrose came to Milan with a good contingent of military forces. It is ludicrous to assume that a Roman general would go anywhere outside his quarters with out a good number of guards. One must assume if he entered the cathedral to quell a riot, he would have entered the cathedral with a sizeable force and they would not have entered quietly. Certainly, it would have been impossible to hear a child above the clang of armor. It would not be a far-fetched argument to assume that people in the cathedral, saw a chance to avoid bloodshed by hailing the general as bishop. If they did, certainly Ambrose could have out and out rejected it, or he could have said, "I will act as bishop, keeping the Nicene bishopric secure until the true Nicene bishop is found." More likely, however, Valentinian I sent Ambrose there: to become bishop. If Valentinian I sent Ambrose to Milan to become the new bishop, then the myth is sheer poppycock.

One way or another, Ambrose became bishop of Milan. But it was not Ambrose's personal disposition to be silent. From all the historical and sociological evidence, we have to conclude that Ambrose was always a belligerent, Nicene Catholic. Ambrose was, after all, part of the elite Constantinian military establishment of the Roman Empire, war-like through and through.

Within the cultural framework of Roman society, Ambrose more than likely waited for a propitious moment to assert the dominance of that Nicene Christianity. According to Williams, the death of Valentinian, and the accession of his son Gratian in 375 was the propitious moment. Gratian's desire to go to war with the Goths in 378 allowed Ambrose to release his wrath against the Arians. Gratian at first carried out his father's toleration of other religions, but he leaned toward a much more war-like view of his Nicene Catholicism, and he was much more amenable to Ambrose's intolerances.

General/Governor as Bishop

Sociologists and historians have long shown us that the seedbed for totalitarian regimes is chaos. We saw that Constantine had hoped to have the fragmented empire united under Christianity and under the Nicene confession so that he could better control it. Such was the case with Ambrose. A more accurate way to describe Ambrose's prowess within the empire is that Ambrose, the military general or governor, was also the bishop. In his new position as bishop, he continued to use the same skills he used to govern Northern Italy as prefect to maintain military control. As a prefect, he knew that he had been obligated to carry out Emperor Valentinian's wishes, even though he might disagree with them or find them reprehensible. He would bide his time until either the emperor was overthrown, or he could scheme to manipulate the emperor to agree with his own opinions. Then he would conveniently be able to manifest his own control.

Clearly, this is the reason Ambrose decided to move from being a general in the military to being a bishop in the church. After all, whether we accept the theory that the people called for his installation as bishop, or that Valentian II desired it, he still could have declined the call. We surmise that he decided that there was more power in the church than there was in the emperor's temporal power. This reason for his decision to take the bishopric of Milan is confirmed by all that transpired after Ambrose became bishop as well as by his own writings. Like the Emperor Constantine in his chaotic times, by dictatorial control of the belief system, Ambrose sought unity in his very own Holy Roman Empire.

AMBROSE, THE CAPTAIN OF THE SHIP

In his volume *Church and State in the Teaching of St. Ambrose*, Claudio Morino asserts that Ambrose "would have preferred to live under a more democratic form of government, but he accepted and promoted absolute monarchy . . ." (Morino 1969, ii.). No evidence exists that Ambrose would have preferred "a more democratic form of government." A passage that Morino quotes from *The Hexameron*, explains Ambrose's view of the empire and contradicts Morino's own statement: "Consequently the head [meaning any ruler], exercising the powers of censor, gives orders to its servants and special instructions to each individual" (Ambrose, *Hexameron* 6.57). There is never any indication in all of Ambrose's writings that the lesser human beings could in anyway direct the ways of the "head." Furthermore, everything about Ambrose's life indicates that when he feels comfortable with his rule, there is no one, no emperor, no pope, nor other bishops, who could influence him or change his thinking.

Nothing in Ambrose's life, rule, or teaching would suggest that he would even come close to preferring a democratic model. Furthermore Claudio Morino suggestion that Ambrose would have preferred democracy is just another Roman Catholic delusion. Democracy was never even a thought by Ambrose or anybody else at that time. This is clear regarding his attitude toward the emperor, his subjects, and everyone else, including his cursed enemy, the heretics.

Unraveling of the Empire Continues

Everything unraveled and became complicated in 378. Gratian's father, Valentinian I, made Valens, his brother and Gratian's uncle, the emperor of the East. Both Valentinian I and Valens were staunch Christians, but Valentinian I was Nicene and Valens was Arian. The Arian Goths revolted because of their mistreatment by the empire. Valens, Gratian's uncle, led the forces of the east to put down the barbarian revolt. The Goths routed Valens's forces, and Valens was killed. This put not only the Eastern Empire, but also Northern Italy in an uproar, for immigrants from the Eastern Empire, including many Arians, then invaded Northern Italy. Among the Arians that moved there were Valentinian II, Gratian's half brother, and his mother Justina, Gratian's stepmother, both Arians. In the upheaval following Valens's death, Gratian moved Justina and Valentinian II to Milan. As far as Emperor Gratian was concerned, even though he was a warlike Nicene Christian, bloodlines ran thicker than the waters of Nicene baptism. Gratian buckled under family pressures and gave his aunt and cousin the Portian Basilica outside the walls of Milan.

The Portian Basilica

Ambrose's response to Gratian's giving the basilica to the Arians reveals Ambrose's authoritarian attitude and his ire. Justina, the Arian, requested a basilica so that the increasing numbers of Arians would have a place to worship, but even more importantly, the Arians would have a bishop. This is important to remember, since in the Christian Empire as Constantine set it up, the bishop received the economic resources to support his people.

To prevent this from happening, Ambrose shrewdly incited his followers to occupy the basilica. In describing this event to his sister, Marcellina, Ambrose wrote:

> At last the command was given: Surrender the Basilica. My reply was, it is not lawful for me to surrender it, nor advantageous for you, O Emperor, to receive it. By no right can you violate the house of a private person, and do you think that the House of God may be taken away? It is asserted that everything is lawful for the Emperor, that all things are his. My answer is: Do not, O Emperor, lay on yourself the burden of such a thought as that you have any imperial power over those things which belong to God. Exalt not yourself, but if you desire to reign long, submit yourself to God. It is written: "The things which are God's to God, those which are Cæsar's to Cæsar." The palaces belong to the Emperor, the churches to the Bishop. Authority is committed to you over public, not over sacred buildings. Again the Emperor was stated to have declared: I also ought to have one Basilica. My answer was: It is not lawful for you to have it. What have you to do with an adulteress? For she is an adulteress who is not joined to Christ in lawful wedlock. (Ambrose, Letter XX.19, *NPNF* 2nd Series, CCEL)

Well, guess what? The mighty emperor backed down and the Gothic Arians did not get their Basilica. In history of Catholicism, Ambrose is commended for this act, but we suspect that commending him would be like feeding a lion a small piece of liver, and then the lion would devour the hand of the feeder and then the feeder.

Gratian's War and *De Fide*

Nonetheless, war with the Goths was still on Gratian's plate. We get the impression that it was not a religious matter for him. He wanted to settle family matters first of all, bringing justice for the death of Valens, his uncle, and second, deal with the threat of the Goths to the empire. Oh, yes, and third, they were Arians. But the Arian situation did not seem to matter that much as we can plainly see from the Portian Basilica affair.

While Ambrose does consider the Goths uncouth barbarians, that did not bother him as much as the fact that they were "vile" Arian heretics. To set the record straight and make sure Gratian was on the right side, Ambrose wrote *De fide* (*Concerning the Faith*), which opens by stating: "Your sacred Majesty, because you are on the verge of going to war, I feel it necessary to write a book, expounding on the Faith."

D. H. Williams suggests that the reason for *De Fide* was really a personal defense. The Arians were gaining strength in Milan and were accusing Ambrose of heresy, so he was writing to defend himself (D. H. Williams, 1996, 144). This may bear some truth. Ambrose could have meant *De Fide* to be a classic rhetorical document that he could have meant to be a defense by offense. But that did not seem to be Ambrose's chief purpose for writing the document. The chief purpose of De Fide, as far as Ambrose was concerned, was to destroy the Arians. It is Ambrose's verbal attack on them. Here we view the real Ambrose, naked of any pretense, and here is the Christianity he represented. Gone is the religion of Jesus of Nazareth whose kingdom is not of this world; who advocated love of enemy; who told Christians to carry the cross of discipleship; who accepted the Samaritan and the gentile; who commanded leaders to serve others. In comes the reign of the kingdom of this world: with the power of the emperor and the bishop as supreme; with the task of the average Christian to serve their emperor, their bishop, their masters, and mistresses; with the task of rejecting and destroying the barbarian, the Arians, and any other enemy of the emperor or the church.

CHRISTIANITY: ENDANGERED OR EXTINCT?

In reality, for Ambrose, the state and the church had become one. Who was in control? Probably both bishop and emperor maneuvered to influence the other. At any rate, for Ambrose, the lines of distinction were totally abolished. The Roman Empire had become his very own Holy Roman Empire. As bishop, he used his spiritual power and the mind-set of an authoritarian general to cajole and tyrannize the Roman emperors with his Nicene faith. Considering the volatile situation in and outside the empire, and the reaction of Ambrose, this is the only interpretation that makes sense.

As a pretext of setting forth his statement of faith, Ambrose wrote *De Fide* (*Concerning the Faith*) to Emperor Gratian. He begins with a typical Roman statement of feigned humility:

> Imitating examples of history of old, you, Holy Emperor Gratian, wish to learn about my faith. You imitate the Queen of the South who came to hear the wisdom of Solomon; you imitate King Hiram who sent messengers to Solomon that he might get to know him. But what can you learn from me, Emperor Augustus? From your infancy you have always devoutly and piously kept the faith. Scripture says: "Before I formed you in your mother's womb, I knew you" (Jeremiah 1:5) and "Before you came out of the womb, I sanctified you." Your sanctification cannot be given to you by anyone else on earth—it is infused into you. God placed it there; you guard it as a divine gift.
>
> Because your majesty is about to go to war, you seek from me a book expounding on faith. For you know that victories are gained more by the faith of the emperor than by the valor of any soldier. Take the example of Abraham. He led three hundred and eighteen men into battle. He reported that he received many victories from battles with his innumerable enemies (Genesis 14:14ff.). And in the name of the sign of the cross of the Lord, he conquered five kings, undergoing the onslaught of their best troops. He was thereby able to triumph by releasing the son of his brother (Genesis 14ff.). Therefore, Emperor Gratian, you, who adore Christ, must also prepare to conquer. Yes, you who seek to know

about my faith must prepare to conquer for Christ. Concerning counsel, I am following the greatest of leaders. Like Abraham, I have three hundred and eighteen priests who I judiciously chose to aid me to orchestrate the victory of the power of faith. I am thereby assuring myself that I will win the rewards by conquering the unfaithful in the world. It seems to me that this is the divine number, so I have chosen this number of oracles to counsel me in the faith, following the example of history (*De Fide* [*Concerning the Faith*], I.i.1-2, CSEL, 78).

There are some things that need to be underscored here, and Ambrose, we believe, was fully aware of them. The first is about the emperor himself. Michael Grant in *The Roman Emperors* describes Gratian in the following terms:

He was an agreeable and cultivated youth, a fluent orator with a keen interest in literature as well as religion. . .Gratian's gifts were accompanied by an excessive preoccupation with sport (and the parade-ground) that distracted him from his administrative duties. He was a young man of remarkable talent . . .eloquent, controlled, warlike and merciful, and seemed likely to rival the best of his predecessors while the down was still spreading over his cheeks. (R. M. Grant 1988, 1997, 267–68)

Simply put, Gratian was a youth when he became emperor. He was only 19 when Ambrose wrote *De Fide* to him. While it would be unfair to compare him with teens of today, biologically, there was no difference. His hormones were in full bloom. He had a sense of strength and omnipotence. While most emperors had strong egos, his youth only intensified his desire to dominate.

In *Concerning Faith* (*De Fide*), Ambrose consciously and deliberately played on those feelings. He began by using the appellation "Augustus." In Ambrose's usage, it implied that Gratian was superior to all human beings. Then he frequently used the appellation "Holy Emperor," a further move to ingratiate himself with Gratian. He encouraged Gratian by connecting him to the Old Testament prophet Jeremiah, quoting Yahweh's statement to Jeremiah: "Before I formed you in your mother's womb I knew you," and "before you came out of the womb I sanctified you" (Jeremiah 1:5). Then Ambrose went overboard in flattering Gratian's supposed holiness, even though Ambrose hopefully knew that he was beginning to stretch reality: "Your sanctification cannot be given to you by anyone else on earth—it is infused into you. God placed it there; you guard it as a divine gift." This whole section was a mockery. Today, it leaves a taste of "disbelief" in the mouth of the reader, not a taste of "faith." (*De Fide [Concerning the Faith]*, I.i. f.)

Then after making examples of Abraham, who somehow conquered five kings with "the sign of the cross," and Joshua who conquered "by recognizing a heavenly militia," Ambrose dares to say: "Therefore, Emperor Gratian, you, who adore Christ, must also prepare to conquer. Yes, you . . . must prepare to conquer for Christ." First, Ambrose attempted to win the emperor to his side; second, unbelievably, he commanded him to take up military arms "for Christ." As far as we know, this is the first time in Christian history that a Christian bishop blessed a military figure before he went to war. He says:

> I must not further detain your Majesty, in this season of preparation for war and the achievement of victory over the barbarians. Go forth, sheltered, indeed, under the shield of faith and bearing the sword of the Spirit; go forth to the victory promised in olden time, and foretold in oracles given by God. (*Exposition of the Christian Faith* II. XVI. 136. *NPNF*, 2nd Series, 10, 241. CCEL)

But within *Concerning Faith* (*De Fide*), Ambrose lays out the specific reasons that Gratian should go to war. The people whom Gratian is to defeat are the "barbaric Goths." But it is not their barbarism that is the Problem for Ambrose, rather it is the fact that the Goths are Arian heretics:

> Treacherous are those who follow after heresies—every one of them different . . . And when they gather together to communally work against the Church of God—even when they do not agree among themselves, I will call all of them by the common name of heretics, demanding our strong response. For heresy is like Hydra of fable. In spite of her wounds she continued to be well. Whenever she had a limb lopped off, she grew a new one afresh.

AMBROSE, THE CAPTAIN OF THE SHIP

To stop her, she needed to be thrown into the fire. Only fire could destroy her. Or, it is like some dreaded and monstrous Scylla, who like vi many Christian sects, divided herself into many forms of perversion, throwing men to and fro in the waves of unholy waters, and making their faith a complete wreck with the fangs of her blasphemous doctrine... (*De fide* [*Concerning the Faith*], I., 46, *CSEL* 78)

Ambrose finds support for his cause by projecting the situation into the apocalyptic Old Testament prophet Ezekiel:

For Ezekiel, in those far-off days, already prophesied the Gothic wars and the decimating of our people, saying: "Prophesy, therefore, Son of Man, and say: O Gog, the Lord says—will you not, in that day, when My people Israel is established peacefully, rise up and come from your place from the far north, taking many nations with you, a mighty army with riders upon horses? Go up against my people Israel, a great and mighty cloud of dust covering the land, in the last days" That Gog is the Goth, who has already come out, and over whom victory in days to come is promised, according to the word of the Lord: "And they shall spoil them, who had been their despoilers, and plunder them, who had carried off their prey, says the Lord. And I will give to Gog"—that is, to the Goths—"a place that is famous, for Israel a high-heaped tomb of many men, of men who have made their way to the sea, only to be entrapped there. And it shall reach round about, and close the mouth of the valley. There the house of Israel shall overthrow Gog and all his multitude, and they will call it the valley of the multitude of Gog: and the house of Israel will overwhelm them, that the land may be cleansed" Nor, furthermore, may we doubt, your sacred Majesty, that we, who have undertaken the contest with alien unbelief, shall enjoy the aid of the Catholic Faith which is strong in you. Plainly indeed the reason for God's wrath has been already made manifest, so that belief in the Roman Empire was first overthrown only where faith in God gave way. (*De fide* [*Concerning the Faith*], II. XVI.137, *CSEL* 78)

Over and over he calls the heretics liars, deceivers, and blasphemers. They are mad; they "overthrow the dominion of the Trinity"; "they are worse than the Jews"; "The Catholic and apostolic Church declares them accursed" (*De Fide (Concerning the Faith)*, I. XI 69; XII 75-78; XIV 119–120; XX 135). There is a major problem with Ambrose's writing, which most contemporary people would acknowledge. It is that Ambrose mixes name-calling with verses from the scriptures while never dealing with Arianism itself.

De Fide, Not Truth, But Rhetoric

Williams points out that Palladius, an Arian bishop, reacted negatively against *De Fide* and published scathing rebuttals of Ambrose. These texts (Scolia) of Palladius were recently studied (R. Gryson, 1980, 1982). In these texts Palladius accuses Ambrose of neither reading nor understanding Arian thought, and then of massively distorting it (D. H. Williams 1996, 148–53). R. P. C. Hanson, in his exhaustive study, *The Search for the Christian Doctrine of God*, supports those accusations of modern scholarship. He asserts that Ambrose

> ...has learned the conventional arguments handed out by the official church ... His account of the doctrines of Arianism is hasty and superficial, and ... these statements are gross travesties of Arian doctrine. Arian thoughts rely, he says, on "clever argumentations" (*versutis disputationibus*) Ambrose appears to know nothing of the doctrines of Arius. (Hanson 1988, 2005, 669–70).

De Fide, or Concerning Faith, certainly was not a good exposition of the Arian faith; it was not even a serious exposition of the Christian faith. It was, however, a serious rhetorical document. Following principles of pagan rhetoric, it did what it was supposed to do: it demolished the opposition and ingratiated him with the emperor (Cameron 1991, 30ff.).

Ambrose, The Emperor's "Father in the Faith"

De Fide did the trick as far as Ambrose's relationship with the emperor was concerned. In 379, Gratian wrote a letter to Ambrose calling him his "father in the faith" (D. H. Williams 1996, 154). This is, in part, what

Ambrose wished to accomplish in *De Fide*. Constantine took advice from the bishops before he interpreted the nature of the faith; Ambrose called the shots with advice from no one.

Ambrose, likewise, made little if any change in his behavior when he advanced from Roman prefect to bishop: in his mind, the Goths were still "bloodthirsty barbarians," even though he knew that the Roman legions were at least as bloodthirsty and violent as the Goths, if not more so; he had to have doubts whether the empire would "be safe with such defenders" because he knew that the Roman soldiers were marauding degenerates (*De Fide* II.XVI.140). Yet he insisted on the ill treatment of the Goths and the other hordes, the Visigoths (the Goths from Western Germany), and Vandals (another East German tribe). These tribes did not take such abuse, and they marched against the empire and helped to destroy it.

The "Council" of Aquileia

A few years after Ambrose wrote the first two books of *De Fide* he engaged in tactics that revealed his manipulative, basically un-Christian tactics. As part of his anti-Arian campaign, he talked the emperor into calling a church council. On September 3rd, 381, this council met in Aquileia in Northern Italy just off the Adriatic Sea. The pretext of the council was to discuss the unity of the faith. However, when the Arian bishop Paladius and his associate, Secundianus, arrived at Aquileia from Bulgaria, they realized that it was not a discussion. In actuality, they were being tried as heretics. There were only 25 bishops present, and none of them favored Paladius and Secundianus. Ambrose talked the emperor into excluding other eastern bishops on the pretext that they were aging and it would not be good for them to travel. His true concern, however, was that there be no support for these Arians from the east (D. H. Williams 1996, 169–79).

Reviewing the Arian texts (scolia), Hanson states that Ambrose's behavior at Aquileia "was characterized by injustice and bullying." He notes these unjust and intimidating characteristics:

1. According to custom the bishop of the area was to moderate the council, but Ambrose demanded that position.

2. None of the Bishops from the east who might have been more favorable to Paladius and Secundianus were invited to the Council.
3. Ambrose tried to force Palladius to sign that he agreed with "a letter purported to have been written by Arius."
4. After Palladius argued that he did not know Arius and would not sign the letter, Ambrose tyrannically took this then as an admission that Palladius accepted the letter.
5. Ambrose then went into a long harangue that Palladius refused to accept "the Trinity."
6. Ambrose then revealed that he had stationed scribes behind Palladius and Secundianus.
7. Seeing that they were set up for heresy trial, both Palladius and Secundianus bolted from the chambers only to discover that guards prevented their exiting. (Hanson 1988, 2005, 668-669)

Ambrose's letter to the emperors describing the conference lends credibility to Palladius's complaints. Ambrose was out to drive the Arians out of existence. Describing the conferences to the emperors east and west (but mainly to Gratian), he wrote, "Therefore according to the directions of your Graces we have met together without the odium of large numbers (*sine invidia multidinis*) . . ." Normally, large numbers would not be "odium," *invidia*, but rather, would assure a good ecumenical council because it would involve the agreement of the universal Roman Catholic Church. Furthermore, his claim that he did not invite the eastern bishops, "who were weighed down with old age (*senectutis gravatus annnis*)" was at very least a deceptive statement since the very next year he invited the same bishops to a conference in Rome. It is clear from the letter to the emperors that the main—if not the sole—purpose of the conference was the discussion of the only "heretics" present: Palladius and Secundianus (Ambrosius, *Epistula X:ii, CSEL* 72). Everything in Ambrose's epistle to the emperor confirms Palladius's suspicions that they were set up for a trial. Ambrose clearly had loaded the deck against them.

The Murder of Gratian

Ambrose's intrigue is observable in several more instances. In 383, Magnus Maximus, the prefect in Britain, a Christian and a strong Nicene

AMBROSE, THE CAPTAIN OF THE SHIP

Christian, murdered Gratian. Ambrose went quickly to Trier to negotiate a temporary peace between Maximus and Emperor Valentinian II, Gratian's half brother. What is so amazing about this fact is that he readily met with the culprit that murdered Gratian, who was "his son in the faith," for whom he supposedly had so much respect, yet he refused to negotiate at all in a lesser matter, the turning of a basilica over to the Arians, and in a future controversy, financial aid to the pagan altar of Victory.

In Ambrose's attempt to establish his dominance within the Roman Empire, procuring peace between ruling powers was supremely important. Furthermore, in the political nature of things in the Roman Empire, a general killing an emperor was common fare, and therefore, politically, Ambrose made the most of it. *Sic transit gloria mundi* (So passes the glory of the world).

The Pagan Altar of Victory

The next significant event in Ambrose's life occurred when Symmachus, a Roman senator, attempted to get Valentinian II to reestablish the pagan Altar of Victory on behalf of the elite pagans of Rome. Ambrose effectively blocked the move by threatening to excommunicate Valentinian II. He wrote to the emperor:

> What will you answer a priest who says to you, "The church does not seek your gifts, because you have adorned the heathen temples with gifts. The Altar of Christ rejects your gifts, because you have made an altar for idols, for the voice is yours, the hand is yours, the subscription is yours, the deed is yours. The Lord Jesus refuses and rejects your service, because you have served idols... (Ambrose, Epistle XVII. 14, NPNF 2nd series. 10, 413, CCEL).

In threatening Valentinian II with excommunication if he reinstituted the Altar of Victory, again Ambrose used the most powerful weapon in the Roman Empire, now Ambrose's Holy Roman Empire.

The Burning of the Jewish Synagogue

The next event of significance in Ambrose's push for authority involved Emperor Theodosius and the burning of a Jewish synagogue in the

CHRISTIANITY: ENDANGERED OR EXTINCT?

east. A Christian bishop incited monks in his diocese to burn a Jewish synagogue in Callicinum, Syria. The emperor rightfully ordered the bishop to pay for the rebuilding of the synagogue and to have the monks punished, but Ambrose arrogantly and tyrannically intervened (with an emperor!). In *Epistle* XL, an address to Emperor Theodosius, Ambrose wrote:

> I prefer for me to be of help to you, rather than me being a companion in evil. Therefore, your clemency ought to be displeased by the silence of priests, rather than delighting in your own freedom. For you are placed in danger by my silence, and you are aided by my speaking to you. Therefore, it is not inopportune that I place myself in your debt in order to force something upon your conscience. By obeying God regarding what I need to say to you, I keep my conscience free before God. But this is not the main reason that I speak to you. I do so primarily because I love you, my Grace. I am careful to preserve your salvation. (Ambrosius, *Epistula ad Augustus Theodosius* XL.iii., CSEL 72).

This was so magnanimous of Ambrose. He is preserving Theodosius' salvation and preserving him from perishing in hell for all eternity. In Ambrose's age, this has to be considered ultimate power, that an emperor of the Roman Empire must be worried about the silence of a bishop. Today, a bishop who criticized a dictator would find himself, like Oscar Romero, dead. This would not be the case with Ambrose. He put the fear of God into the emperor, and the emperor went crawling to him. Furthermore, in this action, "Saint" Ambrose set the standard for future centuries of anti-Jewish sentiments.

In this same epistle (XL) Ambrose was speaking to the emperor of the archbishop of Antioch, and he as bishop of Milan was intervening in a diocese completely on the other side of the Mediterranean. Of course, this was his right as the voice of God for the Catholic Church, for he considered himself as the Pope. He literally says this in the very next thought in this epistle:

> I am not then an officious meddler in matters beyond my province, an intruder in the concerns of others, but I comply with my duty, I obey the commandment of our God. This I do chiefly

from love and regard for you, and from a wish to preserve your well-being. But if I am not believed, or am forbidden to act on this, then in truth I speak from fear of offending God. For if my own danger could deliver you, I would consent to be offered for you, though not willingly, for I would rather that without danger to myself you should be accepted and glorified by God. (Ambrosius, *Epistula ad Augustus Theodosius* XL.iii., *CSEL* 72).

Ambrose and the Pope

Here there is another important element in Ambrose's ascent to power. Not only has Ambrose raised himself above the emperor and others, he acts as the prime authority within the church and spokesperson for God. This, indeed, should play havoc with the Roman Catholic concept of the primacy of Rome. In all of Ambrose's writings, there is no hint that he was subservient to the bishop in Rome. Everything that Ambrose wrote, he wrote as the final authority. Even when he received a notice from Siricius, the pope, that the presbyters, deacons, and other clergy had found certain Christians, "Jovinian, Auxentius, Genialis, Germinator, Felix, Prontinus, Martianus, Januarius, and Ingeniosus," to be heretical, Ambrose found it necessary to investigate and to convict the heretics himself. These accused heretics, followers of Jovinian, were little noted in church history and among scholars. However, they were key to an understanding of Ambrose.

In his Synodical letter to Pope Siricius (also written to 11 bishops), Ambrose wrote:

> They pretend that they are giving honor to marriage. But what praise can rightly be given to marriage if note is not made of the honor of virginity? We do not deny that marriage was hallowed by Christ, for the Divine words say, "And the two shall be one flesh," and one spirit. For certainly our birth precedes our calling. Even so, the mystery of the divine operations is much more excellent than the remedy of human frailty. A good wife is deservedly praised, but a pious virgin is more properly preferred, for the Apostle says, "He that gives his virgin in marriage does well, but he that gives her not

in marriage does better; for the former cares for the things of the world, the latter for the things of the Lord." The former is bound by the chains of marriage, the latter is free from those chains; the former is under the Law, the latter under Grace. Marriage is good, for thereby the human race is able to continue in existence, but virginity is better, for thereby the heavenly kingdom can continue to exist on earth, allowing humankind to discover and attain heavenly rewards. By a woman, care entered the world; by a virgin, salvation. Furthermore, Christ gave us virginity and chastity as His own special gift, displaying it in His own person as His Mother previously had done. (Council of Milan, Ambrose, *Letter* XLII *to Pope Siricius*, 3 [1881 translation] www.roger-pearce.com)

This paragraph expresses the essential complaint Pope Siricius, and then Ambrose, had against "the heretics" Jovinian and his followers. They simply claimed that married people were equal to virgins in God's sight—nothing more. No indication exists that Jovian and his followers were questioning any of the central dogmas of Catholic, Nicaean beliefs. The point is that the text reveals no submission to the Pope's reasoning but rather Ambrose, himself, as either co-equal or the Pope's superior, establishes the reason for declaring these people heretics.

The New Asceticism

Jovinian and his followers threatened Siricius, and Ambrose, in particular. As we pointed out with the Montanists, before Constantine, particularly during the Diocletian persecutions, the church venerated the "confessors/martyrs," those persons under the pain or threat of torture and death who were faithful to their beliefs. As the preeminent scholar Elizabeth Clark points out in *Reading Renunciation: Asceticism and Scripture in Early Christianity*, in the fourth century, asceticism replaced martyrdom for special distinction in the church. Clark sets forth many definitions of asceticism, but she accepts the scholars of the Society of Biblical Literature as the most definitive. These scholars define asceticism in the following way:

Ascetic behavior represents a range of responses to social, political, and physical worlds often perceived as oppressive or unfriendly, or as stumbling blocks to the pursuit of heroic personal or communal goals, lifestyles, and commitments"; "abstention or avoidance" lay at its core. (Clark 1999, 14-15)

Let us put this in perspective of Ambrose's life. We remember that after his father died his mother raised him in Rome. His mother did not remarry but set up a consecrated community. Furthermore his sister, Marcellina, was a consecrated virgin. We recall also that the bishop of Rome (the pope!) would visit the community. From the attitudes of power, honor and shame within the Roman Christian community, a person could not have received a higher honor. However, beside that honor and the fact that they were Aristocrats, Ambrose ratchets up that honor to the ultimate level. He writes three volumes extolling the importance of virgins. Of course, he would have the reader remember that he was likewise celibate. In *Concerning Virgins*, Ambrose bears witness that ascetics, particularly virgins, took the place that martyrs had played in earlier Christianity:

> For virginity is not praiseworthy because it is found in martyrs, but because it itself makes martyrs. But who can comprehend with human understanding that which not even nature has included in her laws? Or who can explain in ordinary language that which is above the course of nature? Virginity has brought from heaven that which it may imitate on earth.

Ambrose goes on:

> Fittingly has the virgin sought a manner of life, which corresponds to that of heaven, for she has found for herself a Spouse in heaven. With her whole heart, she has passed beyond the clouds, air, angels, and stars, and she has found the Word of God in the very bosom of the Father, and has drawn Him into herself. For who having found so great a Good would forsake it? For "Thy Name is as ointment poured out, therefore have the maidens loved Thee, and drawn Thee." And indeed what I have said is not my own, since they who marry not, nor are given in marriage are as the angels in heaven. Let us not, then, be surprised if the virgins are compared to the angels who are joined to the Lord of

angels. Who, then, can deny that this mode of life has its source in heaven, something which we don't easily find on earth, except when God came down into the members of an earthly body? Then a Virgin conceived, and the Word became flesh that flesh might become God. (Ambrose, *Concerning Virgins*, I. III, 10–11, *NPNF* 2nd series, 10, 365. CCEL)

As much as Ambrose praises virgins, the one thing that he does not say is that while virgins are honored, they have no say, except maybe by suggestion, in the running of the affairs of the Church. This has been the case for most of Church history, in Roman Catholic, Greek Orthodox and Protestants churches. Only recently have nuns demanded a say in the affairs of Church. This as we have stated was totally different from the Jesus Movement, the Marcionites and the Montanists.

Ambrose and Slavery

For Ambrose, there is only one thing that matters and this is power, power, and more power. When he walked into the cathedral after Auxentius's death, Ambrose knew the full implications of being Milan's bishop. He was certainly well aware of his potential for power even before he became bishop. But as we stated regarding Ambrose's thoughts on leadership and the military, there was very little in Jesus' teachings that informed Ambrose's thought and behavior. To press the point a step further, his attitudes toward slavery were the typical attitude of the pagan philosophical elite. In 386, 13 years after his installation as bishop, Ambrose wrote to Simplicianus, a philosopher, who became a Christian priest and was instrumental in Augustine becoming a Christian:

Yet the Epistle, which troubled you after you were gone, has to do with the meaning of Paul the Apostle, who calls us from slavery to liberty: "You were bought with a price; do not become the slaves of human beings" (1 Corinthians 7:23). In this, he shows that our liberty consists in the knowledge of wisdom. This passage has been pitched and tossed around by a great number of philosophers who say that every wise man is free, every fool is a slave. This was said long ago by a son of David in the words: "A fool is changed like the moon" (Eccli 27.12). A wise man is not shattered by fear, or changed by power, or elated by good fortune, or overwhelmed by sadness. Where there is wisdom there are strength of spirit and perseverance and fortitude. The wise man is constant in soul, not deflated or elated by changing events. He does not toss like a child, carried about by every wind of doctrine, but remains perfected in Christ, grounded by charity, rooted by faith. The wise man is never idle and experiences no changing states of mind. But he will shine like the Sun of justice that shines only in the kingdom of His Father.

Let us consider the source of that philosophy from which the patriarchs drew their wisdom and learning. Was not Noah the first to curse his son when he learned that Canaan had made fun of his nakedness: "Cursed be Canaan; meanest of slaves shall he be to his brethren," for his brothers, who with wisdom knew that they should respect their father's years. Did not Jacob, that source of all wisdom, who by reason of his wisdom was preferred to his elder brother, pour an abundance of reasoning into the hearts of us all? Although the devoted father felt a father's affection for both his sons, he judged each differently (for love is not estranged from kinship, but judgments are formed according to merit). Hence, he gave favor to one, pity to the other, favoring the wise, but pitying the unwise because he could not rise to valorous deeds by his own strength or advance his steps at will. Thus, he blessed him so that he would serve his brother and be his slave, revealing how the lack of wisdom is brought rightfully low by servitude, that his slavery may be a remedy for him, because the foolish man cannot rule himself, and if he is without a guide he is undone by his own desires.

After due deliberation, the devoted father made him a slave of his brother so that he would be guided by the other's prudence. Thus, wise men become rulers of the indiscreet in order to guide by their power the foolishness of the masses over whom they rule. Thus, they bring unwilling subjects to obey those who are wise and make them submit to the laws. So the devoted father put a yoke on the foolish one as on an unruly man, and he denied liberty to the person whom he decreed must live by another's sword. Such an unwise man should willingly put his wise brother over him so that he might not sin by his temerity, but subject his limitations to a wise man's authority. Thus he might come to repentance. Thus we must make a distinction between some slaves and others. Some are strong of purpose and must be made slaves, others become slaves in a more beautiful way, willingly, because they recognize their weakness, but either way, the yoke is necessarily placed on either type in order to secure for the slave the blessing of subjection. Not nature but foolishness makes the slave. Freeing a foolish slave willy-nilly does not free him, but learning does make a man free. Esau was born free, but he became a slave; Joseph was sold into slavery, but he was raised to power that he might rule those who had purchased him. Yet he did not slight his obligation to work zealously; he clung to the heights of virtue; he preserved the liberty of innocence in the stronghold of blamelessness. (Ambrosius, *Epistula* XXXVII.1-3, *CSEL* 72)

While this is a lengthy quote from Ambrose's letter, it is highly revealing on how instrumental he was in the devolution of Christianity. The letter from Simplicianus to Ambrose is not available to us, but from analyzing Ambrose's letter, we can surmise that what was perplexing Simplicianus is the question concerning how it is possible for Christians to be slaves. What we find in this text is an excellent example of what scholars call intertextuality. Julia Kristeva as describes intertexuality as "[e]very text builds itself as a mosaic of quotations, every text is absorption and transformation of another text." (Cited by Clark 1999, 122).

This is precisely what Ambrose did. When Paul said in 1 Corinthians 7:23, "You were bought at a price; do not become slaves of human beings," Paul was not talking about philosophy freeing the person, but rather God freeing the Christian through Jesus' death on the cross and his resurrection. But for Ambrose, it is the wise who are free. The fool or slow of thought are the slaves and must be supervised by the wise. The Hexameron, not Paul, states that the fool or the slow need somebody to be over them. According to Ambrose slavery was not due to the fallen state of humanity as it would be for Augustine. Slavery for Ambrose was the existing natural order of life. Therefore the hierarchical order of the Roman Empire as it existed and as he was establishing it was divinely ordained.

From a People's History perspective, while Augustine, as we will see, built the structure of imperial Christianity, or Augustianism, Ambrose provided the blueprints, or the framework, for that structure. If Ambrose taught anything to Christians, he taught the clergy of the ages how to advance themselves by being politically astute. He set in stone sexual fantasy and power dynamics that are plagues of the Roman Catholic Church, today.

8

Augustine Versus the Donatists

In the last two chapters, we observed how the church was consumed in a struggle between male egos with disastrous results. In this chapter, we are going to discuss a struggle that would eventually end the dominance of Christianity in North Africa and critically wound the Jesus Movement. This unholy struggle was between just one cleric, Augustine of Hippo (354–430), and the majority of Christians in North Africa.

Influence of Augustine

Augustine, Bishop of Hippo, is one of the most influential theologians in Western Christian thought. Two of his best-known works are *The Confessions* and *The City of God*. But these are just two books from Augustine's massive body of writing. One theologian has stated, "If anyone says he has read all of Augustine's writings, he is a liar." "Writings" is not quite accurate. The word should be "dictations," because most of Augustine's thoughts were written, not by himself, but by his scribes who followed him, writing down everything that proceeded from his mouth.[41] *The Confessions (Confessiones)* and *The City of God (De civitate Dei)*, like most of Augustine's works, touch on the depravity of human beings who must be swept away in the Spirit into

---

[41] Today, it is not so much Augustine's own works that are incapable of being read, because we have better tools to do so. It is the infinite amount of material written about him in English (Irish), German, Italian, French, etc., which is impossible to read.

another realm, God's own realm, in order to be saved. The realm is described in *The City of God*:

> The servants of Christ listen to his voice. Others are indifferent to it, while most turn away, enthralled as they are by the enticements of evil rather than the value of virtue. Whatever be the condition of the servants of Christ, they—whether they be kings, princes, judges, soldiers, civil administrators, rich or poor, slave or free, men or women, or even the most wretched and despised persons on earth, if they must be in such dire positions—are charged to endure in this desolate, earthly republic in order that they might enter into that most holy and august meeting place of the angels, into the republic of heaven, where every issue will become very clear and where the will of God is law. (civ. Dei (*The City of God*), II, xix. CSEL)

While the saints, whether they are kings or slaves endure suffering on earth, they will all be in heaven, but implied in this thought is a hierarchical positioning. Every person is predestined to his or her social position in life. In history, this has justified the oppression of the masses of people by the establishment, set up by the three estates[42] and the divine right of kings.

It is clear from all of Augustine's works that the king had his own high position in the hierarchy, but even he must worship correctly. Worshipping correctly meant that he believed and worshipped according to the Catholic persuasion, the only true faith. For example, he states in *The City of God*:

> If the king worships the true God properly and with sincere holiness, he will hopefully reign both far and wide for many years. His reign exceeds the realm of being merely useful. His piety and honesty, which are great gifts from God, are beneficial for the king himself. They are sufficient to give him the gift of true happiness and a good life here on earth, and then,

---

[42] Generally, in feudal Europe and later, especially in France, the three estates were the clergy, the nobles, and the commoners.

afterwards, ensure for him eternal life. His reign in the kingdom is profitable on this earth not only for himself, but also for his subjects . . . For the good ruler, even though he serves, is free, but the evil ruler, even if he rules, is a slave, not only to one man, but, what is even more grievous, to as many masters as he has debtors. (*civ. Dei* (*The City of God*), IV, iii. *CSEL*)

Augustine established the Roman Catholic faith as the only purveyor and monopolistic dispenser of eternal life that "worships the true God properly in sincere holiness" (*civ. Dei* (*The City of God*), IV, iii. *CSEL*). In doing so, he sets the stage for and justifies persecutions, inquisitions, holocausts, genocides, and cultural oppression. In Epistle 93, Augustine wrote the following message to Vincentius, a dissident Christian bishop. In it, he justified the stark persecution, which the Donatists were facing:

The earlier time of that king [Nebuchadnezzar] represents the former age of emperors [Diocletian and the others] who did not believe in Christ, at whose hands the Christians suffered because of their wickedness; but the latter time of that king represents the age of their successors to the imperial throne [Constantine and the others], who now believe in Christ at whose hands the wicked now suffer because of the Christians. (*Epistula* XCIII. III.ix. *CSEL*.[] Brackets ours.)

The Donatists of North Africa: An Ancient Christian Independence Movement

While most Christians know the name Augustine, they would not know that of the African people called Donatists. Likewise, most of the Christian clergy would not recognize the name Donatist. Even Africans have long forgotten the name. Yet in the fourth through the sixth centuries, according to W. H. C. Frend, this group of Christians dominated the culture of North Africa and was identical with Christianity itself. (Frend 1970, 95–111)

Frend stipulates that North Africans perceived Christianity as a protest movement against the Roman Empire. Christianity was preceded in the third century (200–300 CE) by the African cult, Saturn/Caelistis, which had been a pagan religion in defiance of Rome. Frend states that the elite of the cult became romanized and in so doing, the cult lost popular support. The North Africans then found in Christianity the protest movement that refused to bow its knees to any emperor. This made Christianity overwhelmingly attractive (Frend, 1971, 78–80).

Tertullian (ca 160–220, whom we discuss in chapters 3–5), born in Carthage, was the paragon of the attitudes of North African Christianity. According to Tertullian and likewise the Montanists, acceptance of the Christian faith meant striving to maintain the attitude of Jesus. Pagan sacrifices, of course, were immediately deleted from Christian life. Other Roman traditions that were strictly forbidden were attendance at gladiatorial combats or any form of debauchery or licentious activity. Anything connected with the compromising of Christian belief was to be omitted. This included such things as accepting municipal office or engaging in trades remotely connected with paganism or pagan attitudes.

The Donatists and the Great Persecution

To say the least, such attitudes did not ingratiate these North Africans with the Romans. Frend gives an insightful description of the North African Christian culture:

> The attitude of defiance and rebellion was developed to an extreme degree in Africa. The powers of evil seemed to be personified in the Roman officials and magistrates. Yet the Christian did not take up arms against their enemies. Martyrdom was their means to victory... (Frend: 1971, 107)

Because of this rebellious attitude of the Donatists, the Roman Empire was much more repressive and violent in North Africa during the Great Persecution (303–311) than in any other part of the Roman Empire. Even some bishops and their clergy could not bear the intense pressure. At the command of Roman magistrates, they sacrificed to the Roman gods or offered up their scriptures to be burned in public ceremonies. The Donatists called those who did so *traditores*. One bishop, a suspected *traditor*, ordained a deacon, Caecilian, also suspected of being a *traditor*. Caecillianus was accused of forcibly preventing food from being brought to the Christians held in prison. Caecillianus did not ingratiate himself with the common people. To say the least, he was not popular with the people of North Africa. Furthermore, in the mind of the people, a bishop, deacon, or clergy who turned traditor invalidated his own ordination and was unable to validly ordain anyone.

Bishop Donatus of Niger

The people found a champion in a member of the clergy by the name of Donatus of Niger. They ordained Donatus as bishop in place of Caecillianus, creating a schism. It is from Donatus that the North African Christians received their name, Donatists (see Frend 1971, 3–24; 148–68). Donatus and his followers represented what Frend called "the rigourist" Christians—those Christians who resembled in their discipleship Tertullian and his disciple, Cyprian. Caecillianus represented the tolerant and affluent Christians.

Constantine and the Donatists

The Donatists could tolerate the horrendous persecutions of Diocletian more than they could the next events of history. Barely 3 months after Constantine's "vision" at the Milvian bridge, his killing of Maxentius, and his legalization of Christianity, Constantine sent an epistle to Bishop Chrestus of Syracuse in which he described the state of affairs of the church in North Africa. The following showed his political resentment of the Donatist. He condemned the North Africans for being

> . . . forgetful both of their own salvation and of the reverence due to the most holy religion, [they] do not even yet bring hostilities to an end, and are unwilling to conform to the judgments already passed, and assert that those who expressed their opinions and decisions were few, or that they had been too hasty and precipitate in giving judgment, before all the things which ought to have been accurately investigated had been examined—on account of all this it has happened that those

very ones who ought to hold brotherly and harmonious relations toward each other, are shamefully, or rather abominably, divided among themselves, and give occasion for ridicule to those men whose souls are aliens to this most holy religion. Wherefore it has seemed necessary to me to provide that this dissension, which ought to have ceased after the judgment had been already given by their own voluntary agreement, should now, if possible, be brought to an end by the presence of the many. (Eusebius, *Church History*: X.V.22 *NFPF* 2nd Series, vol. 1, 382, *CCEL*)

Within the same epistle, Constantine indicated that he was going to bring bishops to Rome to judge the dispute, but Constantine clearly had made up his mind. The Donatists were in trouble. To confirm the fact that Constantine had already loaded the dice against the Donatists, he wrote the following epistle to Bishop Caecillianus:

Constantine Augustus to Caecillianus, Bishop of Carthage. Since it is our pleasure that something should be granted in all the provinces of Africa and Numidia and Mauritania to certain ministers of the legitimate and most holy Catholic Church to defray their expenses . . . if you should find that anything is wanting for the fulfillment of this purpose of mine in regard to all of them, you shall demand without hesitation from Heracleides, our treasurer, whatever you find to be necessary (Eusebius, *Church History*: X.6.1 *NFPF* 2nd Series, 1, 382, CCEL).

According to McGiffert (*NFPF* 2nd Series: I, 382–83. CCEL), this is the first evidence of state-sponsored remuneration of the church. The last sentence is a blank check signed and guaranteed by the emperor himself. This letter was the torch, which together with the friction between the rich and the poor in the Roman Empire, brought the powder keg in the empire to the point of explosion.

Constantine showed his cards. He cut through the theological jargon when he spoke of money and riches for the clergy. He was inviting the clergy into the elite and exclusive group, which was smothering the Roman Empire.

To the Donatists this was revulsive. The Church had literally become part of the oppressive Roman Empire. But now there was an added element: thanks to Ambrose, the bishops had the power to condemn people to hell. So Ambrose added to the fear of physical force, the fear of eternal damnation. It is here that we have entering the scene the major player in the era of the Holy Roman Empire, Augustine of Hippo.

The Life of Augustine

So we return to Augustine and the Donatists, which, quite frankly, now becomes a microscopic view of the waning empire. In this context, we pick up on the person of Augustine, parading around in his cloak, and his scribes scurrying after him, writing down every word that came out of his mouth. Augustine was born in 354 in a small Roman town of Thagaste, Numidia, which is called today Souk Ahras in Algeria. In Augustine's day, this was one of the most productive areas for olives, grapes, and grains. It is on a plateau that is sheltered by the Atlas Mountains. Even today, it gets about 60 inches of rain a year, compared to almost none within the Sahara Desert to its south. Furthermore, Souk Ahras is just a few miles from the Chelif River. While this river is not terribly wide, it is the major river in Algeria. During the Roman Empire's control over North Africa, it was the prime waterway for moving agricultural products from the farms of Numidia to the Mediterranean Sea, and then to Italy. Consequently, there was a considerable number of Italians who migrated to Thagaste. Among these, of course, were the military, but also many from the top society to take advantage of the wonderful weather and the great resources. They supplanted the Berber tribes from the land, and enslaved them.

Peter Brown, in his biography, *Augustine of Hippo*, describes the archeological evidence that shows the leisure and comfortable lifestyle of the elite:

> On mosaics we can see the great country-houses of the African Romans: two-storied villas, surrounded by paddocks, fish-ponds, and ornamental wreaths of cypresses. Their owners are shown in the flowing robes of the age, hunting on horseback,

and receiving the obeisance of the peasantry. These rich men were the patroni, the 'protectors' of their community, in town and country alike. As they strode through the forum with their great retinues, the poor man was well-advised to rise and bow deeply to his lord. (Brown 1969, 4)

Patricius, the Absent Father

Augustine's family was not counted among the elite class of Roman citizens. However, Augustine's father, Patricius, was an Italian and a Roman citizen. More than likely, he was sent to Thagaste to help administer the shipping of the food products to Rome and elsewhere in the Roman Empire. While his work may have been functionally important in the scheme of things to the empire, in the honor and shame culture of the society he was a low-level Roman clerk, which meant he was one step above a peasant. He would be in the class called curial, which, according to de Ste. Croix, was the most oppressed of the propertied classes. Augustine, in *The Confessions*, Book II, 3, 5, states that his father, "was but a poor freeman of Thagaste," but "that he went even beyond his means to supply his [Augustine's] . . . necessities . . . for the sake of his studies."

The works of Augustine, and particularly *The Confessions*, tell us little about Patricius. Being a person with a curial position, he was most likely an obsequious person with his superiors. He more than likely resented his position and saw in his bright, eldest son the possibilities of advancing the status of the family. This is precisely what happened. He, however, was not able to see his dream fulfilled because he died when Augustine was sixteen.

Monica, the Controlling Mother

By far, the most influential person in Augustine's life was Monica, his mother. The Roman Catholic Church proclaimed Monica a saint for having brought Augustine to Catholicism, but Monica was no saint. She was self-serving in the sense that she served her family above everything. Yes, she was instrumental in bringing her son to Catholicism, but in reality, if her son was to make any advancement in the Roman Empire after 380, he had no choice but to be Catholic.

CHRISTIANITY: ENDANGERED OR EXTINCT?

Monica was born in the Berber tribe of North Africa. By marrying Patricius, an Italian, she was marrying upward in society. Patricius, on the other hand, was marrying down. This likewise was a sign of his lower-class status. If he had been upper class, he would have sought to marry into a more influential family, or his parents would have arranged that marriage.

Augustine continued the pattern of his father. He chose a Berber woman as his concubine. Because his mother was Berber, she should have been delighted when her son began a relationship with the Berber woman. But Monica was not delighted. She thought the relationship should be ended and moved Augustine to send his concubine back to her home in Africa. Monica, however, was not interested in her son being celibate. She was interested in her son marrying someone of higher status, a woman from a wealthy family, thus moving her family upward. Monica died before she knew the end result of her son's conversion to Catholicism.

Augustine did not marry, but he did infinitely better than Monica's greediest dream. He ended with more people waiting on him and more property under his control than most of the Roman elite.

Augustine, the Bishop

Thus, our story begins with Augustine and Donatus.[43] Augustine was ordained a presbyter in 389, and he was consecrated the bishop of Hippo in 396. Hippo was a city near the Mediterranean Sea in Numidia, which is in present-day Algeria. Naomi Norman, in her article on "Hippo," in *Augustine through the Ages: An Encyclopedia*, reports that today there is no town in this area.[44] The area is predominantly Islamic, and if there are any Christians there, we do not know of them. The great bishop who went around in his robe with scribes in tow left only ruins in his wake. According to Peter Brown, before Augustine became bishop of Hippo the Catholics were "the harassed minority."

---

[43] To get more of a more complete record of Augustine's life, we recommend Peter Brown's *Augustine of Hippo* or James O'Donnell's *Augustine: A New Biography*.

[44] It is worth going to Ms. Norman's article to read how Hippo was in Augustine's day. For the article, see: Alan D. Fitzgerald, *Augustine through the Ages: An Encyclopedia* (Grand Rapids, MI: William B. Eerdmans Publishing Company, 1999), in loc.

AUGUSTINE VERSUS THE DONATISTS

The Donatists were "predominant in both the town and the surrounding countryside." Animosity was rampant between the established Catholics and the Donatists. Brown documents that the Donatist bishop had imposed "a boycott on his rivals: he had forbidden the bakers to bake bread for the Catholics" (Brown, 1967, 2000, 130-32).

The Gulf between the Bishop and His People

Bishop Valerius, Augustine's predecessor, Brown asserts, was an "elderly Greek who spoke Latin with difficulty." He was quite unable to understand the Punic dialect of the country-folk." He had Augustine preach in Latin (Brown, 1967, 2000, 138–39). The elite Latins were very impressed with him. But, of course, the Berbers could not understand him. There was a language difficulty. From Augustine's early years, his mother, Monica, ashamed of her low status, did not speak to her son in her native language—she tried her best to shelter him from contact with the Berbers. So Augustine never preached in Punic or Berber. But he did preach in Latin, the language of the oppressive empire. The people who best understood Augustine were the Romans, the elite in society. T. Kermit Scott, in *Augustine: His Thought in Context*, points out that, besides the fact that all humans face "pain and the tribulation, Augustine showed no signs that his Berber tribe faced any undue oppression from the Roman occupying forces" (Scott 1995, 66–67). As shall soon be very apparent, Augustine considered the suffering the Berber people faced from the Roman forces was due to the fact that they had not turned from their error of maintaining their Donatist Christianity. They had not become good sons and daughters of the Catholic Church and thus, subject to him.

Indeed, there was nothing in Augustine's life with which the average African could relate. His Greek and Roman philosophy were foreign to them. His conversion was heavily influenced by the aplomb and pomp of the Roman Empire. It is no accident that Monica drew Augustine to Milan. She knew, as did Augustine, that Ambrose, the bishop of Milan, was one of the most powerful people in the empire. Therefore Milan would be a good place to promote Augustine's upward mobility. Augustine rejected the closest person to his maternal Berber ancestry, his Berber concubine. Not only was there nothing in the person of Augustine to which the average Berber could relate, but there was everything in him that they would resent. Though he had Berber blood, he was Roman through and through. Even the fact that he was a master of rhetoric did not ingratiate him with the Donatists. It alienated him even more.

Augustine's Attack on the Donatists

If the Donatists could not understand Augustine, neither could Augustine understand the Donatists. In 397, shortly after his ordination as bishop, Augustine began his attack on them. While he knew that people belonging to the Catholic faith were in the minority, he also knew that he had the force of the Roman Empire and its military behind him. Politically, in the long run, he could do nothing but triumph. Previously in 380, not only did Emperor Theodosius I declare that Catholicism was the religion of the empire, but he also outlawed any other religion. Violent repression became standard fare for the Catholic faith; it was now considered normal (de Ste. Croix 1981, 713).

Augustine was willing to use the force of the empire to crush the Donatists. Furthermore, the Donatists neither had the power nor the interest in fighting back. James O'Donnell wrote in *Augustine: A New Biography*:

> That Native African Christianity remained insular, idealistic, and highly suspicious of the Roman government. Its believers awaited the coming of their God patiently, venerated their martyrs, and did not much care what the rest of the world thought or did. For them, the important thing was to grasp and hold the true faith that had been handed down to them. (O'Donnell 2005, 195)

W. H. C. Frend, likewise, gives helpful insights into life in North Africa:

> ...[T]he advance [of the Roman administrative system] should not hide the fact that these communities were little affected even by the outward forms of Roman civilization. Their inhabitants still knew themselves by tribal names, 'Leopard-hunters,'

etc. This is true of Numidia also, where members of great tribal confederations such as Suburbaures and Musulamii retained their identity even when they were coloni of Imperial estate. At the end of the fourth century ... a priest who did not speak the native language was useless. (Frend 1951, 1971, 44)

Frend goes on to state that the archaeological evidence shows that North Africa did not change much through the centuries. The communities in the fourth through the fifth centuries lived in mud huts developed around a communal grain house and a church. Frend concludes, "Everything, indeed, points to the existence of a primitive and equalitarian form of society" (Frend 1951, 1971, 45–46).[45] In short, two different worlds emerged. Augustine's world was hierarchical, the world of emperor, generals, governors, bishops, and wealthy landowners who all spoke an elite language, Latin. The world of the populace was poor and tribal, with chiefs, clergy, and bishops elected by the people who spoke the Berber language. Neither side could understand the other.

The situation continued to get worse, and it was Augustine who kept making it worse. Because of his persecution of the Donatists, his property and his wealth as bishop continued to increase. In a letter to Vincentius, a Donatist presbyter, Augustine defended his acquisition of Donatist property by pointing out that Vincentius would have been overjoyed if the Donatists had won the argument and the Catholic property had been confiscated. Augustine wrote:

> ... [T]he emperor, as you know, in that early case decreed for the first time that the confiscation of the property of those who were convicted of schism and obstinately resisted the unity of the Church should be confiscated. If, however, your predecessors who brought accusations would have won their case, and the emperor would have made such a decree against the community to which Caecilianus belonged, you would have called the emperors the friends of the Church's interests and the guardian of her peace and unity. (Augustine, Epistle *to Vicentenius* 93.4.14. *NPNF* 1st Series, 1, 387. CCEL)

---

[45] They held and promoted the view that all human beings are equal, politically, socially and religiously.

CHRISTIANITY: ENDANGERED OR EXTINCT?

Augustine, together with his fellow bishops, continued to gain increased property rights due to the decree of the emperor. But this is one thing, at least, which should not be held against him. Confiscated property was merely a corollary of his standing with the establishment, not necessarily a sign of greed on his part. Greed does not appear to be part of Augustine's motivation. In a sermon preached on June 29, 411, Augustine chastised bishops, who objected to the inclusion of a Donatist into the ranks of the Catholic Church, whom they believed was insincere in his beliefs and converting only because he did not want his property confiscated. In his harangue, Augustine said:

> Why do you want to judge people's hearts? ... We have worked hard to demonstrate the truth and expose falsehood. God was on our side, and truth conquered. Who knows that this man might eventually become a changed person after he carefully considers the truths of the faith. Why do you want to pass judgment on his motives? (Sermone CCXII. *CSEL*). [46]

Obviously, Augustine was not promoting the seizing of property.

Outside of maintaining a certain flair, which identified him with the emperor's elite, Augustine did not live luxuriously. The reverse is true. His frugality was part of the paradox of the man. Rather, Augustine's greatest fault was this: unlike Jesus, he lived a life far distant from the people he was supposed to serve. Indeed, he was no servant to them at all. Peter Brown gives an excellent description of what Augustine's bishopric was like:

> ... [He] surrounded himself with "servants of God" in black robes. Augustine insisted that his priests live with him in monastic surroundings. They were isolated from the life of the town by the walls of strict monastic rules, which included poverty and celibacy...they preserved the Catholic clergy as a distinct caste, involved neither by marriage nor by economic interest in the life of the town.(Brown 1969, 198).

---

[46] Translation: Edmund Hill and John Rotelle 1999. *The Works of Saint Augustine: A Translation for the 21st Century*,v. III, *Sermons*, 9 . 296. Hyde Park, NY: New City Press.

AUGUSTINE VERSUS THE DONATISTS

Brown asserts also that many members of Augustine's monastery established their own cloistered monasteries, "extending the clergy caste exponentially." This could only help widen the chasm between Catholicism and the Berber Donatists.

Augustine's Monastery

Augustine's monastery was not elitist, as some would become in the medieval period; monasteries whose monks from more prosperous backgrounds studied and the monks from poorer backgrounds did the hard labor. All the monks in Augustine's monasteries did manual labor. In *The Work of Monks* (*De Opere Monachorum*), Augustine belabors for 46 lengthy paragraphs Paul's statement, ". . . The one who is unwilling to work shall not eat" (2 Thessalonians 3:10). Paragraph 19 is a good summary of his tract on manual labor:

> The Apostle [Paul], nay rather the Spirit of God possessing and filling and actuating his heart, always exhorted the faithful who had wealth that the servants of God who wished to hold a higher degree of sanctity in the Church should not lack the necessities of life. They ought to support those who cut themselves off from secular ties, and dedicate their mind to the warfare of godly service. They ought to support those who obey the Apostle's precepts by unshackling themselves from private wealth and sympathizing with the weak. Then these servants of God can labor with their own hands for the common good and submit to their superiors without a murmur. While they labor they must have confidence that they will be supported by the oblations of good believers so that, while they labor in ecclesiastical occupations which bring salvation to others, they may still be able to live and their bodily infirmities and other needs will be taken care of while they do the work which brings salvation to those who lack it. (*The Works of Monks* 19, *NPNF* 1st Series, 3, 514. CCEL

Directly after Augustine made the above statement, he refuted those monks who would argue that they should be about "spiritual matters" and leave working in the field and other mundane tasks to others. To these men Augustine humorously states that since they are "spiritual, they do not need the physical substance of food, and they do not need to eat" (*The Works of Monks* 20, *NPNF* 1st Series, 3, 515. CCE.). Thus, everybody at Augustine's monastery worked in the field all except Augustine. In spite of his admonition to his monks, there is no indication that Augustine ever did any physical labor.

Augustine's Basilica

The basilica, which was part of Augustine's domain and in which he preached, was open-air and huge. O'Donnell states:

> The centerpiece of the modern excavation is the grand basilica, the ground-level remains of a substantial church. The nave was about 120 feet by 60 feet, and at one end a semicircular apse was about 30 feet across. The apse was surrounded by a low bench for the clergy, and at the center of the apse was the marble seat, now lost, of the presiding bishop. An altar table would have stood in front of where he sat (O'Donnell 2005, 13–14).

Here was Augustine sitting on the bishop's chair for liturgical ceremonies, preaching and holding court. Scribal monks writing down his every word surround him. All sorts of people come to him to participate, plead their cases, and get him to intercede on their behalf (Brown 1969, 173). Monica and Patricius would have been infinitely proud of their son, who rose from his lowly family status to rise to such a lofty state.

Placing everything in context, Hippo, in terms of the Roman Empire, was a nonentity. According to Brown, Augustine's lay friends did not live in Hippo, but in Carthage, the big city nearby where real power existed (Brown, 1969, 189ff.). It was only through massive political manipulation that Augustine became the center of power, not only in Africa, but also in the Roman Church itself.

Augustine before His God

Upon reading Augustine's sermons, his letters, and, indeed, any of his works, the reader becomes immediately aware of the fact that Augustine does not underestimate his importance to God and the church. While a pope lived in Rome, to whom Augustine gave lip service, when it came to both doctrine and practice, Augustine, like Ambrose, was the final arbitrator. In *The Confessions*, the reader senses that Augustine has the humility to admit his sinfulness. But then, the whole nature of the narration suggests that the Almighty all along was preparing him for some extraordinary task, for he was the select of the Lord.

Augustine, a "Kinder and Gentler" Bishop?

His task, it would seem, was to proclaim God's judgment on the world of depravity since the fall of the primal parents Adam and Eve, and to proclaim eternal damnation to the sons and daughters of darkness, and eternal life for the Catholic sons and daughters of light. Throughout Augustine's contentions and his dismal judgments, a person would think that if Augustine was a Christian that compassion and love would emanate from his works and that it would be possible to find a "kinder, gentler" Augustine. O'Donnell suggests that while this task is difficult it is possible to find a more "pastoral Augustine" whose sermons are read "with great patience." (O'Donnell 2005, 181-183) The problem with this suggestion is that the texts O'Donnell* cites can be otherwise interpreted. This text is from a sermon delivered by Augustine at the celebration of the anniversary of his ordination:

> The turbulent have to be corrected, the faint-hearted cheered up, the weak supported; the gospel's opponents need to be refuted, its insidious enemies guarded against; the unlearned need to be taught, the indolent stirred up, the argumentative checked; the proud must be put in their place, the desperate set on their feet, those engaged in quarrels reconciled . . .

> In all the vast and varied activity involved in fulfilling such manifold responsibilities, please give me your help by both your prayers and your obedience. In this way I will find pleasure not so much in being in charge of you as in being of use to you. (Augustine, *Sermon* 340 3:11 O'Donnell translation. O'Donnell 2005, 181).

CHRISTIANITY: ENDANGERED OR EXTINCT?

Constantine expressed similar attitudes in his epistle to Chrestus cited earlier:

> Constantine Augustus to Chrestus, Bishop of Syracuse. When some began wickedly and perversely to disagree among themselves in regard to holy worship, celestial power, and Catholic doctrine, wishing to put an end to such disputes among them, I formerly gave command that certain bishops should be sent from Gaul . . . But some are forgetful of their own salvation and of the reverence due to their most holy religion. They continue to remain hostile, unwilling to conform to judgments already decided upon. They excuse themselves by saying that few expressed their opinions, and that those who made the decisions did so too hastily, before carefully examining the facts. Thus those who ought to show brotherly love toward each other, are shamefully, or rather abominably, divided among themselves. They set themselves up for ridicule by souls alien to their holy religion. Wherefore I find it necessary to end this dissension, which ought to have ceased voluntarily after judgment had been given (Eusebius of Caesarea, *Church History* X.5.21 Epistle to Chrestus, *NPNF* 2nd Series, 1, 382. CCEL)

In both cases, "the turbulent have to be corrected"; "the gospel's opponents need to be refuted"; "the argumentative checked"; "the proud must be put in their place." The only real difference was that the Roman Empire has now become the Holy Roman Empire, and Augustine was rising in power. O'Donnell goes on to try to place "the kinder, gentler" Augustine in the context of his pastorate. He gives the example of how Augustine put on the shawl a woman sent him while he sat and wrote a letter answering her questions. He then comments in the letter that he had done so. Kinder and gentler, indeed! Every politician and dictator does such things to gain popular support. The type of "kinder, gentler" Augustine that truly existed is found in the letters he wrote to the Roman civil authorities petitioning them not to execute the Donatists whom they captured.

AUGUSTINE VERSUS THE DONATISTS

But, in each case, if the shawls and robes of kindness and gentleness are ripped away, they actually expose the nude Augustine as a closet brutal man.

These letters reveal Augustine's attitudes, which initiated the formation of the Holy Roman Empire. In a particularly revealing letter written in ca 406 to the proconsul, or governor, of North Africa, Cæcilianus, Augustine wrote:

> To My Noble Lord Cæcilianus, *My Son Truly and Justly Honourable and Esteemed in the Love of Christ, Augustin, Bishop, Sends Greeting in the Lord.* The renown of your administration and the fame of your virtues, as well as the praiseworthy zeal and faithful sincerity of your Christian piety, gifts of God which make you rejoice in Him from whom they came, and from whom you hope to receive yet greater gifts,—have moved me to acquaint your Excellency by this letter with the cares which agitate my mind .(*Letter* LXXXVI.1, *NPNF.* 1st Series, 1, 365. CCEL. *Italics* ours)

Even today in England, nobility are addressed as "lord." But to be true to the linguistics of the Roman Empire, the appellation, rather than being a formality was descriptive of the power that the proconsul, legate, or governor possessed. He was the representative of the emperor. He was indeed the presence of the emperor. Thus, he had the power of life and death over the inhabitants of the province. Calling him "lord" would be more than a formality in Rome at the time. But also, to be true to the linguistics of the Roman Empire, the shock comes when Augustine addresses the proconsul as "My Son truly and justly Honourable and Esteemed in the Love of Christ." As far as we are able to determine, Augustine is the first bishop or Christian authority to address a secular authority in such a familial, condescending, and even patronizing manner. Even two earlier powerful bishops, Athanasius (296–372) and Ambrose (340–397), most notorious in controlling secular authorities, never addressed the authorities as "sons." "My son" places the proconsul in a secondary position in relationship to Augustine. In the Roman hierarchal system, this would place Cæcilianus in a subservient position duty bound to come to Augustine's aid.

Augustine goes on in his letter to commend Cæcilianus:

> My noble lord, and my son, truly and justly honourable and esteemed in the love of Christ, our joy is great that throughout the rest of Africa you have taken remarkably successful measures on behalf of Catholic unity, but our sorrow is proportionately great because the district of Hippo and the neighbouring regions on the borders of Numidia have not enjoyed the benefit of your vigour as a magistrate. Lest this should be regarded as a neglect of duty on my part who bears the burden of the Episcopal office at Hippo, I have considered it my duty to mention it to your Excellency. If you condescend to acquaint yourself with the extreme effrontery of the heretics in the region of Hippo, as you might do by questioning my brethren and colleagues, or the presbyter whom I have sent with this letter—all who are able to furnish your Excellency with such information—I am sure you will deal with this tumor of impious presumption, so that it might be healed by warning [torture] rather than painfully removed afterwards by punishment ... (*Letter* LXXXVI. *NPNF*. First Series, 1, 365.CCEL)

"Warning" is the genteel word used by Romans in polite society at the time for "torture." "Painfully removed . . . by punishment" was another way of saying "capital punishment." It is apparent from his letter that Augustine neither knew nor even met Cæcilianus . . . (Yet he commended Cæcilianus and calls him "my son" and commends him for his "piety.") Still, showing apparent mercy, Augustine asks him to come into the Hippo area, but not to kill the Donatists—at least not as a first action—but merely to torture them. Was it not clear to Augustine—not to mention the Christian Caecilianus—that Christian faith forbade the torture or the execution of anyone?

In this epistle, Augustine appears to be in bed with the most brutal of Roman emperors. Caecilianus is duty bound to come to

AUGUSTINE VERSUS THE DONATISTS

the succor of the bishop by torturing and, as a last resort, by inflicting capital punishment on the Donatists. This is a fact of grave concern for Christianity as events play out in the latter years of the Holy Roman Empire, and then in the crusades, the inquisitions, the burning of the witches, the Reformation, the peasant rebellion, the Anabaptists, Abu-Ghraib, and more. From Augustine onward, the Christian church allows, and sometimes encourages, the empire to torture and carry out capital punishment. This program of oppression is even further spelled out in another epistle, which Augustine wrote to another proconsul by the name of Donatus (not, of course, the Donatus who was the leader of the Donatists) in 409 concerning Donatism. He begins with a greeting similar to that given to Cæcilianus:

> To Donatus, His Noble and Deservedly Honourable Lord, and Eminently Praiseworthy Son, Augustin Sends Greeting in the Lord. I would wish that the African Church were not placed in such trying circumstances as to need the aid of any earthly power. But since, as the apostle says, "there is no power but of God," it is unquestionable that, when you, a sincere son of your Catholic Mother [the church] give her help, that help is in the name of the Lord, "who made heaven and earth." For you, noble and deservedly honourable lord and eminently praiseworthy son...have been raised to the dignity of proconsul, so that power allied with your goodwill may restrain the enemies of the Church from their wicked and sacrilegious attempts against her. In fact, there is only one thing of which we are much afraid in your administration of justice, viz., lest perchance, every injury done by impious and ungrateful men against Christian society be considered a more serious and heinous crime than if it had been done against others. It ought merely to be punished with a severity corresponding to the enormity of the crime . . . We beseech you, in the name of Jesus Christ, not to do more than this. For we do not seek to revenge ourselves in this world . . . It is not their death, but their deliverance from error, that we

seek to accomplish by the help of the terror of judges and of laws, whereby they may be preserved from falling under the penalty of eternal judgment. We do not wish either to see the exercise of discipline towards them neglected, nor, on the other hand, do we wish to see them subjected to the severer punishments which they deserve. Do you, therefore, check their sins in such a way, that the sinners may be spared to repent of their sins. (Letter C. Section 1, *NPNF*. 1st Series, 1. 411. CCEL)

Here again, if the robes of the "kinder, gentler" Augustine are torn away, we see the real Augustine, who set the example for the ages. In this letter he insists he does not want the Donatists killed. In his mercy, he wants to spare them from eternal damnation. It is fine, however, if they are tortured. They may also be deprived of their property and their livelihood, so that they might despair in this life and pine for the eternal life which the Catholic faith would give them. It must also be emphasized that one of the main features of Donatism was its veneration and love of martyrdom, as it was in much of pre-Constantinian Christianity. Consequently, to kill Donatists only entrenched them in their own beliefs and would make them even more honored by the other Donatists.

In the same vein, this apparently "kinder, gentler" Augustine sent another letter to Marcellinus, a legate sent from Emperor Honorius (395–423) to Carthage to attempt to get the Catholics and the Donatists together to work out their differences. The council that Augustine called was, as far as the Donatists were concerned, hardly a mutual exchange of views. It was a kangaroo court with everything stacked against the Donatists. At the end, Marcellinus declared that the Catholics were vindicated and that the Donatists needed to recant.[47]

Of course, this did not sit well with the Donatists. A fringe group of Donatists, the Circumcelliones, went into a rage and attacked the Catholics. Marcellinus, using the Roman troops at his disposal, captured some of the Circumcelliones. In the letter that Augustine

---
[47] *Augustine through the Ages: An Encyclopedia*, "Collatio of 411," pp. 218–19.

wrote to Marcellinus, whom he addressed as "My Noble Lord, Justly Distinguished, My Son Very Much Beloved," Augustine revealed some of the common practices of interrogation:

> Do not lose now that fatherly care which you maintained when prosecuting those to be examined, in doing so you extracted the confession of such horrid crimes, not by stretching them on the rack, not by furrowing their flesh with iron claws, not by scorching them with flames, but by beating them with rods, a mode of correction used by schoolmasters, by parents as they chastise their children, and often also by bishops in the sentences awarded by them. Do not, therefore, now punish with extreme severity the crimes which you searched out with leniency. The necessity for harshness is greater in the investigation than in the infliction of punishment; for even the gentlest men use diligence and stringency in searching out a hidden crime, for in that way they find out those to whom they may show mercy. Wherefore it is generally necessary to use more rigor in making inquisition, so that when the crime has been brought to light, there may be scope for displaying clemency. For all good works love to be set in the light, not in order to obtain glory from men, but, as the Lord saith, "that they seeing your good works may glorify your Father who is in heaven." Therefore let not the power of executing punishment inspire you with harshness, seeing you showed clemency in the examination of the criminals. Do not call for the executioner now when the crime has been found out, after using clemency when you were finding it out. (*Letter* LXXXIII.2, *NPNF*. First Series, 1, 362. CCEL)

That Augustine considered it "lenient" when Marcellinus did not use the "iron claw" or "rack," but simply beat with a rod, is remarkable. All these tortures cause excruciating pain. In our secular world, all these methods would be considered inhumane torture by civilized nations, and in violation of the Geneva Convention.

CHRISTIANITY: ENDANGERED OR EXTINCT?

Augustine and the Teachings of the Donatists

In reality, Augustine had one problem with the Donatists; the same problem that Constantine had. Both Constantine and Augustine perceived the Donatists as schismatic. Augustine's assessment of the Donatist problem is best found in a letter that he wrote in 417 to Boniface, a Roman general, and governor of Africa. He begins the narration by contrasting the Donatists with the Arians, whom he, of course, considers more culpable. He wrote:

> I wish to place, therefore, briefly before your Grace the difference between the errors of the Arians and the Donatists. The Arians say that the Father, the Son, and the Holy Ghost are different in substance; whereas the Donatists do not say this, but acknowledge the unity of substance in the Trinity. And if some of them say that the Son is inferior to the Father, yet they have not denied that He is of the same substance. Yet the greater part of them declare that they hold entirely the same belief regarding the Father and the Son and the Holy Ghost as is held by the Catholic Church. This is not a question in dispute with them. Their problem is that they carry on their unhappy strife solely on the question of communion with the Church. The perversity of their error is their rebellious hostility against the unity of Christ. But sometimes, as we have heard, some of them, wishing to conciliate the Goths, who have a certain amount of power, profess to entertain the same belief as they. But these are refuted by the authority of their own leaders; for Donatus himself, of whose party they boast themselves to be, is never said to have held this belief. (*A Treatise Concerning the Correction of the Donatist* or Epistle CLXXXV *Letter to Boniface* section 1, *NPNF*, 1ˢᵗ Series 4, unambiguous 633. CCEL)

Within the above quoted text there is a hint of what Augustine thought may actually have been transpiring among the Donatists. But considering that Augustine did not even know the Donatists living in the vicinity of Hippo, the numbers of people that were supporting the Goths might have been more than he knew. On the other hand, African Christianity could stand on its own feet—it did not need the

AUGUSTINE VERSUS THE DONATISTS

Gauls. It was founded on sheer defiance of the Roman Empire and now, on defiance of Augustine, Catholicism, and the Roman Empire, which the Donatists considered to be one and the same poison.

Augustine and the Nonviolence of the Donatists

We also know from Augustine that most of the Donatists, with the exception of the Circumcellians, believed in Jesus' teachings of nonviolence. In the same *Epistle 185* written to Boniface, Augustine argues that the Donatists "think that no one can be justified in using violence... (*Epistle 185.2*)" In another letter written in 408 to Vincentius, a Donatist bishop, he wrote, "You are of the opinion that no one should be compelled to follow righteousness . . . (*Epistle 93.2.5*)" Most of this letter he spends defending the Catholic uses of the Roman military to force Donatists to the Catholic faith. However, continual use of force against the Donatists had just the opposite effect. Rather than bringing them into the Catholic Church, for the Donatists it had the positive impact of authenticating their existence. Being persecuted meant to the Donatists that they were the true church and that if they held there ground God would reward them. After all they had suffered through the great Diocletian Persecution from 303-311. They felt that Jesus' beatitude "Blessed are those who are persecuted because of righteousness . . ." (Matthew 5:10) applied to themselves. After all they were the righteous people who were faithful to God and would not bend their knees to the Roman Empire. Therefore, they, the Donatists, were the true church. Conversely, the fact that the Catholics were persecuting them and the fact that the Catholics had bent their knees to the Roman Empire were signs that the Catholics were the false church.

Augustine wrote many letters attempting to refute the Donatists interpretation of the beatitude.[48] In almost every letter Augustine justifies the church's use of violence or the empire's use of violence on the church's behalf to punish "the unrighteous heretics." In reading these letters, we see how Augustine twisted the interpretation of scripture so to allow the church and "Christian" governments a huge amount of perfidy in the name of Jesus. His thinking, along with Ambrose's has been used by "Christianity or Augustinian Constantinianism" to

---
[48] *Epistles 43; 51; 55; 58; 88; 93; 133; 173; 185.*

justify the crusades, the inquisition, the Thirty Years War, the Hundred Years War, etc.

The two following quotes are from two different letters that Augustine wrote ca 417. The first is from the above-cited letter to General Boniface (Tribune). The second letter is to a Donatist bishop by the Name of Vincentius, who had written to Augustine to assert that the use of force was totally inconsistent with the teachings of Jesus.

> But true martyrs are such as those of whom the Lord says, "Blessed are they which are persecuted for righteousness' sake." It is not, therefore, those who suffer persecution for their unrighteousness, and for the divisions which they impiously introduce into Christian unity, but those who suffer for righteousness' sake, that are truly martyrs . . . But if they think that no one can be justified in using violence,—as they said in the course of the conference when they stated that the true Church must necessarily be the one which suffers persecution, not the one inflicting it . . . If, therefore, we wish either to recognize the truth, we must recognize that there is such a thing as the persecution of unrighteousness, which the impious inflict upon the Church of Christ; and there is a righteous persecution, which the Church of Christ inflicts upon the impious. The faithful are therefore blessed in suffering persecution for righteousness' sake; but they are miserable if they suffer persecution for unrighteousness. Moreover, the Church persecutes in the spirit of love, they in the spirit of wrath; the Church persecutes so that she may correct, they that they may overthrow: she that she may recall from error, they that they may drive headlong into error. Finally, she persecutes her enemies and arrests them, until they become weary in their vain opinions, so that they should advance in the truth; but they, return evil for good. Because we take measures for their good, to secure their eternal salvation, they endeavor even to strip us of our temporal safety . . . (*A Treatise Concerning the Correction of the Donatist or Letter CLXXXV Letter to Boniface* section 1, *NPNF*, First Series 4, 634 CCEL)

AUGUSTINE VERSUS THE DONATISTS

The following Augustine wrote to Vincentius, *Letter* XCIII:

In some cases, therefore, both he that suffers persecution is in the wrong, and he that inflicts it is in the right. But the truth is, that the bad have always persecuted the good, and the good have persecuted the bad: the former doing harm by their unrighteousness, the latter seeking to do good by the administration of discipline; the former with cruelty, the latter with moderation; the former impelled by lust, the latter under the constraint of love. For he whose aim is to kill is not careful how he wounds, but he whose aim is to cure is cautious with his lancet; for the one seeks to destroy what is sound, the other that which is decaying. The wicked put prophets to death; prophets also put the wicked to death. The Jews scourged Christ; Christ also scourged the Jews. The apostles were given up by men to the civil powers; the apostles themselves gave men up to the power of Satan. In all these cases, what is important to attend to is this: who are on the side of truth, and who on the side of iniquity; who acted from a desire to injure, and who from a desire to correct what was amiss? (Augustin, Letter to Vicentius, XCIII.II, 8-III,9, *NPNF* 1, 384-385. CCEL)

Summary

Augustine's words are clear and unambiguous documentation of the change in Christianity. Christianity had left the way of the cross and had taken up the way of domination. It was Augustine who theologized, canonized, and institutionalized these changes, so that, as flawed as his reasoning was and as abusive as he was of scripture, his thinking on such concepts as the just war and the validation of wealth became part of the fabric of Christianity. Despite Augustine's writings about being saved by the faith of the universal Catholic Church and love between brothers of the common faith, the Donatists knew quite well that he was talking about submission to the Roman Empire, which they had been opposing long before Constantine had come to power. The Donatists had found in the teachings of Jesus a belief system that resonated with their tribal, communal living. However, for them, the religion shaped by Constantine and Augustine was just repackaging the Roman Empire in just another guise. These Donatists were a reflection of the early church in the sense that they reflected Jesus' teachings on loving one's enemies and living simply. They may have overemphasized martyrdom, but so did the earlier Catholics.

As we learned earlier, in W. H. C. Frend's reporting on his studies and archaeological reports, the Donatists were (egalitarian) community conscious, and they shared authority. The Donatists were the dominant group of North African Christians who were as W. H. C. Frend states, "a protest movement." They were protesting not the message of Jesus, but precisely what Christianity had become: the wealthy, powerful, and arrogant Church of the Roman Empire.

The most fitting way to close this chapter would be to quote from Frend's "Epilogue":

> The Christianity of the sects [Donatism in Africa, Copts in Egypt, Montanism, and Novatianism in Asia] was the real enemy of the Empire. This was not a political enmity, for a different form of human society could not be imagined at the time. But the Emperors were regarded by men like Petilian as the "kings of this world," and the Christian must renounce the society of this world in its entirety. The dissenters thus created a set of values different from those of classical society and also from Catholicism, which sought to harmonize classical and Christian concepts. Christian poverty and martyrdom, for instance, represented not merely virtuous conduct or personal heroism, but were ritual acts, perhaps one might say magical acts, designed to secure for the Elect the vision of Paradise and immediate admittance to the "Vine of the Lord." (Frend 1951, 1971, 334)

9

Augustine Changes the Course of the Church

As Augustine was dying, the Vandals were at his door ready to bury him and the tyrannical reign of the empire that he admired and, in fact, promoted. Augustine was reluctant to say that Christianity was an entity tied to the Roman Empire. In fact, he wrote *The City of God* to refute the charge of pagan philosophers that Rome fell because it became Christian. As much as he tried to disengage the church from the Roman Empire, he was not able to do so. However, he did see the glory and power of Rome as the instrument of God:

> Could these and other similar events, which are found in Roman history, become so well-known, even famous, if the Roman Empire, extending far and wide, had not grown through unbelievable successes? That empire grew large and enduring because of men of glory whose virtues were the reward of their dearest aspirations. These ancient Romans were certainly worthy men. (*civ. dei* (*City of God*) V. xvi. *CSEL*)

The church fathers of the first three centuries, and the apostles, would have had trouble stomaching such language. Even more repulsive, however, is what Augustine continued to say:

CHRISTIANITY: ENDANGERED OR EXTINCT?

The Jews were rightfully given to the Romans as a reward. The Romans, who rested their virtue on earthly things, conquered the Jews who, because of their depravity, slew and rejected the giver of true glory, the one who gave us the eternal city. (*civ. Dei*, (*City of God*) V. xviii. CSEL)

Here again, rampant and stark, Augustine not only unites the will of God to the violent and destructive empire, but he claims for his own the anti-Semitism that obsessed Ambrose. Augustine even takes that anti-Semitism one step further. According to Augustine, in the divine order of things, a function of the empire was to punish the people of Israel "for their great depravity," which was the crucifixion of Jesus. He fails to mention that it was not the Jews but the Romans who were responsible for crucifying Jesus. The Jews did not have the power or authority to do so.

Augustine goes on to continue to stroke the beast that was the empire: "These Romans are examples for us—with some reservations, of course. Indeed, they shame us if we do not show the same effort for the sake of the glorious city of God that they showed for the sake of temporal benefits and an earthly city" (*De civ. Dei*, (*City of God*) I. xviii–xix, CSEL).

The only problem Augustine had with Rome was that it did not glorify God. His statement, however, justifies a whole raft of sins, which the church would commit in the name of Jesus. Among these was his belief that the violence and repression that was used to maintain the Roman Empire should be used to maintain the Catholic faith. Its hierarchical structure and material wealth and glory, according to Augustine, should be and would be the wealth and glory of the church. This glory would be used to build huge and expensive cathedrals on the backs of the poor. Likewise, it would be used on other "earthly treasures" contrary to Jesus' own teaching. This is one of the most amazing phenomena of all history. The movement founded by the radical, poor rabbi of Galilee would become entrenched in the glory and structures of the Roman Empire. It was, of course, Emperor Constantine who broke the door open to the transformation, but it was Athanasius and his supporters who walked in the door at the Council of Nicaea in 325, and Augustine who cut it in stone for the ages.

AUGUSTINE CHANGES THE COURSE OF THE CHURCH

The Council of Nicaea and the Transformation of the Church

At the Council of Nicaea, the Church set up a creed that asserted that Jesus "eternally begotten of the Father, God from God, light from light, true God from true God . . . for us and our salvation came down from heaven" (see Chapter 5: "The Storm Intensifies: Arius, Athanasius and the Age of Arrogance"). The church after Nicaea, and particularly Augustine, interpreted salvation to be only life after death and thus, life eternal.

In the New Testament and in the first centuries of Christianity, the Jesus Movement viewed salvation as a process which began in this life in a holistic way with shared fellowship with other believers, and was a walk through this life to the next. The movement was successful in providing a means of essential survival for the poor and disenfranchised. It was in this world an alternative society to the Roman Empire. This change from salvation beginning in this life to salvation beginning after death, now central focus of Constantine, theologians and Augustine, has to be one of the most fundamental cultural transformation in the history of humanity. It is central to the theologies of most traditional Orthodox churches, Roman Catholic and most Protestant churches.[49] It likewise is central to thought of all those person's in society who confront others with the question like: "How are you going spend eternity?" or "Are you saved?"

The next step in the transformation of the Jesus Movement to the religion of the Roman Empire was hinted at in the phrases of the Nicene Confession. This Jesus, who was God from eternity, "became incarnate."[50] He then suffered and died, and on the third day he rose again. Soon after, he ascended into heaven. Within the creed, there is no mention that Jesus taught anything. There is no expectation that he desired his followers to do anything. The Nicene fathers completely separated Jesus from his teachings and the life Jesus lived between his birth and death. This served Constantine and the future Christian emperors well. They did not have to worry about all their violent escapades, the blood which was shed in their names. Nor did they have to worry about their exorbitant, luxurious

---

[49] There are some denominations that stress a good life on earth. These are called Holiness churches that developed out of Wesleyan and reformed traditions. But even with that these persons who show signs of salvation in this live is not a matter of making life here on earth better but a sign of one's "eternal salvation."

[50] The expression "by the Holy Ghost of the Virgin Mary" was added at the Council of Chalcedon (451).

lifestyles; as long as they held the true Nicene faith, they would be saved.[51] The church had effectively become the church of the rich and the famous not the church of the poor and downtrodden.

By the time the Roman general Ambrose (337–397) was installed as bishop in 374, the all-consuming concern was holding to the correct Nicene faith. Those teachings of Jesus that became exclusively important were the teachings of the end-times and Second Coming—Jesus "will come again in glory to judge the living and the dead." These teachings were used not only to ameliorate the rich and powerful, but to scare people into obedience to "the one, holy, catholic, and apostolic church." Of course, this "one, holy, catholic, and apostolic church," for the next few centuries, would be the Roman or Orthodox faiths. Then in a few more centuries, the "one holy catholic faith" would be changed by the Lutherans to the "one holy Christian and apostolic church," because, according to them, no Catholic could be saved, only Lutherans. However, Lutherans were not able to restore Jesus' teachings by changing only one word of the creed.

Augustine, Prime Corrupter of the Jesus Movement

As we have seen, Emperors Constantine, Theodosius, and some church fathers, such as Athanasius, Ambrose, and Augustine, were corrupters of the Jesus Movement. However, Constantine, Theodosius, Athanasius, and Ambrose were not as influential in forcing Catholicism into the religion of the Roman Empire as was Augustine. His theology had a much more destructive influence on the Jesus Movement and on the history of humankind than all previous and future emperors and theologians.

It simply has been a major, cultural fantasy that has accredited Jesus as being the most influential person in Christian history. That appellation sadly belongs to Augustine of Hippo. He has completely dominated the Christian scene. So strong has his influence been that instead of "Christianity" being the nomenclature for the dominant religion for those who today are called Roman Catholic, Orthodox, and Protestant, the more proper term should be our newly coined word, "Augustianism."

---

[51] This is not true of other ecclesiastical fathers at the time—Eusebius, Chrysostom, Gregory of Nazinanzus, Gregory of Nyssa and Basil of Caesarea. While they placed emphasis on salvation, they also saw that following the teachings of Jesus was essential not only as a sign of salvation but good for all people.

AUGUSTINE CHANGES THE COURSE OF THE CHURCH

Augustine's Theology of Empire

The reason why "Augustianism" is a better appellation for what we now call Christianity is that in Augustine's theology, we find not Jesus, but an amalgamation of Greek philosophy, the way of the world as conceived and lived by the genteel Roman aristocrat, and the Catholic faith. In the terms of T. Kermit Scott, in *Augustine: His Thought in Context*,

> Augustine was a man who fit into Roman/African society, and his thought and manner were those of that culture. Augustianism was able to thrive and survive as the dominant theology of the whole Western world simply because it was grounded in beliefs that made simple common sense to the members of that society, especially those who belonged to the dominant classes of that society in his age. Augustine always identified with that dominant class and adopted and fit in well with the leisurely life of the elite who were its intellectuals. He was truly a fashionable man of his times. As such, he thought it ridiculous to doubt that the Christian God should be anyone but the imperial god establishing his rule throughout the world. That imperial god would grant immeasurable rewards to those who were unquestioningly devoted to him or unspeakable punishment to those who failed to do so. Augustine's god was a Roman emperor par excellence. (Scott 1995, 9)

Whereas that vanguard of philosopher-theologians before Constantine had been tied to Plato, Aristotle, Cicero, and Plotinus, the post-Constantinian Christian, "vanguard" was tied to an amorphous religion based on Plato and Plotinus and an assorted number of biblical texts. Augustine built a Christianity without discourse as he walked around in his robes with scribes in tow, telling them what was the proper Christian faith. According to him, Christianity could not be Christianity unless it was all-powerful. Turning a pile of imperial doctrines, beliefs, and practices and mish mashing them with various philosophical texts and spurious scriptural texts was the essence of Augustine's theology. In this task he failed to make his Catholic faith logically and rationally consistent uniform and universally, compelling faith.

After sixteen hundred years of worshipping the man and his thought, we are finally realizing the impossibility of the task he tried to undertake, and how contradictory his faith was to the very faith of the Jesus

CHRISTIANITY: ENDANGERED OR EXTINCT?

Movement. Up to now, Christians have been blinded by the bravado of this ambitious clergyman.

As hard as Augustine and the empire tried to stamp out differing views and move the empire to one monolithic Catholic faith, they were never able to do so. According to sociologist Rodney Stark, from Jesus' time until Constantine, the average believer was the backbone and support of Christianity. "Amateurs" were the missionaries and the functionaries of the Movement. Then, under Constantine, Christianity became an elite organization, lavishly funded by the state. Hard times were over, much to the delight of everyone. Clergy became the well-dressed, leisurely, well-fed men of the empire. For under the new system, the clergy became wealthy and church positions became highly sought by the rich and famous. The dedicated leaders must have been frustrated by all the phony piety and pretension that they were experiencing in the newly legalized Christianity. The movement to which they were so committed was radically changed. It was as if the Empire hijacked the Jesus, whom they loved, and, of course, this perception would have been correct. Christianization of people shifted from persuasion to coercion. Laws were enacted against pagans and heretics. Pagan temples were confiscated. Monastic Christians became the shock troops to stamp out diversity. The missionary spirit which flowed from and to the common people was squelched. Christian missionaries no longer lived among the people. The total emphasis was placed now on the attempts to "Christianize" the kings and the barons of other lands. For if they were converted, they were the important ones—that was one more country scratched off as Christian. (See Stark 2001, 107–08.)

The problem that Stark points out is that the people were never really converted. Using *The History of the Franks* by the Monk Gregory of Tours, Stark demonstrates this hierarchical conversion. As the story unfolds, Clovis was nagged by his wife to become a Catholic Christian. Then Clovis, one day, found himself in a fierce battle, and he feared not only losing the battle, but his life as well. So he prayed to the Christian God, promising to be baptized if God would allow him to win. He won the battle and eventually was baptized a Catholic along with 3,000 of his army. We can assume that most of these soldiers did not have the foggiest idea of why they were baptized and that they were baptized because Clovis

AUGUSTINE CHANGES THE COURSE OF THE CHURCH

commanded it. After he became a Catholic, the story continues, he and his army carried on a violent campaign to defeat the Arian Goths and Vandals (Stark 2001, 111). In church history he is accredited with bringing an end to Arianism. He would have been granted sainthood, but he carried, out several "unethical practices." What those "unethical practices" have never been specified, but these "unethical practices" were not his waging wars against the Arians. These were considered "a saintly practices."

The fact that Clovis defeated Arianism is, like so much of church history in the era, a myth. Arianism continued unabated in many different forms. The fact that Clovis did not change his behavior as a ruler when he became a Catholic was consistent with the Constantinian/Augustinian system within the Catholic Church. The violent oppression became God working his wrath on the heretics and evildoers. This, of course, was unacceptable to Jesus and his early followers, but now became acceptable behavior within Catholicism and the Constantinian/Augustinian system. According to Scott, it was this elastic nature of Augustinian Christianity that would allow it to triumph in the Roman Empire. He gives three reasons "for the triumph of Augustinian Christianity":

- ... it was an ideology uniquely suited to serve the needs of the dominant classes of the Roman society ...
- It provided a cosmic justification for the existing hierarchical order as rooted in human sinfulness and divine justice,
- and it encouraged every person to accept her or his place in that order. (Scott 1995, 57)

While Scott's description of the triumph of Augustianism is accurate, Augustianism did not triumph over paganism. Paganism continued unabated in Catholicism: gods took the forms of saints, and magical amulets took the forms of relics. Those in the dominant society maintained and even enhanced these magical religious views. What Augustianism did for paganism was to add the element of eternal life. Now in the Catholic religion, the person would live forever in paradise, providing he or she was obedient to the church, to the state, and to his or her masters or mistresses. All his or her earthly sufferings would be over when he or she died.

CHRISTIANITY: ENDANGERED OR EXTINCT?

The Sincerity of Augustine

Although we have challenged much of Augustine's thinking up to this point as being totally inconsistent with Jesus's thinking, we have no doubts that within his culture he was a sincere man. He believed in "a Jesus," but the Jesus he believed in was not the Jesus of the gospels, but rather his Jesus was a figment of his imagination. The "Jesus" in whom Augustine believed was the Lord of glory. Augustine would have accepted the Nicene Creed definition that Jesus was the son of God from all time. For him, while Jesus was truly human, Jesus' teachings were ethereal, or better, divine and not necessarily understood by humans. Augustine saw Jesus as a sublime being, and as such, Jesus' words, as he saw them and interpreted them, soared above the realm of humankind. While most humans would not understand the true meaning of Jesus's teachings and scripture, and while Augustine, himself, would have denied any special brilliance, he makes very clear in his *Confessions* that from the beginning God had endowed him "with a strong desire for truth," "a strong memory," "the gift of speech" and "the training in rhetoric," and, oh yes, a desire for "refined friendship" (Augustine, *Confessiones* (*Confessions*) I, 20). Throughout the *Confessions* Augustine asserts that when he was not walking in *the truth*, God was still, unbeknown to him, preparing him for his task of proclaiming the truth that he hears in his innermost self (Augustine, *Confessiones* (Confessions) XII, 11-18). Those who oppose Augustine's proclamation are "barking dogs" that, he hoped to silence by "the Truth." (Augustine, *Confessiones* (Confessions) XII, 13-18)

He likewise would want his readers and all his audience to know that he had the advantage of an excellent academic background. He was well versed in the knowledge of Plato and Plotinus. Furthermore, he inherited the mores of the greatest civilization on earth, the Roman Empire. All this he brought as a "gift to Christianity." Who on earth was better prepared to take the "Christian message" that was hovering above humankind, and bring it down to the practical living situation of earth? Augustine was convinced that he was handpicked by God to do just that. And Augustine did what he thought that God intended him to do.

Other theologians picked up on Augustine's message and further transmitted it to the ages. It is this "practical Christianity" that we have inherited. It has become the Christianity for all time and for all ages.

AUGUSTINE CHANGES THE COURSE OF THE CHURCH

There is no reason to believe that Augustine was anything but sincere in sculpting this theology. Like the apostles in Acts 6, Augustine was deeply sincere but wrong. His stress on the depravity of humanity was not Jesus' view of humanity. Nor was his view of salvation as eternal life alone.

In previous chapters we have revealed how values of the dominant society had begun to infiltrate and control the Jesus Movement. We will show how Augustine's thinking with all the differences from Jesus' became the *modus operandi*, the religion of the Empire.

Augustine's Writings without the Teachings of Jesus

It is important to remember that the following events transpired before Augustine's conversion and made that conversion utterly necessary and utterly expedient. Emperor Theodosius, after practically dying and receiving baptism, made a miraculous recovery. He then made the Nicene Christianity the religion of the empire. He ruled:

In 380:
- It is our will that the peoples who are ruled by the administration of our clemency shall practice that religion which the divine Peter the apostle transmitted to the Romans . . . [that which] is followed by the Pontiff Damasus and by Peter, bishop of Alexandria . . . [that is] we shall believe in the single deity of the Father, the Son and the Holy Spirit, under the concept of equal majesty and of the Holy Trinity. (*Theodosius Code* 16: 1, 2. Translation Ayres 2004, 251)

In 381:
- That man shall be accepted as a defender of the Nicene Faith . . . who confesses that Almighty God and Christ the Son of God are one in name, God of God, light of light, who does not violate by denial the Holy Spirit . . . that man who esteems . . . the undivided substance of the incorrupt Trinity, that substance which those of the orthodox faith call, employing a Greek word, *ousia*. (*Theodosius Code* 16: 1, 3. Translation Ayres 2004, 252)

CHRISTIANITY: ENDANGERED OR EXTINCT?

In 382:

- We command that all churches shall immediately be surrendered to those bishops who confess that the Father, the Son, and the Holy Spirit are of one majesty and power, of the same glory, and of one splendour, to those bishops who produce no dissonance by unholy distinction, but who affirm the concept of the Trinity by the assertion of three persons and the unity of the Divinity. (*Theodosius Code* 16: 1, 4. (Translation: Ayres 2004, 252)wdc

With these rulings Theodosius cemented the fact that the Nicene Creed would be the Orthodox interpretation of all religion in the Empire. Not only would there be no tolerance of paganism, there would be no tolerance of Arianism, or any other interpretation within what now was becoming the Holy Roman Empire.

In 386 Augustine became a Christian, and of course, Augustine would have subscribed to the Nicene Creed, as Theodosius described it. He would never have been baptized and become bishop and one of the most powerful and wealthy persons in the empire without subscribing to that creed. Yet, Augustine never mentioned the Nicene Creed. As we approach an understanding of Augustine's view, standing as a bulwark against those of Jesus and his teachings, it is important to realize that for Augustine there is no final authority except God and God's scripture, and furthermore, Augustine himself was the final interpreter of both God and the scriptures.

In reading Augustine's work, a person soon realizes that Augustine, like Ambrose, elevated himself into the position of that authority. It did not matter to whom Augustine was addressing, be it a general, a governor, or a heretic, he was addressing them as their superior. The only exception to this was Ambrose with whom he gave his obeisance.

Even the pious Jerome expressed concern when he thought that he was a thorn in Augustine's side and that Augustine might attack him. He wrote to Augustine:

> You never wrote a book against me? How is it that an epistle was brought to me, written by someone, a treatise containing

a rebuke from you aimed at me? How is it that Italy received a treatise of yours which you did not write? How can you reasonably ask me to reply to a treatise which you solemnly assure me was never written by you? I am not so foolish as to think that I am insulted by you, just because your opinion differs from mine. But if challenging me as it were to single combat, you take exception to my views, and demand a reason for what I have written, insisting that I recant my errors... Let not the world see us quarreling like children, and giving material for angry contention in the sight of our adversaries (*Episle of Jerome to Augustine, DOMEÑO VERE SANCTO ET BEATISSIMO PAPAE AUGUSTINO HIERONYMUS. Epistula* LXXII.4 CSEL 34, 258-9)

Augustine's Writings without the Teachings of Jesus

Another indication that Augustine's theology is consistent with the Nicene Creed is that in the preponderance of Augustine's writings there is so little of Jesus' teachings. According to Allan D. Fitzgerald, general editor of *Augustine through the Ages: An Encyclopedia*, Augustine produced over five million words (Fitzgerald 1999, xv). Of these five million, two small books of 34,000 words titled *Our Lord's Sermon on the Mount according to Matthew* (*De Sermone Domini de monte secundum Matthaeum*) are his major works on Jesus' teachings as contained in the three synoptic Gospels. The two books comprise only 65 pages in the massive eight-volume *Nicene and Post-Nicene Fathers* (1st Series) of Augustine. This compares with 13 books of 145 pages of his autobiography called Confessions, and 22 books of 511 pages for his philosophical/theological work, *The City of God*. Another work, *Harmony of the Gospels* (*Consensu evangelistarum*) that is twice the size of the volume of *Our Lord's Sermon on the Mount according to Matthew*, does not deal with how the Christian should understand Jesus' day-to-day teachings, but how all events and teachings in the Gospels logically fit together to reveal the divinity of Jesus.[52]

---

[52] There are some minor works called *Questions on the Gospels* (*Quaestiones Evangeliorum*) and *Sixteen Questions on Matthew* (*Quaestiones Quaestiones XVI in Matthaeum*) which only recently appeared (1990).

CHRISTIANITY: ENDANGERED OR EXTINCT?

Augustine's approach was to reinterpret Jesus and his teachings so as to make their meaning either null and void or only applicable in some rare situations. He used Ambrose's method of interpreting a verse of scripture with the use of some other verse or text. (See Chapter 7 on intertextuality pp. 171-2). In this way, Augustine established the nadir of Christian interpretation of Jesus' teachings.

"Turning the Other Cheek"

A good example is Augustine's intertextual interpretation of Jesus' teaching on "turning the other cheek" (Matthew 5:39). We can presume that Augustine did know what "turning the other cheek" meant. We can also presume that he knew that Christians are called "to turn the other cheek." It is not a difficult concept to understand. Jesus was telling his disciples that they were not to return force with force. Of course all those in the elite society of Rome would have problems with Jesus' teachings. All of Roman society was based on returning violence with violence. It is how Romans controlled their slaves and how those in power suppressed those who would like to be in power. Thus to make the passage acceptable to the Roman elite, Augustine used intertextuality to remove any connection to violence from the interpretation of what Jesus' meant. In so doing, he established the norm for interpretation popular for thousands of years where the meaning of Jesus' teachings had little connection with its true meaning.[53] He stated:

> The things that pertain to mercy pertain for the most part to those suffering from old age or disease, whom people are called to love as they love the children in their charge or the sick whom they love the most. If their health should be compromised, they would suffer as well. The Lord, the Physician of souls, instructs us to cure our neighbors, as he taught his disciples to do. However, if the infirmity should be for their salvation, and if they are called to endure their illness, then it is best to counsel them, lifting their spirits to calmness (*De Sermone Domini de monte secundum Matthaeum*, XIX, 57, *CSEL*, 35).

---
[53] See p. 115, this volume.

AUGUSTINE CHANGES THE COURSE OF THE CHURCH

Augustine then went on: "All depravity[54] comes from turmoil in the midst of weakness[55] of mind. Nothing more innocent exists than those who are perfected in virtue" (*De Sermone Domini de monte secundum Matthaeum*, XIX, 57, CSEL, 35). This statement, even with its piety, in itself was a depravity because it oversimplified Jesus' thought. It sounds good, and it is often true, but Jesus was saying nothing in this text about weakness of the flesh or old age or sickness. He was addressing "turning the other cheek" when somebody slaps you in the face.

Then Augustine, still developing his exposition on "turning the other cheek," brought in the story from Acts 22:22–29. After the crowd heard Paul testify in Jerusalem, they became incensed with him and demanded his life. Paul claims his Roman citizenship to defend himself. Augustine considered this "turning the other cheek":

> Thus, this same apostle, if he had kept silence when men were persecuting him for being Christian, would not have presented the other cheek to those who were smiting the right one. But when he said, "I am a Roman citizen," he turned the other cheek, respecting the dignity which he had in the world. (*De Sermone mounte secundum matthaeum*, xix, 59.*CSEL*)

The Jews in Paul's day, or any other day, would not have had the foggiest idea that Paul's statement would have had anything to do with Jesus' statement concerning turning the other cheek. Augustine used the same occasion to take another swipe at the Jews, saying that the Jews did not persecute Paul for Paul's statement, but rather, "they held contempt for anyone who in his [Jesus'] name is among those who are precious and among the saved" (*De Sermone Domini de monte secundum Matthaeum*, xix, 60. *CSEL* 35). Augustine here did not indicate Paul's anger or even his instinct for self-preservation; rather, he stated that the passage indicated the magnanimous nature of Paul. Paul, according to Augustine, in

---

[54] *Improbitas* means "the condition of being morally bad or unpatriotic, perversity or, as we have translated it, "depravity."

[55] We have translated *imbecillitate* as "weakness of mind." Because of Augustine's Neo-Platonism and his status in the Roman elite, one must assume that "weakness of mind" produces "turmoil," which produces chaos and "depravity."
In the future we will see that heretics are considered ignorant and unable to make correct decisions.

his generosity corrected the perversity of the Jews by not giving them his cheek as an object to strike. We can imagine that the Jews must have been grateful. The point that we are making is that Augustine expounded much verbiage to avoid dealing with the real message of Jesus of "turning the other cheek," and in the process he sanctified Paul's anger and instinct for self-preservation by calling it "magnanimity."

Augustine did not stop here. In furthering his diversion related to "turning the other cheek," he found another text to transfer our attention away from Jesus' stark statement. He turned to Paul's reaction to the high priest in Acts 23:3, when he exploded, "God will strike you, you whitewashed wall!" Augustine stipulated that this might seem like anger, but it really was not, rather it was "prophesy" (*De Sermone Domini de Monte secundum Matthaeum*, XIX, 58. *CSEL*, 35). Augustine did not explain why or how this was not anger but prophesy. We must just assume that he knew because he was the great Bishop of Hippo.

He then continued in a very confused manner to discuss how this prophet, Paul, was not able to recognize the high priest. After all was said and done, the impact of Jesus was still zero because Jesus' words were not discussed, and Augustine's listeners learned nothing about what Jesus meant by "turning the other cheek." This was just one of Augustine's escapades in intertextuality to avoid a "hard saying" of Jesus.

Loving One's Enemy

Augustine did not find the example for loving one's enemy and not returning evil for evil (Matthew 5:38–48) in Jesus' life and his dying on the cross. He saw it rather in Jesus' or God's omnipotence. Then through intertextuality, love became synonymous with punishing the enemy. Leading up to loving one's enemies, Augustine first dealt with the relationship between superiors and inferiors, a very Roman thing to do:

> No, ordinarily it is not right to attempt to counteract with mercy the punishment inflicted by those who are in control of the correction of others. I will say more, it is not even part of mercy to impede those who wish to correct such a one. To do so is not proper unless the person inflicting the punishment is doing so

out of hatred, or if he is clearly overdoing it with great delight. (*De Sermone mounte secundum matthaeum*, XIX, 63.*CSEL*)

Thus, emperors, governors, military personnel, and governments were, for the most part, exempt from the commands of mercy. Likewise, children could be flogged, but not out of "hatred." And what about "love of enemy"? Augustine has avoided it completely. Again, it is not a difficult concept for a brilliant mind like Augustine's to understand. It is not a difficult thing for any unlearned, unintelligent person to understand. Yet, Augustine continued on his oratorical journey:

So do not get excited, unless parents seem to have hatred for a small child and it is clear that by flogging the poor child they are sinning. This of course is an extreme example. Otherwise, if you intervene you sin the more. (*De sermone de mounte secundum matthaeum*, XIX, 63.*CSEL*)

Now while this was a diversion from Augustine's main discussion, we are sure that the modern reader is well aware of the significance. Similar statements can be found in Cicero, Aristotle, and in other classical writers, and, indeed, flogging has been the classic way of disciplining children, but it is not now accepted by most child-raising standards. However, sadly, because of the recognized influence and spiritual expertise of Augustine throughout Christian history, many Christian families continue to observe the practice. Augustine's thoughts are the seeds for child abuse. They were in Augustine's day, too. (For the adverse effects of aversive parenting, see Alice Miller 2002. *For Your Own Good: Hidden Cruelty in Child-Rearing and the Roots of Violence* and see the next chapter of this volume).

"Family discipline" was not the totality of Augustine's meaning. Here, the development of language becomes important. When Augustine spoke of a child or sons, he was not necessarily talking about sons of the biological family or even sons of the Catholic faith. He was also speaking culturally of people who could not be expected to think or act on their own. This could have be anyone on whom the elite would look down their noses or with whom the elite would disagree.[56] Augustine then took

---

[56] See Cragun, *The Ultimate Heresy The Doctrine of Bibilical Inerrancy*, pp. 154-157.

CHRISTIANITY: ENDANGERED OR EXTINCT?

Christian love of enemy further away from the cross and redefined it in terms of empire and in ways that could be utilized by the emperor, future politicians, and future hierarchical institutions.

> For the perfection of love lies in us imitating God the Father, since in so doing we imitate what is written: "Love your enemy: do good to those who hate you; pray for those who persecute you." Take this statement in the context of the prophet: "Whomsoever the Lord loves, he corrects. He whips all his sons whom he accepts." And the Lord says: "The servant who does not know the will of his God is not often tormented by him; the servant however who knows the will of his God is tormented much" (*De Sermone Domini in Mounte*, XIX, 63. CSEL).

In short, as we saw in the previous chapter, when the forces of Rome tortured the Donatists, deprived them of their property and harassed them, they were simply expressing love for an enemy. Those people whose conscience were bothered or were tormented and repented and became Catholics through torture were really the sons of God brought back to "the will of God," that is a true and right relationship with God.

Within the confines of Augustine's thought, Jesus had three basic principles: 1. Jesus' teachings were aimed at stripping away any self-righteousness; 2. thus the person would become prostrate humbly before God (as one would be before the emperor); and 3. the offending person would come to know the Lord and thus see the errors of his way and be converted. So, according to Augustine, corrections were not to be questioned unless in the case of a father beating a small child out of hatred. But what is hatred? And who is to determine it? Even Augustine admitted that all human emotions are suspect. Nonetheless, he asserted that it is better to punish out of love than to leave the person unpunished:

> ... [T]hat you may be the children of your Father, Who is in heaven." This rule must be understood in the words of John: "He gave them the power to become sons of God." Now only one is the natural Son of the Father, and He is the one who did not know sin. We also receive the power of sonship, but only insofar as we implement his instructions. That is why the apostolic discipline

calls our relationship to the Father one of adoption, "an eternal heredity." Our adoption allows us to be coheirs with Christ. We are made sons in a spiritual regeneration, adopted into the kingdom of God, not as aliens, but as sons made and created by him in a relationship gifted to us through his omnipotence. Before we were nothing, but now we are adopted sons able to enjoy participation in eternal life with Him. Notice that he does not say, "Do these things because you are sons," but rather, "Do these things so that you may be sons." (*De Sermone mounte secundum matthaeum*, XXIII, 78–79. *CSEL*)

It is obvious that here again is another giant jump in Augustine's interpretation of scripture. Instead of seeking the meaning within the text of Matthew, Augustine looked for its meaning in the Gospel of John, and then that understanding was wrapped in a Platonized view of John. According to Augustine, the text has to do with eternal life, rather than, as Matthew expressed it, being children of God in this world by loving our enemy. Augustine then continued with Matthew 5:45: ". . . and sends rain on the righteous and the unrighteous." It is a familiar passage today, and it was in Augustine's day. The passage does not need much exposition. However, in his typical distortion of scripture, Augustine used his power as "God's representative":

Or you might say that we receive this visible sun, not through carnal eyes, but, in the wisdom which he speaks: "Bright is the light eternal!" (Wisdom 7:26) And again, "The sun of righteousness will rise with healing in its rays" (Malachi 4:2). And again, "The sun of justice shines on the one who fears the name of the Lord" (Wisdom 5:6). So the rain of the doctrine of truth falls on you. Yes, that rain is available to both the good and the evil, for Christ evangelizes both the good and the evil. The latter is the more probable understanding of these words. In other words, the spiritual sun only shines on the good and the holy. This is what the evil bewail in the Book of Wisdom of Solomon: "And the sun did not rise on us." And the spiritual rain only falls on the good. For the vine, which does not receive the spiritual sun or the spiritual rain signifies the evil, concerning which he said: "I will command my clouds not to send the rain." But whether you understand the passages to read one way or the other, the passage speaks of the great goodness of God which gives us incentive to imitate him if we wish to be a son of God. For who exists who is so ungrateful as to not feel the great comfort bestowed in this life on the righteous and the sinner alike from the light of the sun. But he went much further than to say, "Who makes the sun to rise on the evil and on the good." He added, "which he himself made and established." To create the luminaries, Genesis tells us that He took nothing from anyone. Everything was created from nothing. And, of course, everything which is created out of nothing is his own. Thus, we are admonished with how great a liberality we ought, according to his precepts, to give to our enemies those gifts which we have not created, but have only received from Him. (*De Sermone mounte secundum matthaeum*, XXIII, 79. *CSEL*)

Placed within Augustine's overriding thinking, the sons who are Catholics are given gifts of God, which include the obligation to administer God's punishment against his enemies or evildoers, thus correcting them. If some of these enemies happen to be sons of light, they will repent and come into the Catholic Church. This belief of Augustine, that it was the duty of the Catholic faith and its agents to inflict punishment and chastisement on their opposition, is found in almost everything that he wrote against the Donatists, Pelagians, and Arians. His thoughts on the matter became part of the essential thinking of the Roman Catholic faith. It will be used to justify the crusades, the inquisitions, and the pogroms against the Jews.

The Gospel of John

Of the whole New Testament, Augustine wrote and preached the most on the Gospel of John—over 124 tractates, books, or sermons. The problem, however, is not that he wrote so much on John, but that in what he wrote there is little, if any, of the message of the Gospel. What he wrote became the theological transformation of the Jesus Movement into the institutional church. While the emphasis on John to the exclusion

AUGUSTINE CHANGES THE COURSE OF THE CHURCH

of other Gospels began before Augustine, with him it became doctrine. Furthermore, down the ages, most of the Protestant reformers would uncritically absorb his thought, so that while they may have rebelled against some aspects of Catholicism, they truly were Augustinian. In imitation of Augustine, Luther wrote one small volume on the Sermon on the Mount, and three large volumes of sermons on the Gospel of John; John Calvin, like Augustine, wrote a harmony on the Gospels, but he focused exclusively on the Gospel of John. Today, conservative preachers imitate Augustine in utilizing the Gospel of John, particularly the passage in chapter three which pertains to being "born-again."

If John is the Gospel of Love, Augustine, right from the beginning, put a totally different perspective on the Gospel. He began by discounting many in the congregation. He accused them of being incapable of understanding his homilies. Here is the beginning of one of his homilies:

> Reflecting on what we have just heard in the apostolic reading, we come to understand that a man who is merely living in his animal nature does not perceive those things which come to him from the Holy Spirit [1 Corinthians 2:14]. Therefore, it is clear that in this present congregation of your beloved many are animals, wise only according to the flesh, and not able to arouse a spiritual intellect. I am gravely reluctant to say that the Lord would ever give them the ability to speak or explain the words which I now speak to you which were written by the Evangelist: "In the beginning was the Word, and the Word was with God, and the Word was God." These words, a man who is merely living in his animal nature cannot know. What then am I to do, brothers? Shall I be silent? What sense is it for me to read the words if I am then to be silent about them? Or what sense is it that I hear these words, if I do not explain them? Should I waste my time explaining them, if people are going to sit there like toads, not able to understand them?

> On the other hand, I do not doubt that among your number there are some who are able to not only grasp these words when

CHRISTIANITY: ENDANGERED OR EXTINCT?

I explain them, but who even understood them before I explain them. Therefore I will not cheat those who are able to grasp them.

Nonetheless I fear that most of you have ears, which will not be able to grasp them. I pray that if mercy exists in God, it might come down upon you, and who knows, perhaps the words will penetrate your earthly spirit, and you w ill grasp the message to some degree (*In Johannes evangelium tractatus*, I.1. *CCEL*).

The Christian Berber people were most likely included in the group that Augustine described in his homily on John 1. They were undoubtedly the ones who did not "have ears" to "grasp" the words of Augustine. In fact, they could not understand Augustine at all because he spoke in Latin, and they only spoke Berber. So all they could do was sit there like toads. But the arrogance of Augustine would not quit. He even challenged the fact that John, the author of the Gospel, could understand his own words. He continued on: "I dare to say, my brothers, that perhaps even John himself did not do the reality of God full justice." Augustine, "being kind" to John, goes on:

> He only did the best he could. After all, he was only a man speaking about the things of God. Granted, he was inspired by God, but he was still only a man. Because he was inspired, he had to say something. If he had not been inspired, he might have said nothing. But because he was only an inspired man, he did not say everything that was to be said. Only that which he, as a man, could understand in his spirit, did he say. (*In Johannes Evangelium tractatus*, I.1. *CCEL*)

Undoubtedly, according to Augustine, he (Augustine) had understanding when John did not. What more can we say? Of course this may be rhetorical flourish, but considering his mechanical views of the Scriptures this is not surprising. He stated in *Confessions*, "The Preachers of thy word pass away from this life; but thy Scripture is spread abroad over the people, even to the end of world" (*Confessions*, XIII.29, *NPNF* 1st Series 1, 205) As we stated for Augustine above (p. 207) Jesus' teachings did not just exist in text, but existed ethereally, so The Gospel of

John, written he believed by the apostle John, but more particularly by the Holy Spirit, existed on parchment but also above the heavens. The difference between the words of Jesus and the words of John is that Jesus being God understood his words whereas John being human may not have understood his words, or rather the words of the Holy Spirit. Of course because Augustine was especially anointed he could understand what John could not. This again is just another indication of how far Augustine was from understanding Jesus and how corrupt the movement of Jesus had become. What is so sad is that Augustine theology had such an overwhelming impact on the thinking of the Church when it should have been truly declare as heresy. The reality is that the arrogance of Augustine was the arrogance of the empire and that arrogance took over the religion of Jesus. To some degree, we can understand why. Augustine's mentor and hero of the faith was the Roman general Ambrose. Augustine would have been better off finding his model in the preaching of his contemporary, John Chrysostom (347–407), who was known for his compassion.

Greek Philosophy

But there is much more to be seen in Augustine's homilies on John. In these homilies it is totally apparent that Augustine blended Greek philosophy into his biblical interpretation.[57] In an attempt to defend Augustine from the charge from being a total Platonist Robert J. O'Connell, in *Soundings in Augustine's Imagination*, states:

> Augustine was always determined to think as a Christian even when using and transforming the Platonian philosophy he once thought would serve as a trusty ally in "understanding the faith." We moderns might have more doubts than he did, but even from the first, Augustine himself was obliged to part company with the great man (Plotinus) whenever he detected a conflict between his admired Platonici. Faith always won, and Platonism always lost. (O'Connell 1994, 174)

---

[57] Today, the reader may be surprise to find that much of what is described as biblical faithfulness is nothing more than carrying on the Augustinian tradition of blending biblical texts in Platonic thought.

CHRISTIANITY: ENDANGERED OR EXTINCT?

O'Connell's statement has one problem. It is true that when there was "a conflict between his admired Platonici," "faith always won." However, this faith was something that Augustine constructed, albeit over many years. His faith was a conglomeration of Platonic philosophy, imperial religion, and his personal thoughts wrapped in a veneer of biblical texts. Augustine's high esteem for platonic Greek philosophy is clear from his classic work *The City of God* (written 413–427, Fitzgerald 1999 xliii).

> But there is no conflict on this point between us and these philosophers of the better sort. For they saw and put into their writings, in many ways and at great length, that they (the "gods" or higher souls) derive their blessedness from the same source as we do ourselves, from the casting of an intelligible light, which is God to them and is something other than they are, by which they are illuminated, that they may shine and by participation in it exist as perfect and blessed beings. Plotinus asserts often and strongly, explaining Plato's meaning, that even that soul which they (the Platonists) believe to be the soul of the universe, does not derive its blessedness from any other source than ours, and that its light is something which is not itself, but that by which it is created and by the intelligible illumination of which it shines intelligibly (*De civ. Dei*, X.2, CSEL).

In *Augustine through the Ages: An Encyclopedia*, the editors assert that *The City of God* (*De civitas Dei*) was written between 410 and 427 (Fitzgerald 1999, xliii). This makes the work late in Augustine's life, and it is clear that he saw the philosophers as inspired as much as the biblical writers.

The "Word" of God and the Greek "Word"

In his *Tractatus on John II*, Augustine dealt with the beginning of John's Gospel: "In the beginning was the Word..." (John 1:1). Augustine asserted that the philosophers, i.e., the Platonists, recognized the priority of the word. Augustine wrote that there were philosophers who also believed in John's word:

But there are philosophers of this world who seek the Creator through the creatures that dwell on the earth, for the Apostle says: Since the creation of the world, invisible realities have become known, showing God's eternal power and divinity through the things that he has made. Then it follows: They certainly have knowledge of God. Notice that it does not say: They certainly do not have knowledge of God. Rather, even though they have knowledge of God, yet they do not give him glory or give him thanks. Instead, they persist in speculation which leads nowhere. Their senseless hearts are darkened. Where does this darkness come from? Follow along and hear me clearly: They claim to be wise, but they are fools instead. They see all the things that they have come to see, but they see them with ingratitude. Indeed, they see only what they wish to see, and they dismiss the magnificent facts that the truly wise will attest to. Those who truly know God hear the words that John speaks: through the Word of God all things were made. You will find these same words in books of philosophy, followed by, God has an only begotten Son through whom all things were made. These philosophers are able to see the reality, but they see it from a long way off. They do not know the humility of Christ which would allow them to navigate securely to that which they only see from a distance. In fact, the cross of Christ is dirt to them. Do you sail on the same sea? Do you despise the wood of the cross? Oh wisdom lost! Do you laugh at the crucifixion of Christ which you only see from a distance? In the beginning was the Word and the Word was with God (*In Johannes Evangelium tractatus*, II. CSEL).

O'Connell might have correctly observed that Augustine resisted asserting that the philosophers had knowledge of the Bible. However, as is apparent in the above text, O'Connell fails to see that Augustine believed that certain philosophers, the Platonists, had prior knowledge. But it was similar to the knowledge that John had, "only from a distance." John, the Evangelist, did not understand what he was writing about, neither did the philosophers. But then, in his great wisdom, Augustine did understand. At the same time, Augustine did see differences in philosophers. Some of them could see beyond creation, and they still did not glorify God. But then there were others "who truly know God and hear the words that John speaks."

Augustine clearly linked the word of the Greek philosophers with the word of John. He is not alone. There were other church fathers, such as Justin Martyr, Irenaeus, Origen, and more, who connected the Logos of John with the Logos of the Greek fathers, but none did so as influentially as Augustine. Thus, Augustine equated the dynamic and powerful word of God of the Old Testament, the word (*dabar*) of Yahweh, and the word (logos) of John with the Greek philosophical Logos. They were clearly not the same. The creative word of the Old Testament and John is the creative word of God, who acts whenever he speaks. The Logos of the Greek philosophers was human reason.

Yet, Augustine's interpretation has held dominance in the church, sometimes even within critical interpretation, right up to recent times. There is no dispute, then, that Augustine wrapped Platonic thinking in his theological interpretations.

Very much like O'Connell, Anne Marie Bowery, in her article, "Plotinus, *The Enneads*," in *Augustine through the Ages: An Encyclopedia*, points out the heavy influence of Plotinus (CE 204-270). Also like O'Connell, Bowery asserts apologetically that while Augustine is heavily influenced by Plotinus, "scriptural authority is always present…" She then goes onto state:

> …Augustine's thinking reveals Plotinian influence in these areas: his conception of beauty, his vision of God and belief in divine illumination, his emphasis on the soul, his insistence on purification of the mind as a requirement for understanding truth, the view of evil as privation, the conception of time and eternity, and his desire for spiritual and intellectual community. (Fitzgerald 1999, 655–56)

What Professor Bowery has described as his being influenced by Plotinus is very much core to Augustine's theology. A person thus could not say that the core of Augustine's theology was in any way scriptural. As to the issue of Augustine shaping his thinking around "the authority of Scripture," we have shown that his interpretation would not fit in any way with a literal interpretation or exacting hermeneutics of Scripture. Through intertextuality, taking a verse from here and a verse from there, Augustine made the Bible say precisely what he wanted it to say. Sometimes, "what he wanted it to say" included agreeing with his philosophers; sometimes, it involved the hierarchical thinking of the empire; sometimes, it was simply his own creation.

The Philosophers' Concept of the Soul

Not only did Augustine assume an erroneous Logos, but he also assumed an erroneous concept of the soul. What he has to say about the soul has no biblical basis. Plotinus probably comes closest to Augustine's stance, but he too differed from Augustine. Plotinus stated in his *First Ennead*:

> At the first the soul is evil by being interfused with the body, and by coming to share the body's states, and to think the body's thoughts, so it would be good, it would be possessed of virtue, if it threw off the body's moods and devoted itself to its own Act—the state of Intellection and Wisdom—never allowing the passions of the body to effect it . . . (Plotinus, First Ennead II.3, *Great Books of the Western World*, 17)

Notice the differences Augustine made when he seems to say the same as Plotinus:

> Our soul, my brethren, is ugly because of sin: by loving God, it becomes beautiful. What kind of love is it that makes the lover beautiful? God is always beautiful, never deformed, never changeable. God, who is ever beautiful, loved us first; and how did God love us, if not as ugly and deformed? Not in order to send us away because we were ugly, but rather in order to transform us, to make us beautiful out of our deformity. How shall we be beautiful? By loving one who is always beautiful. The more love grows in you the more beauty grows; for love itself is the beauty of the soul. (*In epistolam Johannis ad Parthos tractatus*, X.40, *CSEL*)

Plotinus and Augustine do differ on certain points. For Plotinus, the soul in and of itself is essentially not evil. When it becomes entrapped in the body it becomes evil. One transcends this evil by overcoming one's passions and beginning to think rationally. Such is not the case with Augustine. In the fall of Adam, all souls become corrupted or ugly. This becomes the doctrine of original sin. This pervades all of Augustine's thinking and would permeate most of the Western Roman Catholic faith, and much of later Protestant thought. It becomes the conceptual force creating the necessity for the baptism of infants, which up to Augustine's time, was rarely, if ever, practiced.

There is another distinction between Augustine and Plotinus. For Plotinus, an individual could become purer by shedding the passions of the body and thinking rationally. This, however, was impossible in Augustine's thought. For Augustine, even the philosophers who had come close failed because they did not glorify God. For Augustine, human reason or rationality could not "beautify the soul." The soul only "becomes beautiful by loving God." On this point Augustine is easily and most frequently misunderstood. We tend to read our own thoughts into his thinking. We do not get much help in understanding Augustine by expressions taken out of context which make Augustine sound wise and appreciative of the human condition: "The more love grows in you the more beauty grows; for love itself is the beauty of the soul." These words stand out of context with words that Augustine wrote seven sentences before. In context, a romantic person would not think that this could express his or her love for the beloved. But out of context, this statement has appeared on wedding and Valentine cards. If they knew the whole of Augustine's thought, romantic people would even be repulsed by Augustine's statement. Most of the authors of the New Testament would likewise find Augustine's words of love repulsive. Words like these are insidious.

Augustine's Love

One of the best analyses ever written on New Testament *agape* was written by Anders Nygren (1890–1978), professor of Systematic Theology at the University of Lund and bishop of Lund, Sweden, and titled in English: *Agape and Eros*. He began the work in 1932 and completed it in

AUGUSTINE CHANGES THE COURSE OF THE CHURCH

1953. In its 741 pages he discusses the use of love in Greek philosophy, in the Old Testament, in rabbinical Judaism, and in the New Testament and in church history:

> It has long been recognized that the idea of agape represents a distinctive and original feature of Christianity. But in what precisely does its originality and distinctiveness consist? If the commandment of love can be specifically Christian, as undoubtedly it can, the reason is to be found, not in the commandment as such ... but in the quite new meaning Christianity has given it ... Christian love ... is universal and all-embracing. "There is neither Jew nor Gentile, neither slave nor free, nor is there male and female ..." [Galatians 3:28] (Nygren 1953, 61–67)

"Agape" love is, then, all-inclusive for the Christian who follows Jesus. It includes even one's enemy. It is Jesus laying down his life for humanity. It is Jesus washing the feet of the disciples. It is Christians serving one another. However, when Augustine took up the concept of agape in its Latin translation, *caritas*, it is not just a translation, but it is a total transformation of the word.

In *Love and Saint Augustine*, the intellectual giant, Jewish philosopher/historian, Hannah Arendt (1906–1975) stated: "Augustine wrote that 'to love is indeed nothing else than to crave something for its own sake,' and further on he comments that 'love is a kind of craving' (*Eighty-Three Different Questions* 35, 1 and 2)." Clarifying Augustine's craving Arendt goes on:

> Every craving (*appetitus*) is tied to a definite object to spark the craving itself, thus providing an aim for it. Love understood as a craving desire, and desire understood in terms of the Greek tradition from Aristotle to Plotinus constitutes the root of both *caritas* and *cupitas*. They are distinguished by their objects, but they are not different kinds of emotions: "just as temporal life is cherished by its lovers, thus we should cherish eternal life, which the Christian professes to love." (Arendt, 1996, 9, 18)

For Augustine, *summum bonum*, the "greatest good" is God, and being with God in eternity must be the Christian's total "desire." To have

CHRISTIANITY: ENDANGERED OR EXTINCT?

eternal life is the ultimate desire of Christians. As a Jew, Arendt makes this profound and objective conclusion:

> Undoubtedly, insofar as Augustine defines love as a kind of desire he hardly speaks as a Christian. His starting point is not God who revealed himself to mankind, but the experience of the deplorable state of human condition, and whatever he has to say in this context is far from original in late antiquity... (Arendt 1996, 21)

Arendt goes on to state that Augustine asserts, "God must be loved in such a way that, if at all possible, we forget ourselves" (*Sermon* 142, 3). "This self-forgetfulness and complete denial of human existence," according to Arendt, "makes the central Christian demand to love one's neighbor as oneself well nigh impossible." One could not find a stronger statement against the "Christian saint."

Nygren, a Lutheran Bishop, does not slam Augustine quite as hard as Arendt, his views are not far removed. The following portion from *Agape and Eros* is a good summary of Nygren's lengthy analysis of Augustine's views of love:

> Even if Augustine's distinction between *Caritas*," and *Cupiditas* does not entirely lack points of contact with New Testament Christianity, there cannot be the slightest doubt that his doctrine of love . . . rests substantially on the foundation of Eros and has very little in common with *Agape*-love.
>
> The contrast between the two forms of love is very much the same in Augustine as in Neoplatonic Eros doctrine: it is the contrast between love directed upward and love directed downward, between love for the eternal and love for the temporal. Into this scheme, built as it is on Eros theory, the Christian commandment of love is now introduced. To do this is not difficult so far as love to God is concerned, since Augustine is convinced that the ascending love which Neoplatonism had taught him is essentially the same as the love required in the commandment: "Love the Lord your God with all your heart." Such an identification, however, can obviously be made only at the expense of the Christian idea of love;

for if Christian love is thought of as a form of "acquisitive love" and interpreted to mean that we seek our own "bonum" in God, then the theocentric character of the Christian commandment of love is undoubtedly lost. Even though God is described as the highest good, this does not alter the fact that He is degraded to the level of a means for the satisfaction of human desire. "Love to God," as interpreted by Augustine, loses a good deal of its original Christian meaning…(Nygren 1953, 499–500)

Both Nygren and Arendt were on the same page in their interpretation of Augustine. We believe they are both irrefutable. But as a philosopher Arendt had a very astute understanding of how Neo-Platonism saturates Augustine's thinking. She points out that, after the thought of Plotinus, Augustine saw man as being from God" and "to God," and that Man "grasps his own being in God's presence." However, Arendt points out that Augustine not only deviates from the biblical understanding of love, but also of Plotinian thinking. In that for Augustine, love really ends up being a selfish endeavors. Of the many passages she cites one of the most revealingis from Augustine's *Homily on the First Epistle of John, VII, 10* where Augustine states,

And just as I do not love the self I made in belonging to the world, I also do not love my neighbor in the concrete and worldly encounter with him. Rather, I love him in his createdness. I love something in him, that is, the very thing which, of himself, he is not: "For you love in him not what he is, but what you wish that he may be."

Another passage Arendt she cites is also worth quoting: "For he truly loves a friend who loves God in his friend, either because God is in him or so that God may be in him (*Sermon* 336, 2)." (Arendt 1996, 95–96)

The Christian, therefore, if he truly loves his neighbor, will lead him to seek his greatest good (*summum bonum*), his eternal salvation. How does this play out in Augustine's theology or his practices? We saw in the last chapter that his *caritas* (love) for the Donatist included torture. As we saw in Augustine's Epistle to Proconsul Donatus in 409: "It is not their death, but their deliverance from error, that we seek to accomplish by the help of the terror of judges and of laws, whereby they may be preserved from falling under the penalty of eternal judgment" (*Letter C*.1, NPNF 1st Series 1, 412. CCEL).

But it was not just the Donatists that needed deliverance. Humankind had to be stripped or broken of pride before it was possible for humans to show *caritas* to God. Torturing a Donatist was showing *caritas* (love) to them, because it might lead them to the true church. The whole essence of almost everything that was Augustine's theology was intended to mold or break the followers so that they would be obedient followers of the Catholic hierarchy. So within the *Tractatus on John* are these thoughts:

> But why was he crucified? The wood of the cross was necessary to teach you humility: for you are puffed up with pride. Even though from a distance you propose to see a fatherland, your way is interrupted by the waves of the ages. No, I am afraid that you will never enter that fatherland unless you bear the cross. You are an ungrateful one! You laugh at him who comes to you to tow you back to port. The way is made wide open to you, but it is through the sea. Upon this sea He has walked in order that He might show you the way through the waves. But you are not able to walk on water; you are not able to carry the cross. Believe now in the cross, and you will be able to do so (*In Johannis evangelium tractatus*, I.4, CSEL).

Augustine and Nicodemus

And this becomes even clearer as we move into Augustine's *Homilies on John*. Particularly revealing is Augustine's "exposition" of the story of Nicodemus as it is found in John 3:1–5:

> For it is time we exhort you, who are still catechumens, that, even though you believe in Christ, you still bear your sins. And no one shall see the kingdom of heaven while he be burdened with sins; and no one shall reign with Christ unless he be forgiven. But forgiven you cannot be, unless you be born again in water and the Holy Spirit. But let us make note of all the words implied here, so that the sluggish may know that they must quickly put

aside all impediments. For if you were carrying some heavy load, either of stone, or of wood, or some other thing that is advantageous to you; maybe it might be corn, or wine, or money, you would quickly get rid of these loads for something better. Yet you are carrying a burden of sins, and are sluggish to get rid of them. You must quickly get rid of these burdens; they are weighing you down; they are drowning you.

True, if I say to a catechumen, Do you believe in Christ, he will answer, "I believe," and he will sign himself; already he bears the cross of Christ on his forehead, and he is not ashamed of the cross of his Lord. Clearly, he believes in His name. But if I ask him, "Do you eat the flesh of the Son of man, and drink His blood?" He will be flabbergasted, because Jesus has not entrusted Himself to him. (*In Johannis evangelium tractatus*, XI.1-5.CSEL)

Within Augustine's theology, "believing in Jesus" was not enough. But eating "the flesh of the Son of man," and drinking "the blood of the Son of man" is essential. According to Augustine, Jesus will not "entrust himself" to the catechumen, a new convert seeking membership within the Church. Of course, Augustine is referring to the Eucharist, which has become totally dependent on the priest—and thus, the priest is the mediator between the disciple and the Logos. Augustine goes on: Because the catechumen has the sign of the cross on his forehead, he is already in the great house; but only as a servant there. From servants, he must become a son.

Of course, when the catechumen becomes a son, he needs an earthly father, a priest to fill that role. In the logical development of his thought, before Eucharist, the act of baptism is necessary for the catechumen to join the church, an action which was also administered, for the most part, by a priest or deacon. Within this frame of baptism by the clergy, Augustine develops his thoughts regarding Nicodemus. Augustine said, "Jesus told Nicodemus: you must be born-again." According to Augustine, our first birth was "according to Adam" or the "flesh" (*In Johannis evangelium tractatus*, XI.6.*CSEL*). But being "born again," Augustine insists is being "born of the Catholic Church" which was being "born of Sarah" (*In Johannis evangelium tractatus*, XI.7.*CSEL*). The knowledgeable Bible student will recognize that Augustine has brought in a totally different biblical concept here in the use of intertextuality. He has brought in Sarah and Hagar from Paul's discussion of justification of faith in Galatians (4:21–31) and Romans 4:1–23 and applied it to the Catholic Church: He that is born of the Catholic Church, is born, as it were, of Sarah, of the free woman; he that is born of heresy is, as it were, born of the bond woman, but of Abraham's seed nonetheless (*In Johannis evangelium tractatus*, XI. 7.*CSEL*).

So the ecclesiastical structure becomes the new family in which the catechumen becomes a servant who will become a son if he is baptized. This means, of course, that the "born-again" Catholic subjects herself or himself to a close dependence upon the bishop or one of his priests. This is quite a stretch from the meaning of the fourth Gospel. While there are few people today who would put such a slant on being "born-again," Bruce Malina and Richard Rohrbaugh give probably the most accurate interpretation of what being born-again meant in their *Social Science Commentary on the Gospel of John*. According to them, in "antiquity" loss of family connections meant loss of land, honor, and status. There was nothing left to loose. A person in such a position utterly needed an extended family to exist. It was the person's religious, social, and economic link to the world. Such a family, which Malina and Rohrbaugh call a "fictive kin group," replaced the biological family. John was referring to such a person being embraced in this Christian family as being "born-again" (Malina & Rohrbaugh 1998, 89).

As we have stated many times within this volume, in the early years within the Jesus Movement, it was this "fictive" family that was essentially responsible for its rapid growth. It was the fellowship of believers where two or three were gathered in the presence of Jesus (Matthew 18:20) and where the servant community of John 13 and 1 Corinthians 12–13 existed, that the church grew in remarkable numbers.

It is apparent in the works of Augustine that this "fictive" family was no longer operative. Instead, an alternative societal structure had come into existence. This structure in most ways and especially ideologically resembled the Roman Empire, and, indeed, would become known as the Holy Roman Empire with the pope in Rome, being the equivalent to the emperor, or in some cases, surpassing the emperor, in power.

AUGUSTINE CHANGES THE COURSE OF THE CHURCH

Augustine: the Priest as Broker of Eternal Life

When Augustine is not damning the heretics, he is talking about eternal life. In *The City of God*, over and over again he insists that eternal life is the supreme good. This is illustrated by the following passage:

> Since, then, the supreme good of the City of God is perfect, and eternal peace, not such as mortals pass into by birth and death, but the peace of freedom from all evil in which the immortals ever abide: who can deny that the future life is most blessed or that in comparison with it, this life, which now we live, is most wretched, even though it be filled with blessings of body and soul and many external things? (*De civ. Dei*, XIX.X.x. . CSEL)

It is clear from the above passage from Augustine that the priest and the Catholic faith become the chief and only dispensers of eternal life. His thinking sets up the mind-set for almost everything that transpires in the next centuries economically, socially, and religiously. According to the economists Robert D. Tollison, Robert F. Hébert, Robert B. Ekelund Jr., Gary M. Anderson, and Audrey B. Davidson, in *The Sacred Trust: the Medieval Church as Economic Firm*, the Roman Church became the monopolistic brokers of the product called "Eternal Life." They wrote:

> The primary service supplied by the medieval Church to its customers was information about and guidance toward the attainment of eternal salvation. At issue here is not the veracity of the Church's theological claims, nor its ability to guarantee the end-product, but rather the fact that whatever knowledge consumers possessed in this regard was provided entirely and exclusively by the Church. An important aspect of this service concerned the afterlife: the idea that the soul continues to exist for all eternity after the death of the body. To a medieval Christian, one's existence on earth was a tiny part of "life"—while the average person might live a mere forty or fifty years in the earthly realm, the soul's existence in heaven or hell would be forever. Each Christian therefore looked to the Church for advice and guidance on actions required to get to heaven .(Tollison, 1996, 26)

CHRISTIANITY: ENDANGERED OR EXTINCT?

It was Augustine's genius that created the Magna Carta for this economic endeavor. But it was not only his thinking that created it, but his practices. The above economists pointed out that the church eventually became the largest land owner in Europe. Augustine and his order took the lead. They became the largest landowners in all of Africa.

10

The Consequences of Domination in the Christian Church from the Second to the Twenty-first Century

Howard Zinn began his epic *A People's History of the United States* with Christopher Columbus and the mayhem that the Europeans inflicted on the natives of the New World. *Christianity: Endangered or Extinct? A People's History of Christianity* Volume 1: *The Gathering Storm* has dealt with happenings fifteen hundred years before Columbus. The descriptions in chapters one through nine in this book are merely the inception of the abuse that was so vividly portrayed in *A People's History of the United States*. Already by 430 CE, we have seen enough. "Heretic" has been thrown around by synods and councils, Justin Martyr, Athanasius, Ambrose, and Augustine. Good people, even fellow Christians, have been victims of intolerance. Marcion, the Montanist women, Arius and the Arians, the Donatists, Christian "Gnostics," and many more have been used and abused by people who should have known better. Jesus has been effectively put on the shelf, if not thrown in the trash can. And this is just the beginning. Next, we will face centuries of violence and mayhem carried out in the name of the Prince of Peace. To name just a few of the calamities that we will face in future volumes will be the continuing persecution of the people who did not believe in the "correct" nature of Jesus, the wars carried out against the Arian nations, the crusades, the inquisitions, the slaughter of the peasants, the Thirty Years' War, the Hundred Years' War, the burning of witches and heretics, and the genocide of natives in the Western hemisphere. The list goes on ad infinitum. How does this translate into our own age?

Obviously changes have occurred in Christianity. As a religion, Christianity has largely stopped killing Christians who have differing views. Furthermore, some of the attitudes and intolerances that created problems in previous ages are still present, and these attitudes and intolerances add to the problems that many denominations are now facing. More importantly, these attitudes prevent the church from maintaining any resemblance to the church of Jesus Christ. There are multitude of ways that these attitudes continue from age to age, but most public problems that are regularly in the news relate to the sexual abuses committed by Christian clergy. Where do these problems fit into the historic problems, and what are their solutions?

The press and ecclesiastical authorities would like to assert that these abuses arise from a few bad apples. However, the problems, no matter how outrageous or minor, are indications of a deep-seated problem that finds its origins in earliest Christianity in a continuing, characteristic, and pervasive abuse of power and domination. The churches that attempt to isolate the incidents of sexual abuse from the problem of historic hierarchical domination are making scapegoats out of their weakest links. We begin with the present sexual problems of the Christian churches.

Healthy sex, of course, is not exploitative power over another. There is nothing more beautiful than a loving, mutual, sexual relationship among adults. But exploitative, nonmutual sex is ugly. Also, sex is ugly when girls or boys are induced into sexual activity, even if they agree to have sex. It can destroy the whole future life of the child. It often sets up a vicious cycle where the victim as an adult may become a victimizer.[58] Furthermore, sex is ugly when accusations of ugly sex are thrown at individuals or groups without reason.

---

[58] Lloyd deMause, in "Universality of Child Abuse," *The Journal of Psychohistory* 19:2, says, "The pedophile, similar to other perverts, suffers from severe lack of love and fears of individuation in his or her early childhood, and both desires and dreads merging with the mother because of an enormous need to reinstate mother-child unity. Earlier childhood abuse of pedophiles is commonly found. As an adult, the pedophile must have sex with children in order to maintain the illusion of being loved, while at the same time dominating the children as they themselves once experienced domination, repeating actively their own caretaker's sadism."

THE CONSEQUENCES OF DOMINATION

This typically happens when one group of Christians suspect another group of Christians of being sexually intimate without factual knowledge. To go even further, sex is ugly when the hierarchy of any of the Christian churches covers up sexual crimes by moving clergy offenders from place to place, where the old offenses become new ones with new people. Sex is ugly when a clergy person self-righteously and publicly condemns a sexual act when he knowingly, willfully, and secretly commits the same act in private.

All of us are conscious of at least the surface problem. An evangelical candidate for president is found out to have affairs with women and his pious, down-home, Christian image lies shattered on the public domain. A Southern governor from one of the most Christian states is missing from duty because he is with his mistress in Argentina. Ted Haggard, ex-president of the National Association of Evangelicals (30 million members) and pastor of New Life Church, a church of 10,000 members, and a vocal adversary of homosexuality, is found soliciting drugs and sex from men in Denver. Also, the "prosperity" Christian evangelists, Jimmy Swaggart, Jim Bakker, and Earl Paulk, are brought down by sexual indiscretions. The University of Chicago's General Social Survey found that 3 percent of the women it interviewed who attended religious services at least once a month had unsolicited sexual advances from clergy, and 57 percent of these clergy members were married (*Christian Century*, October 20, 2009:14).[59] These 3 percent represent the more overt acts of sexual advances, but an immense valley of flirtations and voyeurism lie underneath which take place in an air of innocence and acceptability.

Those seemingly innocent words and actions which are accepted by all are the slippery slope into the sewers of illicit sex. All this points to the essence of what is an enduring problem for the Christian church. With wisdom, Edmund Burke said in a speech in 1775: "What shadows we are, what shadows we pursue!" The clergy and laity have constantly and grossly misunderstood the power of the sex drive in human beings. In his *The History of Sexuality*, Michel Foucault asserts:

> Sexuality must not be described as a stubborn drive, by nature alien and of necessity disobedient to a power, which exhausts itself trying to subdue it and often fails to control it entirely. It appears

---

[59] General Social Survey, along with Pew Research, has long been rated one of the most accurate surveys.

rather as an especially dense transfer point for relations of power: between men and women, young people and old people, parents and offspring, teachers and students, priests and laity, an administration and a population. Sexuality is not the most intractable element in power relations, but rather one of those endowed with the greatest instrumentality: useful for the greatest number of maneuvers and capable of serving as a point of support, as a linchpin, for the most varied strategies (Foucault 1979/1990, 103).

Sexuality is, then, pervasive and, indeed, unavoidable. People use it to maneuver and manipulate others in the human setting in an immense number of ways and situations which should have nothing to do with power, but actually have everything to do with it—flying in the face of elements in society, even church societies, that try desperately to harness it.

Into this mix, we must mention the huge scandal in the Roman Church related to priests abusing minors. In our analysis of the present problem in the Christian Church, the Roman Church comes first to mind simply because it is historically more closely connected to the early church, where the problem began. The Roman Church is also much larger than any other denomination: it is more monolithic, and, in fact, it is facing a much larger problem.

But the problem certainly does not end with the Catholic Church. Protestant churches have also not dealt with the intricacies of sexuality and power. Similar problems bubble just beneath the surface in these churches as well. These problems may not involve abuse of minors as much, but do involve the inappropriate sexuality between adults. These problems do not usually make the headlines of newspapers, but are carefully handled behind the closed doors of administrative committees. These hidden problems of the Protestant churches could possibly be even more numerous than those of the Roman Catholic Church.

The Problem as It Is Experienced by the Roman Catholic Church:
An Insider's View Of The Problem In The Catholic Church

Richard Sipe, Ph.D., an ex-priest, monk and psychologist, who also lectures in seminaries and medical schools on sexuality and the priesthood, describes the scope of the problem, as he sees it, within the Catholic

THE CONSEQUENCES OF DOMINATION

Church. Sipe has great credibility because he has been on the commission established by the Roman Church to investigate the issue of sexual abuse among priests. In *Sex, Priests, and Power: Anatomy of a Crisis*, his assessment of the scandals is startling and profound:

> ... The scandal of priestly sexual abuse of minors, although real and significant in itself, is primarily a symptom of an essentially flawed celibate/sexual system ... that ... is based on false understanding of the nature of human sexuality and primary Christian experience. Maintenance of the system develops, fosters, and protects sexual abuse and violence. To expose the system is to confront Catholic Christianity with the most profound crisis of its integrity since the earliest centuries of its existence. (Sipe 1995, 4)

In the Catholic Church, many dioceses have come to the brink of bankruptcy because of the litigations caused by the actions of their clergy. The large dioceses of Boston, Philadelphia, Los Angeles, New York, and Milwaukee are just a few of the many dioceses that have paid out millions of dollars to settle cases of abuse. In 2002, for 42 days straight, the *New York Times* had on its front page one story or another about sexual abuse in the Roman Catholic Church (Plante ed. 2004, xvii). In an article from *Theological Studies*, a Roman Catholic journal, Professor David E. DeCosse asserts that the most "authoritative" description of the problem is the report of the United States Conference of Catholic Bishops, "The Nature and Scope of the Problem of Sexual Abuse of Minors by Catholic Priests and Deacons in the United States," prepared by John Jay College of Criminal Justice. In this report, DeCosse established the number of priests accused of sexual abuse between 1950 and 2002 at 4,392 or 4 percent of all priests active during that time. The same study established that 10,667 individuals made allegations of child sexual abuse by priests during the same period.

Denial within the System

Canon Law number 277 states:

> Clerics are obliged to observe perfect and perpetual continence for the sake of the kingdom of heaven and therefore are obliged

to observe celibacy, which is a special gift of God, by which sacred ministers can adhere more easily to Christ with an undivided heart and can more freely dedicate themselves to the service of God and humankind . . . Clerics are to conduct themselves with due prudence in associating with persons whose company could endanger their obligation to observe continence or could cause scandal for the faithful (Sipe 2003, 30).

The problem is that celibacy is thought of as a gift from God, but when the future priest, monk, or friar makes his commitment, he is given little training on how to fulfill that vow. After interviewing members of the clergy, Sipe states:

Priests commonly report, however, that the specific challenges to their sexual identities were not confronted in their education and formation. For many, sex was not dealt with as a lived reality in the seminary. Instead, denial, rationalization, and intellectualization are fostered in the process of seminary training. The real questions surface later in the priests' thirties and even forties (Sipe 2003, 30).

Sipe says that the evidence is overwhelming. One of the authors of this book was a Capuchin Franciscan friar, a priest and director of the novitiate. He is now married with two daughters. His own experience is consistent with Sipe's statement above. He puts it this way:

To this day, I consider the Capuchin Franciscans to be a wise group of men. But celibacy is extremely difficult to teach because sexuality is such an all-present drive, in-bred in us for the preservation of humanity. A teacher of celibacy can only give a few guidelines. Then the student must either find celibacy within himself or not. It is not like teaching someone to play the piano or the violin. No teacher of religious, priestly life is able to teach precisely how another person can be celibate. Sexuality is truly a slippery slope. With all due respect to Church Canon lawyers, it cannot be legislated effectively with a few lines in the canons. So what wise Capuchins told me, and what I told others in the

THE CONSEQUENCES OF DOMINATION

novitiate, was "Just find the celibate you within yourself. You can only possibly find it if you are true to prayer, true to your own brothers, and true to the communities in which you live." It was the best advice that anyone could give another who showed an interest in a celibate life.

In all the books I read of holy persons who excelled in celibacy, rarely is any explanation given regarding how these persons dealt with their own sexuality. They simply "sublimated," "used the strength of the power of their service to God" to take care of their sexual urge. It was, like Canon Law says: do it for the sake of the kingdom of God.

In some, even slight failings made them feel guilty. Some could not meet celibacy's demands and left, and rightfully so. Celibacy is certainly possible. I know that many thrived on it. In the course of history, many found it invigorating. Certainly, the Apostle Paul, Francis of Assisi, Mother Teresa of Calcutta, Father Solanus Casey, who was my own Capuchin brother, whose room I inherited at St. Felix Friary in Huntington, Indiana. Many others exist in our midst. They are made for celibacy, and celibacy is made for them. Others are clearly not made for celibacy, and cave in under its demands. These are strong people, but celibacy makes them emotionally dead inside. For example, I knew one older person in the community, hardened by life therein, whose apparently close friend in the community died. I approached him as human beings do in such a situation to console such a one. But he certainly did not need any consoling. He looked me straight in the eye and said, "Oh well, more cold cuts for the rest of us." That was the end of it. He never showed one stitch of emotion. Such priests and religious will get to heaven someday, and pride themselves before the throne of God, saying, "I have been celibate all of my life." And God will say, "Well, that was not my doing. It must've been your own idea."

From my experience, many religious people and priests struggle with celibacy. But their struggles do not, for the most part, hinder their prayers, their ministry to others, or, for the most part, their own integrity. Some others make arrangements with an adult of the same or the opposite sex, and in secret meet with that person as married couples meet. They, in effect, lay celibacy aside as an unnecessary burden—which it is for them. But they are knowledgeable and dedicated to their ministries. They are excellent pastors and touch the hearts of many. Others do not find a partner, but find it very difficult to be celibate, nonetheless. Others, of course, manipulate others, sometimes young girls and boys, to join them in the sex games and ventures that their imaginations construe. At this point, they destroy themselves, risk destroying other human beings, and often run into problems with the civil, legal system. They also make themselves, their dioceses, and religious communities vulnerable to be sued.

Another personal testimony, which is insightful and poignant, is found in the autobiographical statement of Andrew Sullivan, Ph.D. contributor to *The Atlantic Monthly* and *The New Republic*. Sullivan's perspective is that of a gay man. On his web blog he painfully wrote the following. We are including the whole quote because it is so touching and moving that to break it up would do a disservice to Sullivan and his traumatic experience:

The church teaches first of all that all gay men are "objectively disordered:" deeply sick in their deepest soul and longing for love and intimacy. A young Catholic who finds out he's gay therefore simultaneously finds out that his church regards him as sick and inherently evil, for something he doesn't experience as a choice. That's a distorting and deeply, deeply damaging psychic wound. Young Catholic gay boys, tormented by this seemingly ineradicable sinfulness, often seek religious authority as a way to cope with the despair and loneliness their sexual orientation can create. (Trust me on this; it was my life.) So this self-loathing kid both abstracts himself from sexual relationships with peers, idolizes those "normal" peers he sees as he reaches post-pubescence, and is simultaneously terrified by these desires and so seeks both solace and cover for not getting married by entering the priesthood. None of this is conceivable without the shame and distortion of

THE CONSEQUENCES OF DOMINATION

the closet, or the church's hideously misinformed and distorted view of homosexual orientation. And look at the age at which you are most likely to enter total sexual panic and arrest: exactly the age of the young teens these priests remain attracted to and abused. That's the age when the shame deepens into despair; that's when sexuality is arrested; that's where the psyche gets stunted. In some ways, I suspect, these molesters feel as if they are playing with equals—because emotionally they remain in the early teens. I'm not excusing this in any way; just trying to understand how such evil can be committed. Ask yourself: how many openly gay and adjusted priests have been found to have abused minors? Or ask yourself another question: if straight men were forbidden to marry women, had their sexual and emotional development truncated at the age of 13, and were forced into institutions where they were treated by teenage girls as gods, and given untrammeled, private access to them, how much sexual abuse do you think would occur there? Please. This is not hard to understand.

Things have changed since Mr. Sullivan was in the novitiate. Now the process starts much later—usually in college years. But in reality, according to Sipe and others, many of the young men that enter the novitiate or priesthood are still sexually conflicted, and they find difficulties resolving their inner conflict within the system. It makes little difference if a person's sexuality is truncated at the age of 13 or 18. Many of the young men that enter are still sexually conflicted, and within the system it is difficult to resolve the conflict. As Professor Gerdenio Manuel, a psychologist and Jesuit priest, states:

Regrettably, sexuality in religious and clerical life is considered such a private and personal matter that it is often a painfully awkward topic even in its healthy dimensions. Religious congregations of men and women are still trying to search for ways to talk about healthy sexual development in chaste life. And so, when a religious superior or church authority confronts an alleged offender about sexual misconduct, the topic itself breaks their usual boundaries of "propriety." (Plante 1999, 22–23)

CHRISTIANITY: ENDANGERED OR EXTINCT?

Within this framework, Sipe states three components that create the problem:

> First, denial: "The problem does not exist"; "The problem is not important." The person is presumed to be sexless. Second, secrecy: This is presumed to be necessary for confidentiality and in order to "not give scandal." This seals the problem in the institution and perpetuates the very problem which is supposedly eradicated, but does not go away. Third, immediate forgiveness: Any sexual problem is isolated from developmental and relationship implications . . . The sin is submitted to the confessional with ease, all is forgiven, and the person carries on as though nothing has happened. This keeps at bay any questioning of the validity of the flawed system. (Sipe 2003, 98)

Presently, the Roman Catholic Church is reacting, as it does typically, within the power perspective. It first denies that there is a problem, and then when it is forced to acknowledge that there is a problem, it becomes superreactive and protective of its own self, and it does not care who gets hurt in the process. Part of this noticeable reactive element is intended to ward off any possible further litigation, and as Sipe asserts, threatens to totally undermine the power structure of the church. In this reactive stage, some of the best priests, the most learned and spiritual, are being stuffed away in monasteries and friaries and silenced on mere suspicion and spurious evidence. While a multitude of similar cases are available, one of the authors of this work has personal knowledge of a priest who is a good scholar and a spiritual director to many in his position as director of a retreat center. He was accused by a woman of sexually abusing her 25 years ago when she was a young girl. The woman's own sister said at the hearing that it was not so. She testified: "I was with you every moment of that evening, and it just did not happen." Even in spite of this testimony, the friar was forced to leave his ministry and go to a friary where he was refused permission to minister to anyone. The church was thus protected from another possible litigation, but it lost a great priest. To paraphrase a statement made by Caiaphas, the Jewish high priest, regarding Jesus: "It is better that one person be sacrificed than the whole church be destroyed" (John 11:50). And so the problem continues.

Projection

There have been attempts to blame the problem on the media's anticlericalism and persistent cultural anti-Catholicism. Professor Philip Jenkins wrote in *Pedophiles and Priest: Anatomy of a Contemporary Crisis*:

> From a historical perspective, the contemporary abuse problem is reminiscent of images that have been used to stigmatize priests and religious over the centuries. The idea of the supposedly celibate priest as sexual exploiter can be found throughout the medieval and early modern centuries, and it played a prominent role in the culture and politics of the English-speaking world in the eighteenth and nineteenth centuries. Exploring the cultural roots of the clergy-abuse then requires a survey of lengthy prehistory that includes the intertwined but not necessarily identical themes of anticlerical and anti-Catholic hostility. This is certainly not to assert that modern instances of molestation by clergy are similarly fictitious but that ancient stereotypes contributed to the specific construction of "priest pedophilia" (Jenkins 1996, 20).

While there indeed may be anti-Catholicism in the atmosphere, Jenkins also points out that much of the problem can be placed at the feet of the Roman Catholic Church, for it has often wielded its considerable power to suppress information of abuse (Jenkins 1996, 50–54) and now, put innocent priests on the shelf.

In 1993, Pope John Paul II blamed the problem on the United States, which he characterized as an "irresponsibly permissive" society, one that was "hyper-inflated with sexuality." But this does not explain the problem in other Catholic nations of the world.

The Power Problem in the Historical Church

History does not support the contention that sexual abuse, whether Roman Catholic or Protestant, is only a recent problem. It has been a problem within most of the history of Roman Catholicism, Protestantism, and, of course, Orthodoxy, despite the fact that they allow their clergy to be married. In other Christian churches, we are now skimming just the surface of the problem. The actions of recent abusers are part of a continuum of nearly two millennia of aberrant use of power with sex and the accusations of sex. David Cole, bishop of Christ Church Diocese of the New Zealand Anglican Church, states it most profoundly and most accurately in an article in the 2002 *Ecumenical Review*:

> The truth is that sexual abuse and exploitation of women and children has been taking place in a wide range of churches for centuries. What is new, in Western society at least, is that sexuality is no longer regarded as a private matter, but has become an acceptable subject for public discussion. In the Western churches issues of sexual ethics such as contraception, birth control, abortion, reproductive technologies and sexually transmitted diseases have long been widely discussed in church consultations and meetings. The issue of sexual abuse in the church, however, is only now becoming publicly known and the way this is happening is potentially damaging to the church. (Cole *Ecumenical Review* 2002, 3:228)

Cole then goes on at length to lay the problem of sexual abuse on the problem of faulty theological thinking. He states:

> But we must ask what it is about our current theology of sexuality which leads to such scandalous abusive behaviour in the church. It is hardly surprising that such horrors have happened, when so much of the history of the church is littered with examples of thinking about the human body in negative terms: an approach which sees it as base, sinful, subjugated—a thing to be punished and beaten into submission. (Cole *Ecumenical Review* 2002, 3:231)

While we would be remiss in tracing the roots of this Platonizing or Spiritualizing to the early "church fathers" of Justin Martyr, Irenaeus, and others that we discussed in the early chapters of this volume, it was Augustine who was largely responsible for Roman Catholic understanding of human sexuality. Augustine believed that sexual intercourse was necessary for conception of children but that was the only reason to have sexual intercourse. He believed that Adam and Eve, before the fall, conceived without lust and that a truly spiritual couple would conceive without lust (*vetes libidinosus*). Augustine wrote:

> What friend of wisdom and holy joys, who, being married, but knowing, as the apostle says, "how to possess his vessel in santification and honor, not in the disease of desire, as the Gentiles who know not God," would not prefer, if this were possible, to beget children without this lust, so that in this function of begetting offspring the members created for this purpose should not be stimulated by the heat of lust, but should be actuated by his volition, in the same way as his other members serve him for their respective ends? But even those who delight in this pleasure are not moved to it at their own will, whether they confine themselves to lawful or transgress to unlawful pleasures; but sometimes this lust importunes them in spite of themselves, and sometimes fails them when they desire to feel it, so that though lust rages in the mind, it stirs not in the body. (*City of God*, XIV,16, NPNF 1st Series Volume 2, 275-6. CCEL)

In Augustine's view, then, most properly babies should be conceived *nutu voluntatis acta* or by command of will. Sex for pleasure or enjoyment was lust (*libidinosus*) and definitely against God's will. Today most Roman Catholics recognize Augustine's thinking as not being based on any psychological or biological reality, but that has only been in recent years. Many generations have been raised thinking that enjoying sex was a sin. Such thinking, however, is still playing havoc with Roman Catholics attitudes towards sexuality.

The problem of course, as Michel Foucault explains, goes far deeper and is not simply a matter of passion, but it is, rather of power. We have abundantly pointed out in this volume the early grasp of power by the male disciples of Jesus and the later philosophers, but it was Augustine, again who cemented this control in ecclesiastical thought.

Augustine, like most men in Christian history, did not leave domination within ecclesiastical structures, but cemented it into the very fabric of human relations. From every letter that he wrote to women he communicated domination. Augustine wrote:

> The Apostle has made known to us three unions, Christ and the Church, husband and wife, spirit and flesh. Of these the former has authority over the latter, and the latter must wait for instructions from the former. All things are harmonious when the former have pre-eminence, and the latter are subject, in a becoming manner, to the former. Husband and wife receive commands and pattern how they ought to live with one another by obeying Christ and the Church. The command from scripture is, "Let wives be subject unto their own husbands, as unto the Lord; because the husband is the head of the wife;" and, "Husbands, love your wives." But the Church gives instructions to the wife, and Christ instructs the husbands: "As the Church is subject to Christ, so also wives are subject to their husbands in all things." (Augustine, *On Continence* 23, *NPNF* 3, 369. CCEL)

In short, within Christianity, contrary to Jesus of Nazareth, domination becomes the essence of Christianity: Christ over the Church, husband over the wife, spirit over the flesh. Of course, Christ being the head of the Church and the bishop and the priest being the true knowledge of Christ, the clerics become Christ's surrogates and thus they are the the ones to whom Christians must be subject. The best example for Augustine's spirit over flesh was his thinking on impossible, "lustless" conception. Of course, as we stated, this is totally unrealistic and reveals the true bases of Augustine's thought which is Neo-Platonism.

The basic attitude of subjection, Bishops over priests and Christians, Priests over Christians, and Spirit over flesh, has done immense historical, sociological and psychological damage. Of all the subjections that Augustine taught probably the worst was the subjection of wives to their husbands. While he perpetuated this teaching from his ancient Roman culture, he literally hammered it into stone so that it is taught not only in the Roman, Orthodox and many Protestant churches today. The result of this spiritual repression has resulted in psychological and sociological damage to both men and women. It likewise has justified immense

THE CONSEQUENCES OF DOMINATION

amount of violence inflicted on women, for whenever a woman might protest against a male's repression she could be beaten into submission.

Bishop Cole places an excellent historical perspective on the oppression of women:

> In the seventeenth century, the Anglican theologian Richard Hooker clearly believed the wife was inferior to the husband so he could "rule her lusts and wanton appetites." Richard Hooker claimed that women were . . . alleged to be so constituted as to require guidance, control, and protection. They are intrinsically inferior in excellence, imbecile by sex and nature, weak in body, inconstant in mind, and imperfect and inferior in character.
>
> A whole library of recent literature now offers studies about patriarchy and attitudes toward women, which put such blatant sexist dualism in context. The present alarm in our society about domestic violence, rape, and exploitation of women can only be understood if we are prepared to recognize the total inadequacy (not to mention danger) of such dualistic thinking within the Christian church over many centuries—including the present time. Consider the following examples: . . . The council of Toledo in 400 CE declared "a husband is bound to chastise his wife moderately, unless he be a cleric, in which case he may chastise her harder." By 1782 in England, a judge ruled that "a man could beat his wife if the stick was no thicker than his thumb." Until 1861, it was still legal in England for a man to beat his wife before dusk, after which it might disturb the neighbours (Cole *Ecumenical Review* 2002, 3: 231–2).[60]

Both Coles and Sipe, along with a huge number of other commentators, assert that it is power that is the problem in Christian church history. This is a statement that is difficult to deny, but it is only part of the problem. As we pointed out in the Introduction, the apostles in Acts 6 moved

---

[60] Still today, churches such as the Missouri Synod and Wisconsin Synod Lutheran churches, Southern Baptists, and a whole host of Christian churches continue to preach that women need to be "subject to their husbands." Also, the Roman Catholic Church, as well as the Orthodox churches and many other churches, still do not condone the use of artificial birth control.

from the position of servants, even slaves of their brothers and sisters, to the exulted position of being "servants of the Word." The clergy stepped into positions of respect and authority as masters with their servants. They placed themselves in a position where they must be respected. This essentially describes the beginning of the mentality that has resulted in personalities feeling that it is their right to control and subjugate another person or persons. The situation that confronts the churches today is not a new one. The pride and the arrogance personages like Haggard, Swaggert, Baker, and Paulk, make them models of the total problem in Christian Church history. They believed, as did many others, that God preordained them. Their psychological, sociological makeup and the structures of their Christianity predestined them for the tumbles that they took. They and their churches believed that they were "the exulted servants of the Word." They firmly believed that God Almighty sent them, and because they duped themselves into believing that they knew exactly what God expected, they set themselves on a slippery rock in an alligator pit. They were set up perfectly for the great fall that each of them took.

Hierarchical and male-dominated structures in the churches facilitated exploitation and abuse. As Susan Brownmiller implies in her classic book *Against Our Will: Men, Women and Rape*, sexual power has many faces:

> All rape is an exercise in power, but some rapists have an edge that is more than physical. They operate within an institutionalized setting that works to their advantage in which a victim has little chance to redress her [or his] grievance. Rape in slavery and rape in wartime are two such examples. But rapists may also operate within an emotional setting or within a dependent relationship that provides a hierarchical, authoritarian structure, weakens a victim's resistance, distorts her [or his] perspective and confounds her [or his] will. (Brownmiller, 1975, 256)

Brownmiller published her work long before the massive Christian scandals of the present day had surfaced, though they had existed below the surface for centuries. She implies that the ecclesiastical structure, as well as other authoritative structures, facilitated and continues to facilitate the abuser to abuse.

But the problem is more generic than physical, sexual rape. In fact, all too frequently the hierarchical and male-dominated structures of the denominations have used power arbitrarily to break the spirit of individuals and groups that did not follow the established party line. The church throughout history endorsed abuse of power, whether in declaring persons heretics, in cutting them off from their church families by excommunicating them, or by using other oppressive or self-righteous means, like inquisitions, crusades, or by proclaiming those who do not believe exactly what we believe "heretics of the church." All of these are rape in the broad sense of the word: people exerting power and control over other human beings, destroying their personhood.

Sexual assault and inordinate use of power are two monsters in the closet that are closely related to each other. In most of church history, the church has been not only the authoritarian structure, but also the abuser. The inordinate uses of power, which has occurred and continues to occur in Christian church history by church hierarchical authorities toward their minions, often have the same tone as sexual attacks. As much as the church likes to think of itself as asexual, everything about it reeks of sexuality and power. Many persons besides Sipe have pointed to the underlying sexual connotations in the church's liturgy, architecture, and theology. History is redolent with examples of the inconsistencies of popes complaining about the nude figures in the Sistine Chapel while having affairs with concubines. Sipe gives a multitude of other examples.

Inordinate use of power was, and is, rape in the broad sense: burning the works of a theologian so history could never know what that theologian wrote; ostracizing him or her from the community which he or she served and loved; Tertullian calling the very place where Marcion was born barbaric and strange; churchmen calling sincere Montanist women heretics, when their only fault was not doctrinal at all, but they were simply getting on the nerves of arrogant church authorities; Augustine of Hippo calling the congregation he was preaching to "a bunch of toads," unable to appreciate the sublimity of the great words he preached when the congregation did not even know the Latin language in which he insisted on preaching.

Then after the papacy was solidly established in Rome, inordinate use of power was also rape in the broad sense: inviting John Hus, a sincere

CHRISTIANITY: ENDANGERED OR EXTINCT?

theologian, to Rome to talk, guaranteeing him safe passage, only to burn him at the stake when he got to Rome; stripping and torturing women and girls, men and boys in inquisition tribunals because she or he believed or only possibly believed something different than the perpetrators believed; crusading, killing, and then stealing the homes of the people murdered just because they had sincere but different beliefs; the pope choosing only cardinals and bishops who agreed with his narrow line of thinking, so that they will never challenge his thinking; taking away the pen of a brilliant theologian and sending him to a monastery to do penance for the rest of his life, or sending him into retirement to extremely remote areas where no one could communicate with him; a parish council sending their minister to a psychiatrist, and then sending him packing just because he said things in the pulpit or acted in ways that were not in agreement with their own sense of righteousness. We could go on and on, for all of these and others are factual events in hierarchical Christian church history. You will find many of these events and others described in these volumes. This is rape in the broad sense, sheer acts of power, which are destructive of others. Clearly such church perpetrators are comparable to the perpetrators of sexual assault and rape.

Jesus, certainly, was a person with much different values. While the scholars of the Historical Jesus Seminar have long struggled through layers of text to determine who Jesus was and what he said, the historical record, the perception that Jesus was a compassionate and egalitarian leader seems to stand the test of textual criticism.

The followers of Jesus, soon after Jesus died, continued in the spirit of Jesus. They were so busy helping the poor, the sick, and the homeless that their tasks held them together to do the work at hand. With respect for one another and the people they served, they continued the work of Jesus. Should the popes, cardinals, bishops, priests, ministers, and church councils of history follow in his footsteps? Or must we admit that the very nature of "church hierarchy" was, and is, an aberration from its very inception?

The All-Present Reality of Sexuality

As we have seen in almost every chapter in this volume the persons who demanded the most power and control - such persons as Hippolytus, Justin Martyr, Clement, Athanasius, Ambrose, and Augustine - were

THE CONSEQUENCES OF DOMINATION

"celibate". It would seem that throughout the ages in Roman Catholic Church, the bishops and popes may have been celibate, but their sexuality and their desire for power was never dissipated. They used every ounce of their genetic nature to attack, dominate, and destroy those who disagreed with them. Sipe states:

> I have often heard it said, "Power is the lust of the clergy." The core of the dynamic of the asexual marriage is that, to one degree or another, power replaces adult sexual strivings... Fenichel commented: "Asexuality connotes a lack of personal development, an immaturity characterized by a failure to achieve adequate differentiation of sexual identity. It is observed in many persons who use power to dominate others. The gratification experienced from this asexual model of functioning is in some sense a substitute for mature sexual gratification." (Sipe 2003, 98)

Their failure to recognize and honor its reality has led to an immense amount of mayhem in history. The mentality of the church hierarchy and its members has been influenced by thousands upon thousands of incidences of abuse of power, including cover-ups of sexual exploitations, and uncalled for accusations of sexual advances.

Professor Stephen V. Springle, Ph.D., Brite Theological Seminary, a Foucauldian scholar, in an article in *Journal of Religious Leadership*, satirically and painfully wrote what may be the thesis of this book:

> Thanks to the work of Michel Foucault (1926–1984), we know that Christianity arose as a sweeping critique of the culture of desire of our ancestors, the Greeks and Romans. In place of this older edifice and its erotic structures, the Church built a new structure of ascetic self-denial. This was all done, of course, under the warrant given the church by the first fruits of a new creation, Jesus Christ. Yet the cupid vendors were not put out of business by any means. They simply shifted their social location, from the pagan empire to the new Christian empire... Instead of creating leadership on the model of the grand new experiments of the primitive Pauline and Lukan congregations, by the time of the pastoral epistles, the comfortable hierarchy and patriarchy of the empire had

CHRISTIANITY: ENDANGERED OR EXTINCT?

supplanted innovative strategies of community... The Holy Spirit, like a chicken, was cooped by the vendors of control. (Springle, 2007, 75–103)

This is, in our estimation, one of the best and precise descriptions of church history. This volume just fills in the details, as will further volumes of *Christianity: Endangered or Extinct? A Peoples History of Christianity.*

The scandal which the Christian church is facing today with clergy who are accused, charged with, and convicted of nonmutual adult sex, child molestation, and especially their cover-ups, is partially indicative of a greater problem of hierarchical dominance within authoritarian structures, which, at times, includes the added element of total male dominance. Jesus would look askance at the whole structure of the Christian church as it has developed and its total unhealthy understanding of sexuality.

The History of Sexual Abuse within the Church

Foucault states that every attempt at the elimination of sexuality is doomed to failure (Foucault 1990, 1978, I, 41), and church history proves him right. As much as the church fathers tried to repress sexuality, it kept reappearing in a multitude of different forms. This is apparent from the fact that sexual problems consume an inordinate amount of even the church fathers' thoughts. A few examples are in order.

Sipe points out that in one of the earliest councils that was held in Elvira in 304–305, 38 of 81 canons dealt with sex. He further illustrates the hypocrisy of the Roman Catholic Church in that Pope Julius III, who presided over the reforming Council of Trent (1552–1554), had picked up a 15-year-old boy from the streets of Parma, sexually cohabited with him, and then appointed him bishop. According to Sipe, the philosopher Jean-Jacques Rousseau complained to priests that he was sexually molested, and they told him that they likewise were, but he should be silent about it because it would embarrass the community of priests to which they belonged (Sipe 1995, 10).

We would further add to Sipe's list that at the all-important Council of Nicaea (325), where the Nicene Creed was formulated, three of the 20 canons covered sexual matters. Peter Damian (ca 1007–1072), a pious monk from Ravenna, Italy, was horrified at the rampant homosexuality among the clergy

THE CONSEQUENCES OF DOMINATION

and the monks in the monasteries. He wrote (ca 1050) to Pope Leo a scathing report detailing the immorality. The work was called the *Book of Gomorrah* (as in Sodom and Gomorrah). Pope Leo thanked him for the report and then promptly ignored it. Peter Damian was not the only person who complained of the sexual misconduct of the clergy. It seems that in almost every century this was the constant complaint of reforming clergy and the laity. Likewise this was one of the major complaints that led to the Reformation.

One poignant, but often overlooked fact in history is that when Luther returned to Wittenberg from his imprisonment in Wartburg in 1523 to his Augustinian monastery, he found the monastery almost deserted. Only two nuns remained. All the monks, led by Andreas Carlstadt, had deserted the monastery and married Augustinian nuns. (So much for these monks' vows of chastity!) See forthcoming Volume III of *Christianity: Endangered or Extinct? A People's History of Christianity*.

Furthermore, if there is one organization which at least verbally offers healing solutions to people, it is the church. In their churches, young persons who are raised in a religious setting are bound to hear the message about love and believe that it is the solution to the world's problems. But complicating this problem is the fact that this message is most frequently delivered by an authority figure, a clergy person, who indeed sets the model. In many, if not most, cases, he or she is a kindly person, a person of power, who even in congregational churches, is looked up to as a person who gives direction. In many churches, the person wears robes and vestments, which add to his or her authoritative stature. He or she may be called "reverend" or "pastor," or some other name that separates him or her and adds to his or her stature. Within the Roman and Orthodox Church, there is another element which adds to the authority and power of the priest. This element is the celebration of the Mass. The priest is endowed with the power to raise the bread and wine and through the words of institution, make them the body and blood of Jesus.

It is important to take a look at another of Sipe's comments. He sees that the very uncovering of the sexual abuse cases is a threat to the very power structure of the Roman Church:

> When one begins to grasp the implications of priest sexual abuse—that it is a symptom of a failed system of power and

inadequate sexual doctrine—one can understand the confusion and fright of church leaders. The very structure of their existence is disintegrating. The more they analyze the symptoms, the more clearly the diseased function and structure of the system become apparent. Instinctively, some bishops know that they are witnesses to the demise of the celibate/sexual system of power (Sipe 1995, 42).

The problem is that moderns of the twenty-first century, as their ancestors in the 20 centuries previous, have not come to grips with how connected sex and power have become. The power structures wish so intensely to control it, but it cannot do so. Michel Foucault (1938–1984), in *The History of Sexuality*, connects the dots:

> We, on the other hand, are in a society of "sex," or rather a society "with a sexuality": the mechanisms of power are addressed to the body, to life, to what causes it to proliferate, to what reinforces the species, its stamina, its ability to dominate, or its capacity for being used . . . Through the themes of health, progeny, race, the future of the species, the vitality of the social body, power spoke of sexuality and to sexuality; the latter was not a mark or a symbol, it was an object and a target. Moreover, its importance was due less to its rarity or its precariousness than to its insistence, its insidious presence, the fact that it was everywhere an object of excitement and fear at the same time. Power delineated it, aroused it, and employed it as the proliferating meaning that had always to be taken control of again lest it escape; it was an effect with a meaning-value. (Foucault 1990, 147–48)

Foucault shows that because power constantly pursues sex, it has become impossible to separate them, even when it is feared, or "fought with," or "ignored" as in celibacy.

Foucault states that while sexuality is intricately involved with power, it is, as all human endeavors, part of a complex netlike organization with a multitude of points of contact, action, interaction, and discourses. Within Foucault's methodology there is the assumption that in all human discourses, not only sexual, there are multi-levels of understanding, so that what we say and what we mean may have secondary, and even tertiary meanings. But of all communications among humans, the sex drive is one of the most slippery. Sexual power, itself, is not the villain, but rather, the villain is the misuse of that power. Sexual power can be used for the attraction of individuals, for the propagation of the species, for the enjoyment of individuals. It can be shared in a mutual loving relationship. At the same time, it can be used, and it has been used, for human degradation. It can also be used, even unwittingly and without intentional malice, merely to show the power of one's spiritual largesse, the power of one's charm, to satisfy one's own sexual drives at the expense of another or others, or to show, purely and simply, that a person is more powerful than another. .

The Answer of Jesus—Be a Servant: Paulo Friere

The problem in theology and in historical analysis is that Christians have a limited vision and do not see the multi-levels of their own drives, their own faith, and individual beliefs. While this volume deals with many of these issues, one of the simplest ways to grasp the conundrum of our limited visions is by comprehending Jesus' vision of servanthood. Christians speak about being servants. They hear it in homilies and sermons, but most of the time, these words about servanthood are laced with authoritarian and hierarchical overtones. One of the best passages to perceive the discrepancies between the thinking of Jesus and that of many Christians is found in Matthew 20:25–28)

> Jesus . . . said, "You know that the rulers of the Gentiles lord it over them, and their high officials exercise authority over them. Not so with you. Instead, whoever wants to become great among you must be your servant, and whoever wants to be first must be your slave—just as the Son of Man did not come to be served, but to serve, and to give his life as a ransom for many."

For the average Christian, "servanthood" means giving money, food, and housing for "the less fortunate." For the clergy, it means teachings which empowers the congregation; visiting the sick; comforting the mourning; etc. While all these might be beneficial, they still fall short of what Jesus meant by being a servant. These attitudes may, indeed, come from a hierarchical, elite position of helping the poor, the downtrodden, and the inferior. Our education as clergy, professors, professionals, etc., from the first world makes it particularly difficult to understand what the first-century Jesus meant. We believe the best way to understand it is from the eyes of a person who was deeply entrenched in the third world. While there are many avenues into this world, particularly from liberation theology, we choose to enter it through Paulo Freire (1921–1997), who lived through poverty and was imprisoned in Brazil but became a well educated lawyer, educator, and finally, Brazil's director of education. Freire challenges all hierarchical or elite approaches to assisting or serving the poor.

In *Pedagogy of the Oppressed*, Freire writes:

> We have a strong tendency to affirm that what is different from us is inferior. We start from the belief that our way of being is not only good but better than that of others who are different from us. This is intolerance. It is the irresistible preference to reject differences. The dominant class, then . . . does not intend that those who are different shall be equal. What it wants is to maintain the differences and keep its distance and to recognize and emphasize in practice the inferiority of those who are dominated. (Freire 1993, 71–72)

Too frequently in church history and in today's church, the hierarchy tells the laity what to believe, what to do, and what to feel. In today's society and in today's church, attitudes might seem to have changed, but they have not. We speak of enabling or empowering the laity. But this is strictly vocabulary. It still implies a power-down relationship of the enlightened helping the unenlightened. Freire is emphatic on this point: "Leaders who do not act dialogically, but insist on imposing their decisions, do not organize the people—they manipulate them" (Freire 1993, 76). One could say that the essence of most preaching today is manipulation.

Freire goes on to say that attempting to liberate the oppressed without their reflective participation in the act is to treat them as objects that must

THE CONSEQUENCES OF DOMINATION

be saved from a burning building. Indeed, Freire's methodology comes close to Jesus' model of leadership: the leader helps the group to discern their concerns, and then helps them find the resources to deal with those concerns and allows them to come to their own conclusions.

While we would be hard pressed to find such thinking as Freire's in all of recorded history, we should not conclude that it has not existed. We began this volume with a quote from author, Kate Mosse, "History is written by the victorious, the liars, the strongest, and the most determined. Truth is found most often in the silence, in the quiet places." We think everything in this volume has supported that statement. However, we have well documented that as much as the power establishment has tried to suppress the truth, there is always indications in the text or under service of the establishments claims, in archeological, sociological, anthropological and economical evidence that what the "orthodox" establishment claims is not necessarily reality. We think we have documented well the fact that the Jesus Movement continued, albeit in fringe groups that the "orthodox" called heretical, long after Athanasius, Ambrose and Augustine established Catholicism as the religion of the Empire. In future volumes of *Christianity: Endangered or Extinct? A People's History of Christianity*, we will attest to the fact that Catholic thinking, theology, and performance became increasingly more hierarchical, repressive, and violent. There is no way this sordid history of the Catholic Church or as we think it should be called the religion of Augustinian Constantinianism has any relationship to the life and teachings of Jesus of Nazareth. The movement founded by Jesus was and still is the most revolutionary movement in human history. It was founded in love. Jesus called his followers to love God, each other, their neighbors, and their enemies. They were called to live simply. They were called to share their earthly possessions with the poor and one another. They were called to be servants who wash each other's dirty feet and wait on tables.

When Jesus insisted that the disciples hand out the loaves and the fishes, getting the bread and fish into the people's mouths was not his only desire. He was intent on bringing the disciples in touch with the people in order that the disciples might listen to them and experience their feelings, their thoughts, and their lives.

In this day of environmental catastrophes, decreasing resources, and

CHRISTIANITY: ENDANGERED OR EXTINCT?

increasing national and ethnic hostilities, we believe it is time that the world hears the gospel, the good news of salvation for the planet and all people without all the pious platitudes of pompous people. We will continue in the future volumes to unmask the pretensions of Augustinian Constantinianism and to find those lights that in their own way were faithful to Jesus of Nazareth.

Primary Documents

Unless other wise noted all biblical citations are from the New International Version (NIV).

New English Bible (NEB).

Christian Classics Ethereal Network, *Church Fathers,* Public Domain, www.ccel.org. Cited: CCEL

    Coxe, A. Cleveland. *A Select Library of Ante-Nicene Fathers;* Volume 1–10. Peabody, MA: Hendrickson, 1887. Cited: *ANF* CCEL

    Schaff, Philip. *A Select Library of Nicene and Post-Nicene Fathers of the Christian Church.* 1st Series; Volume 1–14. Peabody, MA: Hendrickson, 1886. Cited: *NPNF* 1st Series, CCEL.

    Schaff, Philip, Henry Wace. *A Select Library of Nicene and Post-Nicene Fathers of the Christian Church.* 2nd Series; Volume 1–14, 1890. Cited: NPNF 2nd Series

Corpus Scriptorum Ecclesiasticorum Latorium. Carolus Halm 1866. Cited *CSEL.*

Ambrose,
    NPNF 2nd Series; Volume 10.
        Concerning the Basilica.
        Concerning the Faith
        Concerning Virgins.
        Epistles:
        To Emperor Theodosius.
        To Simplicianus.
        To Pope Siricius.
    Epistula ad Augustus Theodosius XL, *CSEL* 72
    De fide ad Gratianum Augustum, CSEL 78.

Ammianus Marcellinus, *Rerum Getarum Libri (The Book of Deeds),* ed. J. C. Rolfe, London 1935/40

Apocalypse of John, ca 90.

Apocalypse of Peter, ca 100–150 CE.
Apollonius, Apostle of Eusebius H. E., ca 300 CE.
Aristides, *Apology*, ANF 9.
Athanasius, *De Decretis* NPNF 2nd Series, 4.
Augustine of Hippo.
    De Civitate Dei, CSEL, 40. *The City of God, NPNF* 1st Series, 2.
    Confessiones, *CSEL* ; Vol. 33. *The Confessions, NPNF* 1st Series, 1.
    De Consensu Evangelistarum, CSEL, 43. *Harmony of the Gospels, NPNF* 1st Series, 6.
    De Sermone Domini in monte secundum Matthaeum, CSEL, 35.
    Epistula 100 Vol. 34.
    Epistula 130, CSEL Vol. 44.
    In Joannes Evangelium Tractatus, Patrologiae Cursus Completus Latina Vol. 34, *Tractates on the Gospel of John, NPNF* 1st Series, 7.
    In Epistalum Joannes ad Parthos Tractatus,Evangelium Tractatus, Patrologiae Cursus Completus Latina, 35. *Tractates on the Epistles of John, NPNF* 1st Series, 7.
Cyprian, *On the Unity of the Church*, ANF, 6, ca 248–258 CE.
    The Didache: Faith, Hope, & Life of the Earliest Christian Communities, 50–70 C.E., Aaron Milavec. New York/Mahwah, NJ: The Newman Press, 2003.
Epiphanius, *The Panarion of Epiphanius of Salamis*, Book 1 (Sects 1–46), trans. Frank Williams. Leiden: Brill, 2009.
Epistle of Barnabas, ANF, 1.
Eusebius, *History of the Church, NPNF,* 2nd series, 1. Life of Constantine,, *NPNF,* 2nd series, 1
Hippolytus, *Refutation of All Heresies*, ANF, 5.
Irenaeus, *Against Heresies*, ANF, 1.
Jerome, *Epistula* LXXII.4 CSEL 34. Letter XLV, *NPNF*, 2nd Series, 6
    Lives of Illustrious Men, NPNF 2nd Series, 3
Justin Martyr, *The First Apology, ANF*, 1.
    Dialogue with Trypho, ANF 1.
    Hortatory Address to the Greeks.
Marcion, *Antithesis* (First Paragraph).
Odes to Solomon, The Other Bible. Edited by Willis Barnstone. San Francisco, CA: HarperSanFrancisco, 1984.

Plato, *Phaedrus*, trans. Benjamin Jowett, *Great Books of the Western World*, 10. Chicago: *Encyclopaedia of Britannica*, 1952.

Pliny. the Younger, *Letters/Pliny*; with an English translation by William Melmoth; revised by W. M. L. Hutchinson, 2 volumes. *Loeb Classical Library*; Volumes 55 & 59. London. W. Heinemann; Cambridge, Mass.: Harvard University Press, 1961–1963.

Plotinus. *The Six Enneads*, tr. by Stephen MacKenna and B. S. Page. *Great Books of the Western World*, 17. Chicago: *Encyclopaedia of Britannica*, 1952.

Scholasticus, Socrates. *The Ecclesiastical History. NPNF,* 2nd Series, 2.

The Seven Ecumenical Councils, *NPNF*, 2nd Series, 14.

The Shepherd of Hermas, ANF 2.

Sozomenus, Salaminius. *The Ecclesiastical History. NPNF*, 2nd Series, 2.

Tertullian, c.160-c. 220, Latin Texts derived from Roger Pearse's Tertullian Project, English from *ANF* 3 & 4.

Adversus Marcionem, I–V, 207–208 CE. *Against Marcion*.

Adversus Valentinianos (Against Valentinian).

Apologeticum, (Apology).

De Carne Christi (Concerning the Body of Christ).

De ieiunio adversus Psychicos

De Prescriptione Hæreticorum (Concerning the Rule of Heretics).

Adversus Praxean (Against Praxeas), ca 197–218 CE.

De Anima (Concerning the Soul), ca 206–218 CE.

De Virginibus Velandis (Concerning the Virgin), ca 206–218 CE.

De Pudicitia (Concerning Modesty), ca 197–205 CE.

Emperor Theodosius I, 346-395. *Imperatoris Theodosii Codex in liber sextus decimus, Theodosian Law Code*, trans. Lewis Ayres (2004) in Nicaea and Its Legacy: *An Approach to Fourth-Century Trinitarian Theology*. Oxford: Oxford University Press.

Secondary Documents

Anderson, Bernhard A. *The Old Testament and Christian Faith: A Theological Discussion*. San Francisco: Harper and Row, 1963.

Arendt, Hannah. *Love and Saint Augustine*. Chicago: The University of Chicago Press, 1996.

Arnal, William. "Doxa, Heresy, and Self-Construction" in *Heresy and Identity in Late Antiquity*, edited by Eduard Iricinschi, and Holger M. Zellentin. Tübingen, Germany: Mohr Siebeck, 1988.

Aune, David. *Prophecy in Early Christianity and the Ancient Mediterranean World.* Grand Rapids, Michigan: William B. Eerdmans, 1983, 1996.

Barnes, Timothy 1971. *Tertullian: A Historical and Literary Study.* Oxford: Clarendon Press. 1993.Athanasius and Constantius: Theology and Politics in the Constantinian Empire. Cambridge, MA: Harvard Press.

Bauer, Walter 1877, 1960. *Orthodoxy and Heresy in Earliest Christianity,* translated by a team from the Philadelphia Seminar on Christian Origins, and edited by Robert A Kraft and Gerhard Kroedl. Philadelphia: Fortress Press.

Blackman, E. C. 1948. *Marcion and His Influence.* London: SPCK.

Blackwell, Basil 1965. *Martyrdom and Persecution in the Early Church: A Study of a Conflict from the Maccabees to Donatus.* Oxford: Oxford University Press.

Bonhoeffer, Dietrich1927, 2010. *Communio Sanctorum*, Volume 9, *The Works of Dietrich Bonhoeffer*, Ferdinand Schlingensiepen, and Isabel Best, eds. trs. Edinburgh: T & T Clark.

Bourdieu, Pierre1972, 1977. "Doxa, Heresy, and Self-Construction in Heresy and Identity in Late Antiquity," in *Heresy and Identity in Late Antiquity*, ed. by Eduard Iricinschi and Holger M. Zellentin. Tubingen, Germany, Mohr Siebeck.

Bowe, Barbara Ellen 1988. *A Church in Crisis: Ecclesiology and Paranaesis in Clement of Rome.* Minneapolis, MN: Fortress Press.

Boyarin, Daniel 2001. "Justin Martyr Invents Judaism." *Church History* 70 (3).

Brown, Peter 1978. *Augustine of Hippo.* Berkley, CA: The University of California.

1967, 2000. *The Making of Late Antiquity.* Cambridge, MA: Harvard University Press.

Brown, Raymond E. 1993. *The Birth of the Messiah: A Commentary on the Infancy Narratives in the Gospels of Matthew and Luke.* Revised edition. New York, Doubleday,.

Brownmiller, Susan 1975. *Against Our Will: Men, Women and Rape.* New York: Simon and Schuster.

Burns, J. Patout Jr. 2002. *Cyprian, the Bishop*. London: Routledge.
Burrus, Virginia 2000. *"Begotten Not Made": Conceiving Manhood in Late Antiquity*. Stanford California: Stanford University Press.
Bruce, F. F. 1988. *The Canon of Scripture*. Downers Grove, IL: InterVarsity Press.
Butler, Rex D 2006. The New Prophecy & "New Visions": Evidence of Montanism in The Passion of Perpetua and Felicitias. Washington, DC: Catholic University of America Press.
Cameron, Averil 1991. *Christianity and the Rhetoric of Empire: The Development of Christian Discourse*. Berkeley, CA: University of California Press.
Carrington, Philip. *The Early Christian Church*, vol. 2. Cambridge: Cambridge University Press, 1957.
Carroll, James. 2001. *Constantine's Sword: The Church and the Jews*. New York: Houghton, Mifflin, & Harcourt.
Catholic Encyclopedia. (www.advent.org.)
Chadwick, Henry 2001. *The Church in Ancient Society: From Galilee to Gregory the Great*. Oxford: Oxford University Press.
Chauvet, Louis-Marie 1997. *The Sacraments: The Word of God at the Mercy of the Body*. Collegeville: Liturgical Press.
Clabeaux, John James 1989. *A lost edition of the Letters of Paul: A reassessment of the text of the Pauline corpus attested by Marcion*. Washington, DC: Catholic Biblical Association of America.
Clark, Elizabeth A. 1999. *Rising Renunciation: Asceticism and Scripture in Early Christianity*. Princeton University Press.
Cohn, Norman 1970. *The Pursuit of the Millenium: Revolutionary Millenarians and Mystical Anarchists of the Middle Ages*. 3rd ed. Oxford: Oxford University Press.
Cole, David 2002. "Reclaiming the Sacredness and the Beauty of the Body: The Sexual Abuse of Women and Children from a Church Leader's Perspective." *Ecumenical Review* 54 (3): 228–34.
Cragun, Rodger L.1996. *The Ultimate Heresy: The Doctrine of Biblical Inerrancy*. Two Harbors, MN: Boreal Lights.
Crook, Zeba 2009. "Honor, Shame, and Social Status Revisited." *Journal of Biblical Literature* 128 (3): 591–611.

Cross, F. L. 1932. *The Early Christian Fathers*. London: Gerald Duckworth and Company.

de Mause, Lloyd 1991. "The Universality of Incest." *The Journal of Psychohistory*. Fall, Vol. 19 (2). 1998 "The History of Child Abuse." *The Journal of Psychohistory*. 25 (3).

De Soyres, John 1868, 1965. *Montanism and the Primitive Church*. Cambridge, Deighton and Bell and Co.; Lexington, Kentucky: The American Theological Library Association, Reprint.

Dunn, Geoffrey D. 2004. *Tertullian*. New York: Rutledge, Taylor and Francis Group.

Eck, Werner 1999. "The Bar Kokhkba Revolt: The Roman Point of View." *The Journal of Roman Studies*, 76–89.

Ehrman, Bart D. 2003. *The Orthodox Corruption of Scripture*. Oxford: Oxford University Press. 1993. *Lost Christianities: The Battle for Scripture and the Faiths We Never Knew*. Oxford: Oxford University Press.

Elliott, T. G.1996. *The Christianity of Constantine the Great*. Scranton, PA.: University of Scranton Press.

Esler, Philip F. ed. . 1995. *Modeling Early Christianity: Social-Scientific Studies of the New Testament in Its Context*. London: Routledge.

Fiorenza, Elizabeth Schüssler 1981. *In Memory of Her: A Feminist Theological Reconstruction of Christianity*. Crossroads Publishing Company.

1997. "Jesus and the Politics of Interpretation." *Harvard Theological Review*

Fitzgerald, Allen D. 1999, et al. *Augustine through the Ages: An Encyclopedia*. Grand Rapids, Michigan: William B. Eerdmans Publishing Company.

Fitzmeyer, Joseph. *The Gospel according to Luke (I–IX)*. Garden City, New York: Doubleday, 1981.

Foucault, Michel 1972. *The Essential Works of Foucault, 1954–1984*. New York: New Press,.

2006a. Vol. 1, *Ethics, Subjectivity and Truth*.

2006b. Vol. 2, *Aesthetics, Method and Epistemology*.

2003. Vol. 3, *Power*.

1979/1990. *The History of Sexuality*, translated by Robert Hurley. New York: Vintage Books.

Friezen, Stephen 2001. *Imperial Cults and the Apocalypse of John: Reading Renunciation in the Ruins.* Oxford: Oxford University Press.

Frend, W. H. C. 1965. *Martyrdom and Persecution in the Early Church: A Study of a Conflict* from the Maccabees to Donatus. London: Oxford: Basil Blackwell.

1971. *The Donatist Church: A Movement in Protest in Roman North Africa.* London: Oxford University Press.

1984. *The Rise of Christianity.* Philadelphia, PA: Fortress Press.

Gibson, Elsa 1978. *Montanus, Priscilla, and Maximilla. The "Christians for Christians" Inscriptions of Phrygia.* Missoula, Montana: Scholars Press.

Gillman, Ian, and Hans-Joachim Klimkett 1999. *Christians in Asia before 1500.* Ann Arbor: University of Michigan Press.

Glover, T. R. Tr. *Tertullian: Apology De Spectaculis* with an English Translation. London: William Heinemann, Ltd., 1931.

Grant, Robert McQueen 1957. *Second Century Christianity, a Collection of Fragments.* London: SPCK.

1970. *Augustus to Constantine: The Emergence of Christianity in the Roman World.* San Francisco: Harper Collins Inc.

Gregg, Robert E., and Dennis E. Groh. *Early Arianism: A View of Salvation.* Philadelphia: Fortress Press, 1981.

Hahneman, Geoffrey Mark. *The Muratorian Fragment and the Development of the Canon Book.* Oxford: Oxford University Press, 1992.

Hanson, R. P. C. *In Search of the Christian Doctrine of God: The Arian Controversy,* 318–381. Grand Rapids, Michigan: Baker, 1988.

Harnack, Adolph von 1921, 1990. *Marcion: The Gospel of the Alien God. Marcion, Das Evangelium vom fremden Gott,* Leipzig, Hinrichs, 1921, translated by John E. Steely and Lyle D. Bierma. Durham, North Carolina: Labyrinth Press.

1900, 1976. *History of Dogma. Lehrbuch der Dogmengeschichte,* 1886, 1900, 1912, 1920, tr. Neil Buchanan. Gloucester, MA: P. Smith. .

Harrison, J. R. 2004. "In Quest of the Third Heaven." *Vigiliae Christianae,* 58.

Hill, Charles 1999. "The Epistola Apostolorum: an Asian Text from the Time of Polycarp." *The Journal of Early Christian Studies,* VII, 1, p. 20 ff.

Hoffman, R. Joseph 1984. *Marcion: On the Restitution of Christianity.* Chico, CA: Scholars Press.

Hollerich, Michael 1990. "Religion and Politics: Reassessing the First Court Theology." *Church History*, 59.

Hood, Kathryn E. 1996. "Intractable Tangles of Sex and Gender in Women's Aggressive Development: An Optimistic View," 310–35 in *Aggression and Violence: Genetic, Neurobiological, and Biosocial Perspectives*, David M. Stoff and Robert B. Cairns, editors. Mahwah, NJ: Lawrence Erlbaum Associates.

Iricinschi, Eduard, and Holger M. Zellentin, editors. "Making Selves and Marking Others: Identity and Late Antiquity Heresiologies," in *Heresy and Identity in Late Antiquity*. Tübingen, Germany: Mohr Siebeck, 2008.

Jeffer, James. *Conflict at Rome: Social Order and Hierarchy in Early Christianity.* Minneapolis, MN: Fortress Press, 1991.

Jenkins, Philip. *Anatomy of a Contemporary Crisis.* New York: Oxford University Press, 1996.

Jones, A. H. M.1963. "The Social Background of the Struggle between Paganism and Christianity," in *The Conflict between Paganism and Christianity in the Fourth Century*, essays ed. by A. Momigliano. Oxford: Claredon Press.

Kahlos, Maijastina 1997. "Vettius Agorius Praetextatus and the Rivalry between the Bishops in Rome in 366–367," in ARCTOS 31: 41–54.

Kearsley, Roy1998. *Tertullian's Theology of Divine Power.* Edinburgh, Scotland: Rutherford House.

King, Karen 2003. *What Is Gnosticism?* Cambridge, MA: Belnap Press of the Harvard University.

Klinghardt, Matthias 2008. "The Marcionite Gospel and the Synoptic Problem: A New Suggestion." *Novum Testamentum* 50.

Knox, John. *Marcion and the New Testament: an Essay in the Early History of the Canon.* Chicago: University of Chicago Press, 1942.

Knust, Jennifer Wright. *Abandoned to Lust: Sexual Slander in Ancient Christianity.* New York: Columbia University Press, 2006.

Lampe, Peter. *From Paul to Valentinus: Christians at Rome in the First Two Centuries.* Translator, Michael Steinhauser; editor, Marshall D. Johnson. Minneapolis, Minnesota: Fortress Press, 2003.

MacMullen, Ramsey 1997. *Christianity and Paganism in the Fourth to the Eighth Centuries*. New Haven, Connecticut: Yale University Press.

Madigan, Kevin 2003. "Christus Nesciens? Was Christ Ignorant of the Day of Judgment? Arian and Orthodox Interpretation of Mark 13:32 in the Ancient Latin West." *Harvard Theological Review* 96 (3).

Malina, Bruce J. 1995. *On the Genre and Message of Revelation: Star Visions and Sky Journeys*. Peabody, MA: Hendrickson Publishers.

and Richard Rohrbaugh 1998. *The Social and Scientific Study of John*. Minneapolis, MN: Fortress Press.

and Richard Rohrbaugh 2003. *The Social Scientific Commentary on the Synoptic Gospels*. Minneapolis, MN: Fortress Press.

Markus, Robert A. *The End of Ancient Christianity*. Cambridge: Cambridge University Press, 1990.

McGinn-Moorer, Sheila 1997. "The Montanist Oracles and Prophetic Theology." *Studia Patristica*, Vol. XXXI.

1989. "The New Prophecy of Asia Minor and the Rise of Ecclesiastical Patriarchy in Second Century Pauline Traditions," Ph.D. Dissertation, Northwestern University.

McLynn, Neil. *Ambrose of Milan: Church and Court in a Christian Capital*. Berkley, CA: University of California Press, 1994.

Metzger, Bruce 1992. *The Text of the New Testament: Its Transmission, Corruption and Restoration*. Oxford: Oxford University Press, 1964, 1968, 1992.

Meyendorff, John. *Imperial Unity and Church Divisions: The Church 450–680 A.D.* Crestwood, NY: St. Valdimir's Seminary Press, 1989.

Miller, Alice. *For Your Own Good: Hidden Cruelty in Child-Rearing and the Roots of Violence*, translated by Hildegard and Hunter Hannum. New York: Farrar-Straus-Giroux, 2002.

Moll, Sebastian . 2010.. *The Arch-Heretic*. Tubingen: Mohr Siebeck.

Moorhead, John. *Ambrose: Church and Society in the Late Roman World*. London and New York: Pearson Education, Ltd., 1999.

Morino, Claudio. *Church and State in the Teaching of St. Ambrose*, Translation of *Chiesa e stato nella doctrina di S. Ambroglio*. Berkley: University of California Press, 1969.

Moyer, Elgin S. *Who Was Who in Church History*. Chicago: Moody Press, 1968.

Nygren, Anders. *Agape and Eros.* Philadelphia: The Westminster Press, 1953.

O'Connell, Robert J. *Soundings in Augustine's Imagination.* New York: Fordham University Press, 1994.

O'Donnell, James J. *Augustine: A New Biography.* New York: HarperCollins Publishers, Inc., 2005.

Osborne, Kenan, O. F. M 1999. *Christian Sacraments in a Postmodern World.* Mahwah, NJ: Paulist Press,.

Osiek, Carolyn 1983. *Rich and Poor in the Shepherd of Hermas: An Exegetical-Social Investigation.* Washington, DC: The Catholic Biblical Association of America

1999. *The Shepherd of Hermas.* Minneapolis, MN: Augsburg Press.

Petrement, Simone 1984. *The Separate God: The Christian Origins of Gnosticism,* translated by Carol Harrison. San Francisco: HarperSanFrancisco,.

Plante, Thomas G., ed. 1999. *Bless Me Father for I Have Sinned: Perspectives on Sexual Abuse Committed by Roman Catholic Priests.* Westport: Praeger.

Rainy, Robert D. D. 1902. *The Ancient Catholic Church: From the Accession of Trajan to the Fourth General Council* (A.D. 98–451). New York: Charles Scribner's Sons.

Rankin, David 1995. *The Secondary Role of the End Time in Montanist Doctrine.* Cambridge University Press.

1995b. *Tertullian and the Church.* New York: Cambridge University Press.

Robeck, Cecil M. Jr. *Prophecy in Carthage: Perpetua, Tertullian, and Cyprian.* Cleveland, Ohio: The Pilgrim Press, 1992.

Rohrbacker, David 2002. *Historians of Late Antiquity.* London: Routledge.

Salzman, Michele 2002. *The Making of a Christian Aristocracy.* Cambridge, MA: Harvard University Press.

Ste. Croix, G. E. M. de 1981. *The Class Struggle in the Ancient Greek World.* Ithaca, NY: Cornell University Press.

Scott, T. Kermit 1995. *Augustine: His Thought in Context.* Mahwah, NJ: Paulist Press.

Segal, Alan F. 2002. *Two Powers in Heaven: Early Rabbinic Reports about Christianity and Gnosticism.* Netherlands, E. J. Brill.

Selvidge, Marla 1990. *Women, Cult, and Miracle Recital: A Redactional Critical Investigation on Mark 5:24–34*. Lewisburg NJ: Bucknell University Press.

Sherrat, B. "Montanism," in *Pentecostal,* Vol. 1 (1:27).

Sider, Robert Dick. *Ancient Rhetoric and the Art of Tertullian.* Oxford: Oxford University Press, 1931.

Swete, Henry Barclay 1912, 1966. *The Holy Spirit in the Ancient Church: A Study of Christian Teaching in the Age of the Fathers.* Grand Rapids, Michigan: Baker Book House.

Rainy, Robert D. D. 1902. *The Ancient Catholic Church: From the Accession of Trajan to the Fourth General Council (A.D. 98–451).* New York: Charles Scribner's Sons.

Scott, T. Kermit 1995. *Augustine: His Thought in Context.* Mahwah, NJ: Paulist Press.

Ste. Croix, G. E. M. de 1981. *The Class Struggle in the Ancient Greek World.* Ithaca, NY: Cornell University Press.

Segal, Alan F. 2002. *Two Powers in Heaven: Early Rabbinic Reports about Christianity and Gnosticism.* Netherlands, E. J. Brill.

Sipe, A. W. Richard 1995. *Priests and Power: Anatomy of a Crisis.* NewYork: Brunner-Rutledge,.

2003. *Celibacy in Crisis: A Secret World Revisited.* New York: Brunner-Rutledge.

Smits, Ken 2008, O. F. M. Cap. "Has Ecumenism Gone into a Coma?" *Weekly Recap.* January 25, 2008.

Springel, Stephen V. "In the Market of the Cupid Vendors: Foucauldian and Post-Foucauldian Critiques of Ecclesial Power and Leadership." *The Journal of Religious Leadership,* 6, (2) Fall, 75–103, 2007.

Stark, Rodney 1997. *The Rise of Christianity.* San Francisco: Harper Collins.

2001. "Efforts to Christianize Europe, 400–2000." *Journal of Contemporary Religion,* 16, 1, 106–23.

Smits, Ken 2008, O. F. M. Cap. "Has Ecumenism Gone into a Coma?" *Weekly Recap.* January 25, 2008.

Stead, G. C. 1980. "In Search of Valentinus in the School of Valentinus." Volume I, *Rediscovery of Gnosticism,* editor, Bentley Layton. Leiden, Netherlands: Brill.

Stevenson, J. 1960. *The Early Christian Fathers*. London: Gerald Duckworth and Company.

Swete, Henry Barclay 1912, 1966. *The Holy Spirit in the Ancient Church: A Study of Christian Teaching in the Age of the Fathers*. Grand Rapids, Michigan: Baker Book House.

Tabbernee, William 1997. *Montanist Inscriptions and Testimonia: Epigraphic Sources Illustrating the History of Montanism*. Macon, Ga.: Mercer University Press.

2003. "Portals of the Montanist New Jerusalem: The Discovery of Pepouza and Tymion." *Journal of Early Christian Studies* 11 (1):87–9.

2009. *Prophets and Gravestones: An Inspirational History of the Montanists*. Hendrickson Publishers.

Thomassen, Einar 2004. "Orthodoxy and Heresy in Second Century Rome." *Harvard Theological Review*, (3), .

Tollison, Robert D. 1996, Robert F. Herbert, Robert B. Ekelund, Jr., Gary M. Anderson, and Audrey B. Davidson. *The Sacred Trust: the Medieval Church as Economic Firm*. New York: Oxford University Press.

Trevett, Christine 1996. *Montanism: Gender, Authority and the New Prophesy*. Cambridge, United Kingdom: University of Cambridge.

Trombly, Frank 1999. "Ammianus Marcellinus and Fourth-Century Warfare: a Protector's Approach to Historical Narrative," in *The Late Roman World and Its Historian: Interpreting Ammianus Marcellinus*, Jan Willem Drijvers and David Hunt, eds. London: Routledge.

Tyson, Joseph 2006. *Marcion and Luke-Acts: A Defining Struggle*. Columbia, South Carolina: University of South Carolina.

Vaggione, Richard Paul 2000. *Eunomius of Cyzicus and the Nicene Revolution*. Oxford: Oxford University Press.

Wall, Robert W. 2004. "The Function of the Pastoral Letters within the Pauline Canon of the New Testament: A Canonical Approach," in *The Pauline Canon*, Stanley E. Porter, editor. Leiden, Netherlands: Brill.

Williams, D. H. "Sociological Analysis of the Montanist Movement." *Religion*, 19, 1989.

Williams, David Salter 1989. "Reconsidering Marcion's Gospel." *Journal of Biblical Literature* 108 (3):477–96.

Williams, Michael Allen 1996. *Rethinking "Gnosticism": An Argument for Dismantling a Dubious Category.* Princeton, NJ: Princeton University Press.

Williams, Rowan. *Arius: Heresy and Tradition.* London: SCM Press, 2001.

Wilson, Robert Smith. *Marcion, a Study of a Second Century Heretic.* London: James Clarke & Company Limited, 1933.

Wilson, Stephen G. *Related Strangers: Jews and Christians 70–170 C.E.* Minneapolis, MN: Fortress Press, 2006.

Zinn, Howard 1980. *People's History of the United States.* New York: Harper Row, Publishers, Inc.

and Anthony Armove 2004/2009. *Voices of People's History of the United States.* New York: Seven Stories Press.

www.ingramcontent.com/pod-product-compliance
Lightning Source LLC
Chambersburg PA
CBHW050339230426
43663CB00010B/1915